A Place of Our Own

JUDAIC STUDIES SERIES

Leon J. Weinberger
General Editor

Publication of this book was made possible in part by the generous support of
the Community Development Foundation for Reform Judaism and Elmer and
Fanny Morris.

A Place of Our Own

The Rise of Reform Jewish Camping

Essays Honoring the Fiftieth Anniversary of Olin-Sang-Ruby Union Institute, Union for Reform Judaism, in Oconomowoc, Wisconsin

edited by MICHAEL M. LORGE and GARY P. ZOLA

THE UNIVERSITY OF ALABAMA PRESS

Tuscaloosa

Typeface: Minion

∞

The paper on which this book is printed meets the minimum requirements of American National Standard for Information Science—Permanence of Paper for Printed Library Materials, ANSI Z39.48-1984.

Library of Congress Cataloging-in-Publication Data

A place of our own : the rise of Reform Jewish camping : essays honoring the fiftieth anniversary of Olin-Sang-Ruby Union Institute, URJ, in Oconomowoc, Wisconsin / edited by Michael M. Lorge and Gary P. Zola.
p. cm. — (Judaic studies series)
Includes bibliographical references and index.
ISBN-13: 978-0-8173-1486-6 (cloth : alk. paper)
ISBN-10: 0-8173-1486-5 (alk. paper)
ISBN-13: 978-0-8173-5293-6 (pbk. : alk. paper)
ISBN-10: 0-8173-5293-7 (alk. paper)
1. Jewish camps—United States—History. 2. Reform Judaism—United States. 3. Jewish religious education—United States. 4. Olin-Sang-Ruby Union Institute (Oconomowoc, Wis.) I. Lorge, Michael M. II. Zola, Gary Phillip. III. Series.
BM135.P53 2006
296.8′341—dc22

2005027018

Contents

Acknowledgments

Olin-Sang-Ruby Union Institute (OSRUI)—like many other communal institutions that influence the course of an individual's life—evokes intensely personal emotions. And yet, OSRUI is also a communal institution with a history of its own that is larger than any one individual. Campers, staff members, and faculty not only experience camp, but they are also active participants in its history. Consequently, every individual who has spent time at OSRUI is, in a real sense, an expert on the camp's history—at least in some specific aspect of the camp's evolving legacy. However, just as one individual's life was permanently and indelibly affected by spending time at camp, so too were hundreds of others similarly influenced.

We therefore acknowledge that for those who have a personal relationship with OSRUI, any interpretation of the camp's rise and early growth will likely fall short of expectation. Since this volume is not an exhaustive narrative history of OSRUI, there are hundreds of names, events, and programs that go unmentioned. For example, we do not recount with any detail the vast number of Jewish professionals who contributed selflessly to the camp. Nor do we list the names of many individuals whose professional careers and endeavors were influenced by their experiences at OSRUI. Hundreds of song leaders, counselors, and specialists left their mark on the camp, yet their names will not appear in this book. Nevertheless, we are keenly aware of the crucial role that these unnamed individuals have played in the camp's history. Therefore, we begin this volume with a word of sincere acknowledgment for the wonderful and unique contributions that so many extraordinary men and women have made to the development of OSRUI and, more generally, to Reform Jewish camping.

It is a pleasure to recognize the many institutions and individuals who lent their support to the publication of this book. We are grateful to those who shared their personal recollections and primary source documents with us. In this regard, over the past three years we contacted more than sixty-five people to solicit their reminiscences about the first few decades of OSRUI. We are grateful to all those who responded to our letters, interviews, and telephone calls. They provided us with crucial information in the form of anecdotes, historical information, documents, and stories, some of which are included in the introductions to each chapter. In particular, we make specific mention of the following people: Dr. Irwin Barrington, Rabbi Howard Bogot, Phillip L. Brin, Danny Buchler, Sally B. Cole, Etty Dolgin, Rachel Zohar Dulin, Fradle (Pomp) Freidenreich, Debbie Friedman, Thomas Heiman, Irving B. Kaplan, Rabbi Ronald Klotz, Rabbi Barton Lee, Jerry Lidsky, Anne Lidsky, Eudice G. Lorge, Rabbi Ralph D. Mecklenburger, Dr. Oscar Miller, Rabbi Hayim Goren Perelmuter, Rabbi Michael Perelmuter, Kathy Bayer Rabinovitz, Rabbi Gerald Raiskin, Dr. Lawrence Ross, Rabbi Don Rossoff, Rabbi Herman E. Schaalman, Ellie Schwartz, Sue Ellen Lorge Schwartz, Rabbi Mark S. Shapiro, Rabbi Allan Smith, Rabbi Donald M. Splansky, Greta Lee Splansky, Rabbi Michael A. Weinberg, Rabbi Arnold Jacob Wolf, and Dean Zemel.

There are many individuals within the Union Institute community who were instrumental in this effort. They urged us to undertake this project, provided crucial information, and gave us useful feedback as we developed the work. These include, first and foremost, Gerard W. Kaye, who for the past thirty years has directed OSRUI and played a singularly important role in its remarkable development, and Rabbi Herman E. Schaalman, the camp's unflagging champion, who has served as a spiritual compass for those who pass through the camp's gates. We also acknowledge the encouragement that we received from members of the OSRUI board, Clive Kamins in particular, and those who served on OSRUI's Fiftieth Anniversary Celebration Committee.

Our conceptualization of this volume was greatly enhanced by the many fine suggestions we received from Professor Jonathan D. Sarna of Brandeis University and Dr. Frederic Krome of the Jacob Rader Marcus Center of the American Jewish Archives. We also recognize the work of Neesa Sweet, who helped us with many aspects of our work over the past three years. In addition, Carol Rubin provided valuable editorial assistance.

To a great degree this book could not be completed without primary source documents. These data came from OSRUI's Program Books and the Rabbi Ernst M. Lorge Personal Papers. The OSRUI Program Books are collections of program materials produced at Union Institute each summer, beginning with the summer of 1956. Rabbi Lorge's collection on OSRUI contains camp correspondence and governance records, which constitute an invaluable source for those researching the camp's early history. All of these documents have now been transferred to the Jacob Rader Marcus Center of the American Jewish Archives.

We are indebted to the staff and administration of the Jacob Rader Marcus Center of the American Jewish Archives (AJA), who never failed in their efforts to support our research. In particular, we wish to express our thanks to Kevin Proffitt, Dorothy Smith, Christine Schmid, Alison Stankrauff, Devhra BennettJones, Camille Servizzi, Elise Nienaber, Ruth Kreimer, and Phil Reekers. We offer special recognition of Lisa B. Frankel, Director of Programs and Administration, and Eleanor Lawhorn, the Marcus Center's executive secretary, for their unwavering support and encouragement.

It is a pleasure to acknowledge the support and resources of the partners at Laser, Pokorny, Schwartz, Friedman & Economos, Chicago, Illinois, especially the friendship and counsel of Jules M. Laser, in the completion of this publication. In particular we note the contributions of the firm's support staff.

Without the Hebrew Union College–Jewish Institute of Religion, there would not be an American Jewish Archives. For more than fifty years, HUC-JIR has supported and generously endowed the AJA's efforts. Special thanks are due to HUC-JIR's president, Dr. David Ellenson, and provost, Dr. Norman J. Cohen, who have been unflagging in their support.

There are no words to adequately express our gratitude for the support we have received from our spouses, Susie and Stefi. Both of us met our spouses at Union Institute, and we are blessed with wives who share our passion for Jewish life, Jewish education, and Jewish camping. Without their support and suggestions it would not have been possible to complete this book. Our thanks also to our children: Alyssa, Ilana, Ari, and Sari Lorge and Mandi, Jory, Jeremy, and Samantha Zola. We hope that the years they have spent at OSRUI and GUCI (Goldman Union Camp Institute) will provide for them the friendships and passion for Judaism that it provided to us.

Finally, we dedicate our contributions to this volume in memory of Sue Ellen Lorge Schwartz (1947–2003), whose tragic death occurred while we were in the midst of this project. Sue Ellen embodied the spirit and passion of Union Institute in her work at camp in the 1960s and 1970s, in her love for Israel, and in her dedicated work as a school social worker at Solomon Schechter Day School in Skokie, Illinois. It is noteworthy that she included in her own biographical statement, which she provided when requested for speaking engagements, an acknowledgement that her years at Union Institute had an impact on her chosen profession and commitment to Jewish life.

—Michael M. Lorge and Gary P. Zola

...in ... the establishment of the Reform movement ... Dr. Gary P. Zola's chapter, "Jewish Camping and Its Relationship to the ... Summer Camping Movement in American ..."

Preface

As part of the commemorative activities marking the fiftieth anniversary of Olin-Sang-Ruby Union Institute (OSRUI), the Anniversary Celebration Committee wanted to publish a history of the camp. After some consideration, the editors began to envision a collection of thematic essays that provided readers with an interpretive history on the rise and development of Reform Jewish camping as seen through the lens of the movement's first camp: OSRUI.

Union Institute's first brochure heralded the purchase of the camp "on the shores of beautiful Lac La Belle" by stating, "The success we have had in past years with our short-term meetings, conclaves, and special Summer Institutes, has now led to the establishment of *a place of our very own*" (italics added). From that point on OSRUI became a programmatic and liturgical crucible ever enhancing and advancing Jewish expression in the Reform movement. To celebrate its fiftieth year, we explore these remarkable influences, which grew dramatically in spite of limited financing and initial recognition.

This volume concentrates on three focal points. First, some of the chapters examine OSRUI's early history and its place in the evolution of Jewish camping in America. Collectively, these essays reconstruct the various factors that culminated in the establishment of the Reform movement's first summer camp in 1952. Dr. Gary P. Zola's chapter, "Jewish Camping and Its Relationship to the Organized Camping Movement in America," analyzes how organized camping in America influenced the development of Jewish camping. This same theme receives more detailed focus in Jonathan D. Sarna's essay, "The Crucial Decade in Jewish Camping." Sarna contends that OSRUI's beginnings parallel the establishment of other Jewish denominational or ideologically driven camps, marking a significant new phase in the history of Jewish camping. Finally, Michael M. Lorge and Gary Zola contribute a chapter on the confluence of ideas and the coalescence of events that led Chicagoland's Reform Jewish community to establish Union Institute in Oconomowoc, Wisconsin. The chapter also traces the history of OSRUI during the first two decades of its existence.

Second, this volume contains essays that focus respectively on a specific dimension of Reform Jewish camping: music, prayer, education, and Hebrew language. To one extent or another, these four topics define the distinctive character of Reform Jewish camping. The essays contributed by Judah M. Cohen ("Singing Out for Judaism: A History of Song Leaders and Song Leading at Olin-Sang-Ruby Union Institute"), Rabbi Donald M. Splansky ("Creating a Prayer Experience in Reform Movement Camps and Beyond"), Rabbi Hillel Gamoran ("The Road to Chalutzim: Reform Judaism's Hebrew-Speaking Program"), and Dr. Michael Zeldin ("Making the Magic in Reform Jewish Summer Camps") demonstrate how each of these themes took root in the movement's first camp and how they directly influenced the programmatic development of the movement's entire camping program. To underscore this point, the editors have added headnotes to each of these chapters containing interpolated excerpts from personal memoirs and from the camp's historical papers.

Finally, as the first official camp of the Reform movement, Union Institute in Oconomowoc played a unique role in charting a course for how Reform Jewish camping would ultimately evolve. In reflecting on the content of the entire volume, one senses that much of the contemporary tenor of Reform Judaism today—that is, the movement's approach to music, prayer, education, and Hebrew language—can be traced to the history of experimentation and innovation that characterized the movement's camping program. Indeed, what began as a "place of our own" for a local effort to enrich Jewish living developed into a significant Reform Jewish camping culture which has unequivocally influenced the character of the movement as a whole and continues to do so.

(Note: The Union of American Hebrew Congregations (UAHC) officially changed its name to the Union for Reform Judaism (URJ) in November 2003. For consistency and historical accuracy, the URJ will be referred to in this book as the UAHC.)

1 Jewish Camping and Its Relationship to the Organized Camping Movement in America

Gary P. Zola

Organized camping is a uniquely American cultural phenomenon.[1] Camps and camping programs constitute a familiar and widespread feature of contemporary American life. In fact, according to the American Camping Association (which succeeded the Camp Directors Association in 1935), today there are more than twelve thousand day and resident camps of varying types throughout the country. More than ten million children and adults participate annually in the organized recreational and educational opportunities offered by these camps each summer.[2] Organized camping is so ubiquitous that some may be surprised to discover that 125 years ago camping was still in its infancy. In fact, during the early stages of this uniquely American educational institution's history, camping's trailblazers persistently promoted the new institution's many social benefits. Once considered merely a creative experiment in structured outdoor living and learning, organized camping has today become a staple of American life. Not only is the idea of organized camping an American original, but outdoor camping—American style—has also been exported to all parts of the world.[3]

Our understanding of American history during the twentieth century would unquestionably benefit from a full-scale historical analysis of organized camping as a social movement. As one camping and recreation expert noted, during the first century of the movement's existence in America, there were some who contended that organized camping was a nostrum for almost any unsatisfactory social condition one could name. Although such a historical reconstruction is beyond the scope of this essay, it is possible to provide a brief overview of the various factors that influenced the beginnings and early growth of the American camping movement.[4]

Organized Camping in America

The origins of American camping have been traced back to a schoolmaster named Frederick William Gunn, who founded his "Gunnery Camp" in August of 1861, the summer following the outbreak of the Civil War. Gunn's "encampment" brought some students from his school to the out-of-doors to experience the life of the soldier and to learn firsthand about nature. It is difficult to determine whether or not American camping grew from the seedling that Frederick Gunn planted. Most historians agree, however, that the beginnings and early growth of camping as a bona fide social movement in America occurred during the last two decades of the nineteenth century under the influence of American Progressivism. A remarkable number of American camping pioneers were either educators, physicians, or members of the clergy whose ideas about camping were shaped by the social reforming ideals that characterized that period in American history.

By 1880, 25 percent of the American population lived in cities. Urbanization at the fin de siècle was accompanied by wondrous advances in technology, transportation, and manufacturing. These developments resulted in the creation of many new jobs, and, consequently, many people experienced a better quality of life. However, urbanization brought hardship to many others in the form of unsanitary living conditions, exploitation of labor, and the growth of organized crime. During the last decades of the nineteenth century, a variety of social reforming initiatives emerged in response to the negative consequences of urbanization and industrialization. It was at this time that the Social Gospel movement, an upsurge of interest in fostering a more socially involved, socially active Christianity, arose. At the same time, many people were drawn to the "back-to-nature" and "Fresh Air" movements as necessary antidotes to the negative consequences of industrialization.[5]

These two impetuses coalesced among those who discovered that fresh, unpolluted air and natural surroundings not only renewed their physical health but also revitalized their spiritual lives. Thousands of middle-class Americans retreated from their urban homes and combined religious revival meetings with the pleasures of outdoor living. This increased interest in the natural environment fueled the development of summer camping programs, which featured both organized physical activities and the salubrious effects of life in the out-of-doors. A modest number of organized camping programs took root during the last two decades of the nineteenth century.[6]

The establishment of a series of professional camping associations in the first two decades of the twentieth century, such as the General Camp Association (1903), the Camp Directors Association of America (1910), and the National Association of Directors of Girls' Private Camps (1916), testifies to the fact that organized camping in America was fast becoming a movement of some consequence.[7] By 1918 the editors of *Red Book* magazine began to promote the American camping movement in its pages. Claiming to have the "largest Educational Department of any magazine in the country," *Red Book* assembled a writing staff composed of "college men and women with wide cultural experience" who would provide reading materials that were "designed to inspire parents with the higher ideals of child education." Articles on the state of American camping supplemented the magazine's educational initiatives. During the mid-1920s, Henry Wellington Wack, associate director of *Red Book*'s "Camp Department," visited hundreds of camps and wrote extensively on his experiences.[8]

In 1924 the three aforementioned camp associations merged into a new, amalgamated Camp Directors Association, further underscoring the continuing vitality of the American camping movement. Organized camping in America has experienced a steady rate of growth throughout the course of the twentieth century, and by the end of the twentieth century an estimated one out of nine American children participated in some type of camping program during the course of their lives. On the basis of these statistics it is fair to assert that the camping movement has become a significant sociocultural phenomenon on the American landscape. Indeed, organized camping has become such a familiar feature of American life that it is difficult to believe that little more than a century ago the movement was only in its infancy.

Embedded within the early history of the American camping movement one finds a complicated matrix of diverse ideologies, principles, and philosophies that shaped the social value and communal benefit of the camping experience. It is possible to organize the majority of these theories and ideals into five broad categories that have collectively shaped the overall growth of organized camping in America. As the organized camping movement expanded, a significant number of social and religious groups came to realize that the benefits of organized camping could be adapted to suit their own group's specific needs and objectives. The history of American Jewish camping provides us with a case study of this historical phenomenon.

Organized Camping's Educational Function: Learning Through Doing

The idea that organized camping was rich with educative potential may be traced back to the movement's embryonic phase, when Frederick William Gunn, who directed his own private school in Connecticut, decided to conclude his school's summer semester by taking his pupils to the shore of Long Island Sound for a two-week out-of-doors experience. During their sojourn in the wilderness, Gunn exposed his students to vigorous hiking, firm discipline, sleeping in tents outdoors, and strenuous sporting activities. Gunn was an educator, and he saw this camping experience as a "supplement to formal education."[9]

Reflecting on their camping experience with Gunn, the alumni of this pioneering venture in organized camping remembered that their teacher had an educational agenda in mind; he wanted them to become self-reliant, self-confident adults. Gunn's first student-campers also learned about the Civil War, which had begun a few months earlier. Like soldiers, these boys lived in tents, discussed current events, and listened to stories around the campfire. This was learning by doing. Gunn wanted to do more than compel his pupils to memorize facts; he aspired to develop character. By taking his students into the wilderness, where together they would experience the "hazards, emergencies and challenges" of life in the natural environment, Gunn believed he would promote the development of "solid, self-reliant manhood."[10]

In the 1880s and 1890s, when the organized camping movement was first taking shape, many of its pioneering proponents were Progressivist educators. People such as Luther Halsey Gulick, George Louis Meylan, and Laura Mattoon were personally associated with the era's most prominent educational ideologues: John Dewey and William H. Kilpatrick. Dewey developed his own pragmatic philosophy called "instrumentalism," which asserted that human intelligence is a tool used for overcoming obstacles and problems that confront us. Similarly, Kilpatrick advocated innovative educational strategies such as the use of projects and stimulating activities to enliven the classroom. The programmatic content of many of the early camps bespeaks their founders' familiarity with these Progressivist ideas.[11]

By the 1920s, educational theories emphasizing the link between learning and play had evolved. For its early proponents, the camping environment became a natural laboratory where like-minded reformers were able to put their educational theories into action. These men and women developed educational philosophies of organized camping, which they published and distributed in the form of books and pamphlets. The camping experience was more than an escape into a world of recreation and entertainment. Camp, as one of its early advocates wrote, was to be "a laboratory of life."[12]

The educational value of camping achieved a remarkable endorsement in 1998, when the New York Public School System initiated its Breakaways program, with its focus on year-round learning. Students experienced up to twenty-eight days of nontraditional learning during the summer and school-year breaks. The Breakaways program incorporated the camp experience into the school curriculum, thereby creating a new model for public education in the nation's largest public school system. This innovation was the fulfillment of an ideal that may be traced back to the incipiency of organized camping in America. The idea of "learning by doing" has continuously remained a foundational value in camping. To this day, the American Camping Association describes itself as a "nonprofit educational organization."[13]

As we have seen, the founders of organized camping in America recognized camping's great educational potential. The acquisition of knowledge, however, was not an end in and of itself; rather, education was a means to improve the quality of human existence. Just as camps facilitated new modes of learning, so too could these unique, out-of-door experiences enhance the quality of human life. These ideas found their source in the intellectual milieu of the Progressive Era.[14]

The owners and directors of the many camps established during the camping movement's formative era were committed to the idea that time at camp could literally transform a youngster's life, regardless of whether that child was rich or poor. As we will see, there were camps that catered to a wealthy clientele as well as those that concerned themselves with the impoverished classes. There were camping advocates who undertook to meliorate the spirit of idleness and languor that appeared to be eroding the character of their youth. At the same time, there were those who sought to better the lives of the underprivileged: the children of factory workers, immigrants, and the many unfortunate young people who experienced the "tyranny of the cities."[15]

In 1876, for instance, Dr. Joseph Timble Rothrock, a man who went on to distinguish himself in the professional field of forest management, established a camp outside of Wilkes-Barre, Pennsylvania, for "weakly boys." The camp sought to develop healthy minds and bodies. Rothrock theorized that by "mingling exercise and study" his camp succeeded in improving a youngster's health while concomitantly conveying a wealth of "practical knowledge."[16] And when Ernest Balch established Camp Chocorua in 1881, he contended that the program would cure the "miserable existence of wealthy adolescent boys in the summer when they must accompany their parents to fashionable resorts and fall prey to the evils of life in high society." The camp's primary raison d'être, Balch insisted, was to foster the "development of a sense of responsibility in the boy both for himself and others."[17]

In 1884 Winthrop T. Talbot purchased the grounds of Ernest Balch's Camp Chocorua. Renaming it Camp Asquam, Talbot's program initially catered to a wealthy clientele. Later, Talbot realized that his camp could be a "corrective to negative city influences," and he noted the importance of having privileged children spend time together with their underprivileged peers. Camping, Talbot observed, helped these boys to become better people by smoothing "the rough corners of the embryo aristocrat, the budding of the crude, well-meaning able boy."[18]

Originally there were separate camps for boys and girls. True coeducational camping did not begin to appear until the 1920s, though there were some early examples of girls' camps located adjacent to an associated, though separate, camp for boys. Indeed, organized camping programs for girls appear in the earliest stages of camping's history. Laura Mattoon, a Wellesley graduate, established Camp Kehonka for girls in 1902. In addition to teaching her campers to appreciate poetry, nature studies, and the art of good conversation, the girls who attended the camp were also exposed to hiking, swimming, outdoor cooking, and wood-chopping. Mattoon wanted her camp to be a place where young girls could convert "wishbones into backbones."[19]

It was at this same time that many "Fresh Air" and Settlement movements established organized camping programs that aspired to improve the lot of the needy. Initially the supporters of these camps were convinced that simply by giving underprivileged children two weeks of fresh air, sunshine, and good food, they could overcome the negative effects of their impoverished living conditions. Before long, these camps began to supplement their summer program by offering the campers educational and vocational enrichment. In dedicating the Hull House Camp in 1908, Jane Addams declared: "For fresh air, yes, but fresh air breathed in joy and freedom, and opening up a new world."[20]

Some settlement camps combined the camping experience with summer employment opportunities, and for many of the settlement camps, Americanizing the immigrant was a desideratum. This concern sparked camping program initiatives related to hygiene, family life, and civic responsibility. In sum, the American camping movement gained strength from the belief that outdoor experiences would provide underprivileged American children with a "foothold of opportunity."[21]

By the 1920s, many had been persuaded that camping programs were helping to develop "better people, better lives" in America. Living in nature, becoming self-reliant, and learning to work cooperatively would nurture and enrich the individual human traits of perseverance, courage, courtesy, moral rectitude, and ambition. The best in human nature is released in the natural environment, and that beau ideal can be "made so infectious that the entire camp group develops it."[22]

Organized Camping Spiritual Function: Heightening Religiosity

Since many of the early leaders of the organized camping movement in America were members of the clergy, it should come as no surprise that many of the first camp programs promoted the values of learning, personal growth, and increased spiritual awareness. As one pioneering veteran of camping noted: "a camp should be educational, not only in the development of character, but also in a close study of all that God created for our enjoyment." To be sure, many of camping's pioneering ideologues were deeply religious men and women who believed that organized camping was an excellent tool for the enhancement of a young person's religious spirit.[23]

One vital link that joined religion and organized camping may be traced back to the work of the Young Women's Christian Association (YWCA) and Young Men's Christian Association (YMCA), both of which organized summer camp programs in the early 1880s. At these "Y" camps, religious practice became a seamless component of the daily program. Daily devotions, such as prayers over meals and at bedtimes, were commonly observed at the Y camps. A conscious effort was made to root the camp's overall communal spirit in the soil of Christianity's ethical tradition. It is interesting to note that despite the important role of religion in the development of the Y, many of the camps were pluralistically Protestant, fostering a nondenominational, universalist approach to religious life. As one YMCA camp brochure explained, "Because the Christian ethic plays an important role in the [camp's] activities, all boys are welcome regardless of color, creed, or ethnic background."[24]

The YMCA and YWCA camps significantly influenced many of those who fostered the early development of organized camping. Luther Gulick, for example, the son of a Christian missionary who originally trained as a medical doctor, spent the first half of his professional career working for the YMCA. Gulick quickly earned a reputation for being a magnetic speaker and writer. By the turn of the century he had become a leading figure in the field of recreation and physical education. Spiritual nourishment for young people was vitally important, Gulick taught, because adolescence was a particularly "unstable" time in the development of a human being's moral compass. He summarized the inner conflict as the struggle between being "self-centered or God-centered." The camping experience, Gulick argued, would help a youngster overcome self-centeredness. Despite his deep personal religiosity, he embraced ecumenism and eschewed denominationalism. Alumni of Gulick's camp remembered it as having a "singular religious air" despite the fact that it was free of any denominational doctrine.[25]

This universalistic approach appealed to many of the pioneers of organized camping. At Camp Chocorua, Ernest Balch established a "simple woodland chapel area." So popular were the camper-led services at Camp Chocorua that even neighboring townspeople attended. The program at Laura Mattoon's Camp Kehonka also featured informal worship services. She issued a camp prayer booklet titled "Services for the Open" that eventually was used in camps around the world. As another pioneer of camping observed, a well-run camp program should be successful in giving children "a conception of their Maker through an understanding of nature."[26]

Early on, the religious impulse in American camps expressed itself in the custom of requiring campers to read a self-selected excerpt from the Holy Scriptures or some other type of uplifting literature during rest period. Sometimes a religious role model took shape in the person of a charismatic camp leader who inspired youth with uplifting words. This type of inspiring religious educator helped young people to acquire the "courage to achieve what should be and the patience to endure what is." This feat was accomplished at camp neither by "preach[ing], nor exhort[ing] nor bully[ing] youth into a state of piety," but by encouraging campers to face "the fundamental problems of life." As one camp aficionado noted, "there never was a more welcome religion than that which American boys and girls unconsciously imbibe at flag-raising . . . and taps in some of the beautiful camps along our trail."[27]

The link between spiritual formation and organized camp was strengthened further by the development of youth movements among the various Protestant denominations during the early years of the twentieth century. Church youth groups began to organize weekend and summer camping programs variously called "retreats," "conferences," "assemblies," "conclaves," and "institutes." These programs were held in various locales, including camping sites. One illustration of this phenomenon is reflected in the history of Conference Point Center near Lake Geneva, Wisconsin. This retreat center was first established in 1873 by the Reverend Joseph Collie, a graduate of Beloit College and a pastor at the Congregational Church in Delavan, Wisconsin. By 1884 various religious groups were using Collie's campgrounds. During the week of August 6–12, 1886, a conference at Camp Collie was held to organize the formation of the National Young Women's Christian Association (YWCA). A gentleman by the name of E. H. Nichols purchased this camp in 1906 with the idea of using it as a camp site for the Cook County Sunday School Association, with which he was actively involved. In 1907 the International Sunday School Association sponsored its first organized training school for Sunday school leaders at Nichols Camp.[28]

Some of these religiously based camping initiatives sparked the creation of interdenominational camping programs, such as those sponsored by the International Sunday School Association. In other cases, youth conferences held at camps led dioceses and even individual churches to establish their own "church camps." The cultural, educational, and inspirational programs developed by the Chautauqua movement contributed to the early growth of church retreats and conferences. Denominational and interdenominational camps flourished because outdoor living proved to be a fertile environment for the enhancement of religious life among young people.[29]

Organized Camping's Historical Function: Instilling Respect for Heritage

The American camping movement's well-known association with the folklore of the Native American peoples may be traced back to Ernest Thompson Seton (1860–1946). Seton produced stories and paintings that ennobled wildlife and nature. He was also an aficionado of Native American folklore, and his various writings on that subject delighted thousands of American boys and girls in the first quarter of the twentieth century. In 1902 Seton organized a camp for boys on a large, wooded estate near Cos Cob, Connecticut. This camp became the headquarters of a national boys' organization called the Woodcraft Indians (later called the Woodcraft League). Seton was personally associated with many of the early proponents of organized camping. These reformers were deeply influenced by Seton's enthusiasm for Native American life. The Woodcraft Indians camp program emphasized a respect for the natural environment, food preparation, and the skills humans need to survive out-of-doors.[30]

Luther Gulick and his wife, Charlotte (Lottie) Gulick, were personally acquainted with Seton and impressed with his ideas. Gulick's leadership role in the national YMCA enabled him to make the Y camps a laboratory for testing Seton's theories about the beneficial impact that Native American stories and teachings would have on children. Seton's ideas caught on, and soon American Indian folklore, song, decorative design, symbolism, and religion became an integral part of Y camps. This trend also had an impact on scouting camps and, eventually, scores of privately owned camps that opened during the first two decades of the twentieth century.

Luther and Charlotte Gulick played a central role in this facet of camping's growth. In 1908 they purchased a camp on Lake Sebago, near South Casco, Maine. Charlotte organized a small summer camp program for her own daughters and a handful of girls. Her camp sought to apply the child-centered teaching methods that her husband advocated. She named her girl's camp WoHeLo, a Native American–sounding word that she invented by taking the first two letters of three words: work, health, and love. Luther, who played an active role in the establishment of the Boy Scouts of America in 1910, was eager to create a parallel organization for girls. The success of Charlotte's innovative camp for girls inspired her husband to spearhead the organization of Camp Fire Girls in 1911. By exposing young city girls to the joys of nature, communal living, and physical activity, Camp Fire Girls sought to inspire girls to strive for greater achievements in life.[31]

The Native American motif was not intended merely to enlighten campers with the cultural heritage of the original inhabitants of the land. Men like Seton and Gulick believed that Native American folklore, song, decorative design, and mythopoetry helped young people to understand the "adolescent crisis" that modern American culture had largely forgotten. According to Gulick, "here in the United States . . . there is one population that has not lost the heavenly secret of adolescence . . . the tribal Indians." These communal experiences with Native American culture ultimately would produce a better-adjusted adult who would be furnished with the emotional tools needed to "rebuild American homes."[32]

In addition to the emotional benefit that would come from exposure to Native American culture, there existed the somewhat ironic view that Native American experiences would foster among young people a deeper respect for the pioneering spirit in American culture and the nation's frontier mentality. In the increasingly urbanized America of the early twentieth century, these seemingly forgotten values needed reinforcement. Many early camp leaders believed that if young people were exposed to a heritage that rejected modern life's artificialities, they would be more inclined to embrace the values of the authentic American pioneer. As one naturalist summarized, "Nature Lore is the open air school of Americanism. . . . May we always have the way of the wilderness for those who seek it. This is our American heritage to be guarded by every schoolmate of the woods."[33]

In short, camp organizers soon realized that Native American culture could generate successfully an appreciation for America's cultural heritage and for timeless values whose very existence appeared to be in jeopardy because of the degeneracy of contemporary society.

Organized Camping Communal Function: The Betterment of Society

Many early advocates of camping in America believed that idleness and helplessness posed grave threats to American society. Expanding leisure time was being filled with "cheap, inane, vicious and even brutalizing diversions," and as a result of this debilitation, "America was living largely upon the inherited mental and physical vigor of [its] ancestors." The camping experience, as one proponent claimed, was a remedy for that problem. "Industry and wholesome, constructive recreation are the effective antidotes for many national ills."[34]

As we have seen, two of the most influential and pioneering figures in the history of the American camping movement, Luther and Lottie Gulick, vigorously promoted the idea that the camping movement would improve the overall quality of American society. After working for many years as the director of physical education for the YMCAs in New York, Luther Gulick entered the same position for the New York City Schools in 1903. In this capacity, the influence of his ideas about camping and outdoor recreation continued to grow. Many social welfare organizations admired Gulick's vision, and he was increasingly involved with boards and committees that were interested in the welfare of youth and the betterment of society. For example, in 1907 Gulick joined the staff of the then–newly established Russell Sage Foundation, which had been created to assist in "the improvement of social and living conditions in the United States." Through all of these related activities, Gulick and his wife associated with some of the most respected social activists of that era, including Jane Addams, Jacob A. Riis, Ernest Thompson Seton, Lincoln Steffens, Lillian Wald, and many like-minded Progressive activists from the Fresh Air and Settlement movements.[35]

Luther Gulick was among the first to assert that the organized camping movement could ultimately transform American society. Camping, he insisted, would prepare children for "the business of living in this new world." An increasingly industrial and urban society was the "new world" to which Gulick alluded. Progressivist educators like Gulick and others sought ways to address the perceived decline in self-reliance, self-sufficiency, and individual initiative that accompanied the transformation of American society during the Gilded Age. These Progressivist educators wanted to teach children how to appreciate "the deeper needs of work and its place in life." For Gulick, camping—like physical education, playgrounds, parks, and organized recreational activity— was another arrow in the quiver of social improvement that could help actualize "the new and splendid social world." The camping experience would spawn "a social system based upon better human conduct in all spheres of life."[36]

By 1925 camp enthusiasts effused about the social benefits of organized outdoor living. Camping, it was noted, taught American children how to live together in harmony. Progressive educators argued that "the perpetuity of our democratic society depends upon a consciously developed means of carrying on our affairs as a group." In American society, where the individual participates in shaping the policies of the government, all citizens need to develop a concern for the commonweal. As one educator wrote, "we must learn to *live together* before we as individuals can gain fullness of life through formal education" (italics in original). Organized camps, their proponents claimed, were potentially "important social and educational factors" in the upbringing of American children. All of American society stood to benefit from "this organized exodus toward the sun and stars and unvitiated air; this opening up of the windows, transoms and doors of our airtight dwellings—this deliberate pilgrimage back to the hills and valleys beyond the din and dirt of great cities."[37]

Organized Camping and American Jewry

American Jews have been drawn to the organized camping movement from its earliest days. Just as organized camping is a distinctly American phenomenon, so too does American Jewish camping embody a remarkable fusion of cultural phenomena, both American and Jewish. The five aforementioned themes that guided the overall development of camping in America also directed the growth of Jewish camps in this country. By examining three distinct periods of development in the history of American Jewish camping, it is possible to illuminate the many ways in which the nature of Jewish camping in America has been profoundly influenced by the ideological themes that affected the growth of American camping.

Jews, Social Reform, and the Emergence of Organized Camping in America

Camp Lehman (renamed Camp Isabella Freedman), established in 1893 by the Jewish Working Girls' Vacation Society of New York, may have been the first

Jewish camp in the United States. As the Jewish Working Girls' Vacation Society camp suggests, American Jewry's earliest encounters with the American camping movement were in fact outgrowths of the Settlement, Fresh Air, and other social reform initiatives that arose during the last decade of the nineteenth century. By the dawn of the twentieth century, hundreds of thousands of East European Jewish immigrants had jammed into New York, Philadelphia, and other large urban centers along the eastern seaboard and in the Midwest. The living conditions these Jewish children endured exemplified the appalling social problems associated with the urbanization process. This squalor motivated Jewish social reformers to act. Like other American Progressives, these reformers wanted to establish settlement camps specifically for the children of Jewish immigrants.[38]

During the first decade of the twentieth century, a wide variety of Jewish social welfare organizations established summer camps where outdoor living would boost the quality of life for thousands of Jewish youth. The Educational Alliance in New York founded a camp in 1901 that would later (in 1902) be incorporated as Surprise Lake Camp. In Cleveland a committee of the United Jewish Charities established the first of many Fresh Air Camps in 1904. The National Council of Jewish Women founded Camp Wise (1907) "for needy children, mothers, and babies." Americanizing the Jewish immigrant was also a prominent theme in the work of the Jewish settlement houses and immigrant aid societies. There were notable successes in this effort; Surprise Lake Camp took pride in the fact that the renowned entertainer Eddie Cantor had been one of its first campers. As an official publication of the National Conference of Jewish Charities noted in 1904, summer camping provided "an affordable antidote to urban congestion and the anomie of the slums."[39]

In addition to the Jewish camps that were sponsored by social welfare organizations, a host of privately owned camps cropped up during the first few decades of the twentieth century. Like other Americans, many Jews were also inspired by the back-to-nature movement, which one historian has termed "the call of the wild."[40] Though privately owned, many of the founders of these camps were Progressivist thinkers who embraced the same philosophical ideals that had captured the imaginations of the pioneers of American camping. Like founders of many of the best-known American camps of this era, those who established private Jewish camps were innovative educators and deeply committed social reformers. And like many other Americans of this period, the Jewish founders of camping were enthusiasts of the outdoors movement. As such, they believed that the camping experience would help children to become more self-sufficient, self-aware, and self-reliant. Thus, organized camping programs would produce better people, and, ultimately, better people would foster a better society. Privately owned Jewish camps aspired to transform their campers and, in doing so, to bring about a renaissance of society. When Carrie

Kuhn and Estelle Goldsmith founded Camp Woodmere in 1916, they insisted that their camp imbued the young people with the "fundamentals of good citizenship."[41]

Many of the early founders of private Jewish camps embraced the ideals relating to the use of Native American culture in camp programs. After all, American Jewish children were as much in need of the important values that Native American folklore imparted as were non-Jewish children: love of nature, respect for the wisdom of ancestors, and renewed joy in everyday living. In 1936 the director of Surprise Lake Camp noted that "young boys like to imagine themselves in the places of the natives of this country, the Indians. They like to play at games in which the cunning and swiftness of the Indian is [sic] brought out . . . they are thrilled when they are taught tracking." During the first decades of the twentieth century, many privately owned American Jewish camps took Native American–sounding monikers: Cayuga, Dalmaqua, Jekoce, Kennebec, Kawaga, Ramapo, Seneca, Tamarack, Wakitan, Wehaha, Winadu, and others.

Although some Jewish camps continue to feature the Native American motif as a component of their programmatic content, Jewish educational camps increasingly replaced that motif with themes from Jewish history and culture. Bunk and cabin groups were dubbed Jerusalem, Tel Aviv, or Petakh Tikvah instead of Delaware, Mohawk, or Arapaho. As we will see below, in the 1920s and 1930s Jewish educational camps began assuming Hebrew rather than American Indian names. The Zionist camps, especially, incorporated Hebrew words and aspects of Jewish life in the *yishuv* (settlement) as an important feature of the camp's program. Just as the Native American motif could be used to give American children a healthy respect for a precious though unappreciated cultural legacy, so too could the use of Jewish historical and cultural themes at camp bring Jewish children a renewed respect for their unique heritage. Clearly, the desire to instill a healthy sense of respect for the values of a historic and noble past—in some cases by employing Native American culture and in other instances Jewish culture—played a significant role in the ideological development of the American Jewish camping movement.[42]

Another significant parallel with the pioneers of American camping is the fact that some of the earliest founders of private Jewish camps were rabbis or lay leaders who not only believed that organized camping would improve the lives of Jewish children but who, like other proponents of organized camping, also believed that camping programs were effective vehicles for providing Jewish children with educational enrichment and spiritual enhancement. George Alexander Kohut, a rabbi, scholar, and educator, established Camp Kohut for Boys in Maine in 1907. Kohut conceived of his camp as "an educational as well as a recreational institution." Camp Kohut's boys were taught swimming, sailing, fishing, sports, and various recreational activities. However, Sabbath services were held at camp in what Kohut termed "God's temple"—a grove of apple trees. Kohut used Sabbath services to teach his campers that they were obligated to worship God and participate in prayer services. He engaged them in a discussion of many relevant topics: the "problems of the Jew in the modern world, the special problems of [immigrant] adaptation to American life, and the family problems of the first generation of American-born."[43]

In 1916 Kohut's camping program inspired another young rabbi, Bernard C. Ehrenreich, to establish his Camp Kawaga in Minocqua, Wisconsin. In an early brochure for Camp Kawaga, Ehrenreich informed curious parents that "camp life is an educational institution." He was referring to universal learning. Like Camp Kohut, Kawaga did not advertise itself as an institution that promoted Jewish education. Still, Ehrenreich followed Kohut's lead in offering his camp-ers a spiritual message that was universalistic in tone and content. His campers remembered his oft-repeated credo: "Take the 'G' from GREAT, the 'O' from OUT, and the 'D' from DOORS and the GREAT OUT DOORS can be trans-lated into the name of GOD."[44]

All in all, it is evident that during its first stage of growth, American Jewish camping was spurred into existence by the same objectives and ideals that prompted the rise of the broader American camping movement. Yet these first Jewish camps were Jewish primarily because of their constituency, not because of their mission. By the end of the 1920s, however, a new phase in Jewish camp-ing emerged.

The Emergence of Jewish Educational Camps and Camps with an Explicitly Jewish Mission

Between 1880 and 1920 nearly three and one half million East European Jews immigrated to the United States. This mass migration transformed the demo-graphic and cultural character of American Jewry, particularly in the country's major urban centers. The rise of camps with programming dedicated to an explicitly Jewish educational aim was one aspect of the overall Jewish organi-zational efflorescence that occurred in response to this communal metamor-phosis.

In the early years of the twentieth century, many Jewish leaders began to contemplate new and innovative means to improve and strengthen Jewish edu-cation in America so as "to preserve a distinctly Jewish life amidst the conflict-ing influences of the [general American] environment." Efforts to acculturate and Americanize the East European immigrants had been tremendously effec-tive, and many Jews began to drift away from Jewish life. Interest in the syna-gogue and in Jewish ritual practice declined. One Jewish educator, Samson Benderly, was deeply concerned about these trends. Although he had studied to become a medical doctor, Benderly's passionate interest in Jewish education prompted him to abandon his original career plans in order to direct the country's first Bureau of Jewish Education, which was established in New York in 1910. Benderly insisted that a revitalized Jewish educational system could yet be an effective force in safeguarding the future of Jewish life in America. To accomplish this objective, Benderly asserted that American Jewish education should worry less about "the amount of knowledge obtained, as the creation of a Jewish atmosphere." The success of Benderly's ideas in New York's Bureau of Jewish Education encouraged the development of similar bureaus in major Jewish communities throughout America.[45]

It is interesting to note that these developments occurred as the Progressive Era in American history drew to a close. Although aspects of Progressivism's social reforming extended into the 1920s, as one historian concluded, at the close of World War I "the United States [was] a new country." In the aftermath of the Great War, the harsh social divisions that had been present in American society for decades came into bold relief. The 1920s witnessed an upsurge in racial tensions, fear of the immigrant, strains in labor relations, and other issues relating to the status of new immigrants. These tensions affected American Jewry, which faced even higher levels of prejudice both at home and abroad. Moreover, in the post–World War I era, Zionism became a mass movement, and America's newly enlarged Jewish population identified with this cause. All of these factors contributed to the need for new and innovative communal initiatives that would reinforce Jewish identity and bolster loyalty to Jewish communal life. It is in this social context that the rise of Jewish educational camping with explicitly Jewish aims took root.[46]

The influence of European Jewish youth movements began to affect the programmatic content of many Jewish camps during this particular phase in the history of Jewish camping. Countless Central and East European Jews who immigrated to America during the interwar years had been actively involved in a variety of European Zionist youth organizations before their arrival to these shores. These immigrants carried such experiences with them when they settled in America. As we will see, many of these people eventually played a significant role in the continuing development of the American Jewish camping movement.

The dawn of a new phase in the history of American Jewish camping began when the Central Jewish Institute (CJI) was founded in 1916 in Yorkville on New York's Upper East Side by the Orthodox synagogue Kehilath Jeshurun. The CJI soon became an independent Jewish community center whose primary objective was to vitalize Jewish education by integrating Judaism within the context of Americanism. The CJI operated schools for children, youth clubs, and cultural activities for adults. In 1919 the organization began a program of summer camping that ultimately evolved into the Cejwin (CEntral JeWish INstitute) Camps in Port Jervis, New York. With the establishment in 1919 of Cejwin and Camp Boiberik, a secular camp with an emphasis on Yiddish language sponsored by the Sholem Aleichem Folk Institute, American Jews slowly began to recognize the educative potential of organized camping.[47] Before this era, Jewish camping essentially consisted of camps that were run either under the auspices of a Jewish communal institution or privately owned camps that catered to a Jewish clientele. After the successful establishment of Cejwin and Boiberik, camps with a distinctly Jewish mission began to multiply in the 1920s.[48]

Some of the camps established during this period actively espoused a particular Jewish ideology, and their educational mission existed to serve the needs of its ideological point of view. Thus, camps arose that promoted Yiddish language, Zionism, Hebrew learning, socialism, and so forth. A cadre of progressive Jewish educators—many of whom had either studied with or been directly influenced by the same progressive educators who inspired the trailblazers of the American camping movement—pioneered the development of camps with a specifically Jewish mission:[49] Albert P. Schoolman, one of the Progressivist Jewish educators, took the helm of the newly established Camp Cejwin in 1923, and he maintained his association with the camp for nearly a half century. Cejwin is generally viewed as the first successful Jewish educational camping venture in American Jewish history.[50] A few years later, Jewish educators Isaac B. Berkson and his wife, Libbie S. Berkson, collaborated with Alexander M. Dushkin and his wife, Julia Dushkin, in the founding of Camp Modin (1922), which focused on Jewish learning and living. The dean of this new band of progressive Jewish educators, Samson Benderly, also established a camp—Camp Achvah (1927)—with its special emphasis on the development of future Jewish educational leaders. Shlomo Bardin, a charismatic Zionist youth leader, founded a Summer Camp Institute (1941) under the sponsorship of the American Zionist Youth Commission and with financial backing from Supreme Court Justice Louis D. Brandeis. The institute was named for Brandeis upon his death in September 1941. Shlomo Shulsinger established Camp Massad (1941), with an educational program that concentrated on teaching Hebrew language skills.[51]

The pragmatic success of Jewish educational camping was reinforced by the theoretical writings of American educators and sociologists whose research suggested that camping programs strongly influenced the attitudes and habits of campers. Those individuals who staffed or attended one of these Jewish educational camps knew, on the basis of their own personal experience, that the theorists were correct. Camps with an explicit Jewish mission effected a Jewish transformation, and a dedicated band of Jewish camping enthusiasts emerged. The highly regarded author Chaim Potok captured the all-consuming atmosphere that characterized camps with a Jewish mission: "We lived, it seemed to me, in a permanent state of exhilaration born of a sense of high purpose and accomplishment. We were educating the next generation of American Jews in a living Judaism."[52]

Jewish educational camping programs proved to be invaluable tools for the strengthening of Jewish life in mid-twentieth-century America. As American Jewry left its urban, immigrant neighborhoods and resettled in the suburbs, Jewish identity became ever more compartmentalized. The all-encompassing atmosphere of Jewish neighborhoods and Jewish homes gave way to the allures of society at large. Jewish camping programs offered young people a chance to experience an immersion in Jewish environment. These camps "naturalized the very notion of Jewishness," and in doing so they fostered "several generations of young American Jews knowledgeable about and confident in their Jewish identity, whether as cultural Jews, observant Jews, secular Jews, yiddishists or Zionists."[53]

The Emergence of Jewish Camps Serving the Religious Movements of American Judaism

The number of organized camping programs in the United States mushroomed from approximately one hundred in 1910 to nearly thirty-five hundred in 1933. During this same period of camping's efflorescence in America, dozens of new Jewish camps—benefiting from the success of the first and second generation of Jewish educational camps—sprang up. In 1929 one Jewish publication enthusiastically described organized camping as the most successful "instrument for inspiring and remaking individual young Jewish lives."[54]

By the mid-1940s American Jewish camping had become a familiar sight on the landscape of American Jewish life. A significant proportion of the expanding number of Jewish camps were privately owned. Many of these private camps limited their Jewish content to a brief weekly Sabbath service and some degree of sensitivity to Jewish dietary law. However, the number of camps with a distinct Jewish mission also grew during this period. Many of those who had been campers and staff members in the first generation of Jewish educational camps went on to become champions of Jewish camping. In some instances, those who created the first Jewish educational camps seemed to be consciously striving to bolster the next generation of camp enthusiasts. As one longtime Jewish camp director observed, "there was a sense of one generation keeping an eye on and completing the other."[55]

It is clear that at least some of these efforts bore fruit, since many pioneering Jewish educational camps established in the 1920s and 1930s spawned the development of a second generation of Jewish educational camps in the 1940s. It was during this decade that various leaders of American Judaism's religious streams began to recognize how organized camping could augment Jewish learning, develop leadership skills, and concomitantly strengthen ideological ties to their respective religious movements. Jonathan D. Sarna has dubbed this "the crucial decade of Jewish camping." Rabbi Moshe Davis, for instance, was one of Camp Massad's founders in 1941. He went on to play a central role in the establishment of Conservative Judaism's Camp Ramah in 1947. Similarly, many of those who had been influenced by early Jewish educational camps were instrumental in the development of the Hebrew program at Reform Judaism's first Union Institute (established in 1952). During this same period of time, several large synagogues began to acquire camp sites of their own.[56] Though religious Zionist camps go back to the 1930s, after the 1950s camps associated with the Orthodox and Hassidic movements also came into existence.[57] During the last quarter of the twentieth century, both the Conservative and Reform movements continued to establish new camps. In 2002 the Reconstructionist movement opened its first camp. In sum, at the dawn of the twenty-first century, there were Jewish camps in America that reflected the entire spectrum of Jewish religious practice and learning. The unfolding success of the organized camping movement and its ideological rationale fostered the concomitant growth of Jewish camping, which continued to adapt the institution to serve its own specific purposes.[58]

Conclusion

Just as organized camping has today become a widely accepted social and educational institution in America, so too has Jewish camping become an established feature in the lives of many American Jews. In 2003 Jewish religious movements (Orthodox, Conservative, Reform, and Reconstructionist), Jewish Community Centers, Zionist organizations, Jewish youth organizations, and various other Jewish institutions collectively sponsored approximately 120 not-for-profit Jewish overnight camps in North America. In addition, hundreds of privately owned camps now cater primarily to a Jewish clientele. It has been estimated that fifty thousand Jewish youth attend the nonprofit camps on an annual basis, and an additional ten thousand individuals serve on staff for these camps. Clearly, Jewish camping is touching the lives of a significant number of Jewish young people in North America. Many contemporary leaders of American Jewry are convinced that Jewish camping experiences will contribute significantly to a young person's desire to participate in Jewish communal life as an adult.[59]

As we have seen, the history of Jewish camping is firmly rooted in the soil of a distinctly American phenomenon: the organized camping movement. The beginnings of Jewish camping in this country came as a by-product of the social and ideological trends that enveloped the nation during the Progressive Era. By the end of World War I an ardent group of progressive Jewish educators began to realize that organized camping programs could promote Jewish learning and strengthen the bonds of Jewish identification. It was at this very time that millions of first- and second-generation East European Jewish immigrants were integrating into American culture. Whereas many of the founders of the first generation of Jewish camping sought to Americanize Jewish children, the pioneers of the next generation of Jewish camps—camps with an explicitly Jewish ideological mission—were determined to reinforce Jewish identity.

By World War II, Jewish camping—like American camping in general—had become an accepted feature of American culture. Today, in addition to a steady proliferation of private camps that served Jewish clientele, a diverse array of nonprofit Jewish educational camps have been established. Just as America exported the idea of organized camping around the globe, so too has American Jewish camping been a model for the creation of Jewish camping programs throughout the world. In fact, when American Sikhs contemplated the establishment of their own educational camping program, they used the American Jewish camping program as their model.[60]

Finally, Jewish camping's historic relationship to its American counterpart even extends to the descriptive rhetoric that has been used to characterize the institution's overall significance. In 1922 Charles B. Eliot, former president of Harvard University, concluded, "The organized summer camp is the most important step in education that America has given the world." More than a half-century later, Gerson D. Cohen, chancellor of the Jewish Theological Seminary of America, matched Eliot's flattering sentiments when he ebulliently remarked that Jewish summer camp has constituted "the greatest contribution made by American Jews to modern Jewish life." The zeal that Charles Eliot and Gerson Cohen share in evaluating the significance of organized camping is reflective of a shared exuberance that has characterized camping enthusiasts from the movement's earliest days. As Jewish camping in America evolved and matured, it eventually assumed its own unique character based on the recognition that the proven successes of the American camping movement's ideology could be tailored to serve a distinctly Jewish mission, thereby making Jewish camping a genuine hybrid of organized camping in America.[61]

Notes

1. A distinction must be made between the use of the term "camping," which may refer broadly to any outdoor living experience, and the term "organized camping," which alludes to a specific type of *group* living experience in the context of the natural environment. The American Camping Association has defined "organized camping" as a "sustained experience which provides a creative, recreational, and educational opportunity in group living in the out-of-doors. It utilizes trained leadership and the re-

sources of natural surroundings to contribute to each camper's mental, physical, social, and spiritual growth." In this essay the word "camping" is used as an abbreviated reference to the term "organized camping."

2. Connie Coutellier, "Today's Camps," on the Web site of the American Camping Association, http://www.acacamps.org/media_center/view.php?file=camp_trends_trend_fact_sheet.html. See Eleanor Ells, *Eleanor Ells' History of Organized Camping: The First 100 Years* (Martinsville, IN: American Camping Association, 1986), 3.

3. See Ells, *History of Organized Camping*, vi, and Daniel Cohen, "Outdoor Sojourn: A Brief History of Summer Camp in the United States," in Jenna Weissman Joselit and Karen S. Mittelman, *A Worthy Use of Summer: Jewish Summer Camping in America* (Philadelphia: National Museum of American Jewish History, 1993), 10.

4. Phyllis M. Ford, "Camping—A Social Movement or an Institution," in Ells, *History of Organized Camping*, 138–39.

5. Susan Curtis, *A Consuming Faith: The Social Gospel and Modern American Culture* (Columbia: University of Missouri Press, 2001); Gary J. Dorrien, *The Making of American Liberal Theology: Imagining Progressive Religion, 1805–1900* (Louisville, KY: Westminster John Knox Press, 2001); Donald K. Gorrell, *The Age of Social Responsibility: The Social Gospel in the Progressive Era, 1900–1920* (Macon, GA: Mercer University Press, 1988); Robert T. Handy, *The Social Gospel in America, 1870–1920* (New York: Oxford University Press, 1966); and Ronald C. White, *Liberty and Justice for All: Racial Reform and the Social Gospel, 1877–1925* (Louisville, KY: Westminster John Knox Press, 2002). See also, Robert E. Adler, *Science Firsts: From the Creation of Science to the Science of Creation* (New York: John Wiley, 2002).

6. Andrew Chamberlin Rieser, *The Chautauqua Moment: Protestants, Progressives, and the Culture of Modern Liberalism* (New York: Columbia University Press, 2003), and Wendy Rose Bice, *A Timeless Treasure: 100 Years of Fresh Air Society Camp* (Bloomfield Hills, MI: Fresh Air Society, 2001).

7. On the history of organized camping in America, see especially Ells, *History of Organized Camping;* Henry W. Gibson, "The History of Organized Camping in the United States," in *Camping* magazine (1936); and Julian H. Salomon, "Organized Camping," in *Regional Review* 4, nos. 4–5 (April–May 1940), available at http://www.cr.nps.gov/history/online_books/regional_review/vol4-4-5b.htm. See also, D. Cohen, "Outdoor Sojourn." For information on the first camps for different ethnic communities in the United States, see the Public Broadcasting Service's Web site on camping, http://www.pbs.org/wgbh/amex/kids/summer/features_summer.html. All of these works assert that the organized camping movement is a uniquely American cultural phenomenon.

8. Henry Wellington Wack's summer camp travels were published in three separate volumes: *Summer Camps—Boys and Girls* (New York: Red Book Magazine, 1924); *The Camping Ideal: The New Human Race* (New York: Red Book Magazine, 1925); and *More About Summer Camps: Training for Leisure* (New York: Red Book Magazine, 1926). For the quotes cited above, see the publisher's note in *Camping Ideal*, 9.

9. Ells, *History of Organized Camping,* 7.

10. Cohen, "Outdoor Sojourn," 10, and Ells, *History of Organized Camping,* 5–6.

11. On Luther Gulick, Laura Mattoon, and their association with social reformers, see Helen Buckler, Mary F. Fiedler, and Martha F. Allen, eds., *Wo-He-Lo: The Story of Camp Fire Girls, 1910–1960* (New York: Holt, Rinehart and Winston, 1961). On George Louis Meylan and his connection to Dewey and Gulick, see Ells, *History of Organized Camping,* 22–24. On John Dewey, see George B. Cotkin, "John Dewey and Pragmatic Education," in *American Reform and Reformers: A Biographical Dictionary,* ed. Randall M. Miller and Paul A. Cimbala (Westport, CT: Greenwood Press, 1996), 138–49. On Kilpatrick, see Robert Merrill Bartlett, *They Work for Tomorrow* (Freeport, NY: Books for Library Press, 1970).

12. Ethel Josephine Dorgan, *Luther Halsey Gulick* (New York: Bureau of Publications Teachers College, Columbia University, 1934), 114. Regarding the influence of educational psychology on the development of organized camping in America, see Ells, *History of Organized Camping,* 2–54, and Buckler, Fiedler, and Allen, *Wo-He-Lo,* 5–10.

13. See ACA's Web site, http://www.acacamps.org/research/todayscamps.htm.

14. See Allen F. Davis, *Spearheads for Reform: The Social Settlements and the Progressive Movement* (New York: Oxford University Press, 1967).

15. Ells, *History of Organized Camping,* 29–54. For quote, see p. 32.

16. Cohen, "Outdoor Sojourn," 10; Ells, *History of Organized Camping,* 7–9. On Joseph Trimble Rothrock, see Eleanor A. Maass, *Forestry Pioneer: The Life of Joseph Trimble Rothrock* (Lebanon, PA: Pennsylvania Forestry Association, 2002).

17. Ells, *History of Organized Camping,* 7–9, and Salomon, "Organized Camping," 3–4.

18. Ells, *History of Organized Camping,* 32–33.

19. Ibid., 13; Buckler, Fiedler, and Allen, *Wo-He-Lo,* 68.

20. Ells, *History of Organized Camping,* 50–53 (with quotes on p. 53).

21. Ibid. On the Fresh Air movement, see Bice, *Timeless Treasure.* On the Settlement House movement, see Mina J. Carson, *Settlement Folk: Social Thought and the American Settlement Movement, 1885–1930* (Chicago: University of Chicago Press, 1990), and Harry P. Kraus, *The Settlement House Movement in New York City, 1886–1914* (New York: Arno Press, 1980). The success of these camps ultimately sparked the development of camps for children with special needs. On the beginning of camps for special populations, see Ells, *History of Organized Camping,* 53–54.

22. Wack, *Camping Ideal,* 35, and *More About Summer Camps,* 227.

23. Ells, *History of Organized Camping,* 35, 28.

24. For quote, see Ells, *History of Organized Camping,* 48–50 (quote on p. 49). On the history of YMCA camping, see Eugene A. Turner, *100 Years of YMCA Camping* (Chicago: YMCA, 1985). Ecumenism did not always include Judaism, as Jenna Weissman Joselit has noted. See Joselit and Mittelman, *Worthy Use of Summer,* 17.

25. Dorgan, *Gulick,* 58, 113.

26. Ells, *History of Organized Camping,* 8, 13, 35.

27. Wack, *Camping Ideal,* 254, and *More about Summer Camps,* 226.

28. The name of the property became Conference Point Camp in 1908. See "History of Conference Point Center: The Meeting Place of Inspiration, Williams Bay, Wisconsin," http://www.conference-point.org/history.htm.

29. See Ells, *History of Organized Camping,* 63–65. On the Chautauqua movement, see Rieser, *Chautauqua Moment,* and John E. Tapia, *Circuit Chautauqua: From Rural Education to Popular Entertainment in Early Twentieth-Century America* (Jefferson, NC: McFarland & Company, 1996). On the International Sunday School Association, see Anne M. Boylan, *Sunday School: The Formation of an American Institution, 1790–1880* (New Haven, CT: Yale University Press, 1988); Gerald E. Knoff, *The World Sunday School Movement: The Story of a Broadening Mission* (New York: Seabury Press, 1979); and Robert W. Lynn and Elliot Wright, *The Big Little School: Two Hundred Years of the Sunday School* (Birmingham, AL: Religious Education Press, 1980).

30. On Seton, see H. Allen Anderson, *The Chief: Ernest Thompson Seton and the Changing West* (College Station, TX: A&M University Press, 1986); Magdelene Redekop, *Ernest Thompson Seton* (Don Mills, Ontario: Fitzhenry & Whiteside, 1979); and John Henry Wadland, *Ernest Thompson Seton: Man in Nature and the Progressive Era, 1880–1915* (New York: Arno Press, 1978).

31. Buckler, Fiedler, and Allen, *Wo-He-Lo,* 3–28, 44, and Dorgan, *Gulick,* 112–25.

32. Ibid., 43, and Wack, *Camping Ideal,* 149.

33. See William Gould Vinal, "Nature Lore in Camps," in Wack, *Camping Ideal,* 212–13.

34. Wack, *Camping Ideal,* 51, 39–40.

35. For quote, see Buckler, Fiedler, and Allen, *Wo-He-Lo,* 5. For more on the Gulicks, see Dorgan, *Luther Halsey Gulick.* For a brief history of the Russell Sage Foundation, see http://www.russellsage.org/about/history/. On the Fresh Air and Settlement movements, see Louise W. Knight, "Jane Addams and the Settlement House Movement," and Eric C. Schneider, "Charles Loring Brace and Children's Uplift," both in Randall M. Miller and Paul A. Cimbala, *American Reform and Reformers: A Biographical Dictionary* (Westport, CT: Greenwood Press, 1996), 1–14 and 55–70.

36. Buckler, Fiedler, and Allen, *Wo-He-Lo,* 7–8; Wack, *Camping Ideal,* 35.

37. Wack, *More about Summer Camps,* 24–25; *Camping Ideal,* 29, 32.

38. Ells, *History of Organized Camping,* 52. On the overall history of Jewish camping in America, see Daniel Isaacman, *Jewish Summer Camps in the United States and Canada, 1900–1969* (Philadelphia, PA: Dropsie University, 1970). See also, Jenna Weissman Joselit, "The Jewish Way of Play," in Joselit and Mittelman, *Worthy Use of Summer,* 14–28; Burton Cohen, "The Jewish Educational Summer Camp," in Haim Marantz, ed., *Judaism and Education: Essays in Honor of Walter I. Ackerman* (Beer Sheva: Ben Gurion University, 1998), 245–52; and Nancy Mykoff, "Summer Camping," in *Jewish Women in America: An Historical Encyclopedia,* ed. Paula Hyman and Deborah Dash Moore (New York: Routledge, 1997), 1359–64. In the Klau Library at Hebrew Union College–Jewish

Institute of Religion, Cincinnati, Ohio, there are a number of rabbinic theses on the subject of Jewish camping, including Eric J. Bram, "Toward a Systematic Approach to Training Staff for UAHC Camp-Institutes" (1985); Jeffrey S. Clopper, "The Place of Modern Hebrew in Three Major American Camping Programs: The Habonim Labor Zionist Youth Movement, the Conservative Movement, and the Reform Movement" (1995); Ronald Klotz, "Toward a Survey of the Union of American Hebrew Congregations' Camp Educational Programs" (1977); Benjamin J. Leinow, "Toward a Year-Round Sample Camping Program" (1966); and Herschel I. Strauss, "Toward the Development of an Informal Camp Program for the Young Adolescent in Understanding American Reform Judaism, Emphasizing Values Clarification" (1975). Also, there are many independently published histories of private camps as well as personal memoirs that constitute an invaluable resource for reconstructing the history of Jewish camping in America during the first half of the twentieth century. For example, see David Lyon Hurwitz, "How Lucky We Were," *American Jewish History* 87 (March 1999): 29–59; Frances Fox Sandmel, *The History of Camp Kennebec* (North Belgrade, ME: 1973).

39. See *Jewish Charity* 3, no. 7, as quoted in Joselit, "Jewish Way of Play," 16. On Camp Surprise Lake, see "This Week in Jerusalem: 100 Years of 'Camp Surprise Lake'— Oldest Jewish Summer Camp in N. America," in *Jewish World,* http://www.jafi.org.il/agenda/2001/english/wk3-7/11.asp. Surprise Lake Camp takes pride in the impressive array of alumni who went on to popular acclaim in the arts, including Larry King, Jerry Stiller, Walter Matthau, Robert Abrams, Neil Diamond, Neil Simon, Gene Simmons, and Joseph Heller. See "Surprise Lake Camp," http://www.hvgateway.com/surprise.htm. On Fresh Air Camps, see "History of the Fresh Air Society," http://www.tamarackcamps.com/About/Default.aspx?S=AT&P=OH&PP=No. On Cleveland's Camp Wise, see "A Brief History of Camp Wise," at Camp Wise Web site, http://www.campwise.org/about/mission.html.

40. See Roderick Nash, ed., *Call of the Wild* (New York: G. Braziller, 1970).

41. Mykoff, "Summer Camping," 1362. See Jonathan D. Sarna, "The Crucial Decade of Jewish Camping," in the present text.

42. Joselit, "Jewish Way of Play," 19. For a list of Jewish camps with Native American names, see *Directory of Summer Camps* (New York: National Jewish Welfare Board, 1947). On the ideological development of Native American culture and its use at camp, see Wadland, *Ernest Thompson Seton,* esp. 447–61.

43. Camp Kohut's first summer took place on Hope Island in Casco Bay, Maine (not too far from Portland). The following year, 1908, the camp moved to Oxford, Maine (between Portland and Lewiston). See Rebekah Kohut, *His Father's House: The Story of George Alexander Kohut* (New Haven, CT: Yale University Press, 1938), 103–15. For quotations, see 112–13.

44. On George Alexander Kohut, see ibid. On Bernard C. Ehrenreich, see Harold S. Wechsler, "Rabbi Bernard C. Ehrenreich: A Northern Progressive Goes South," in *Jews of the South,* ed. Samuel Proctor, Louis Schmier, and Malcolm Stern (Macon, GA: Mer-

cer University Press, 1984), 45–64; and Byron L. Sherwin, "Portrait of a Romantic Rebel," in *Turn to the South: Essays on Southern Jewry,* ed. Nathan M. Kaganoff and Melvin I. Urofsky (Charlottesville: University Press of Virginia, 1979), 1–12.

Camp Kawaga's Web site preserves one of Ehrenreich's spiritual poems: "Game and Hike and Swimming ended / lake aflame with setting Sun / Campfire glow and twilight blended / Bugle call the day is done / In the hush a boy's voice falters / Uttering an evening prayer / Stars and lakes and woods his altars / GOD is very near him there." See "Camp Kawaga History," http://www.kawaga.com/information/history_full.htm.

45. Lloyd P. Gartner, *Jewish Education in the United States: A Documentary History* (New York: Teachers College, Columbia University, 1969), 127–31.

46. Albert Bushnell Hart, as quoted in Mary Beth Norton, et al., *A People and a Nation: A History of the United States,* 5th ed. (Boston: Houghton Mifflin Company, 1998), 626. See also, Gary Phillip Zola, ed., *The Dynamics of American Jewish History: Jacob Rader Marcus's Essays on American Jewry* (Lebanon, NH: Brandeis University Press/ University Press of New England, 2003).

47. See overview of the records of Rabbi Jerome Abrams on the Ratner Center Archives of Conservative Judaism's Web site, http://www.jtsa.edu/research/ratner/ conrec/pp_abramsjerome.shtml, September 29, 2003.

48. On the history of Cejwin, see Isaacman, "Jewish Summer Camps." See also, Alexander M. Dushkin, "A. P. Schoolman—The Story of a Blessed Life," in *Jewish Education* 36 (Winter 1966): 71–76, and *Living Bridges: Memoirs of an Educator* (Jerusalem: Keter, 1975). See also, Alfred P. Schoolman, "The Jewish Educational Summer Camp, A Survey of Its Development and Implications," *Jewish Education* 17 (June 1946): 6–15. For information on the founding of Camp Boiberik and its early program, see Leibush Lehrer, *The Objectives of Camp Boiberik: In the Light of Its History* (pamphlet 1962), in the Jacob Rader Marcus Center of the American Jewish Archives, Cincinnati, Ohio; and Fradle Friedenreich, "Yiddish Secular Education in the U.S. and Canada between the Two World Wars" (unpublished manuscript in the AJA).

49. Isaac Berkson, Samson Benderly, Alexander Dushkin, Albert Schoolman, and Shlomo Bardin were all influenced by Columbia University's famed educational Progressives—John Dewey, George Counts, and William H. Kilpatrick. See Ronald Cronish, "The Influence of John Dewey on Jewish Education in America," PhD thesis, Harvard Graduate School of Education, 1979. To gauge the deep reverence these Jewish educators felt for men like Dewey and Kilpatrick, see Isaac Berkson, "John Dewey and the Community-Centered School" in *Jewish Education* (Spring 1950): 3–5, and (honoring Kilpatrick) "Democracy and Jewish Culture," in *Jewish Education* (October– December 1937): 125–27.

50. See overview of the records of Rabbi Jerome Abrams on the Ratner Center Archives of Conservative Judaism's Web site, http://www.jtsa.edu/research/ratner/ conrec/pp_abramsjerome.shtml, September 29, 2003. Abrams's records note that Cejwin was founded by the CJI's Women's Auxiliary in 1919. Tillie Hyman, widow of

Samuel I. Hyman, founder and president of the CJI, was particularly active in the founding of the camp.

51. Walter Ackerman, "A World Apart: Hebrew Teachers Colleges and Hebrew-Speaking Camps," *Hebrew in America: Perspectives and Prospects*, ed. Alan Mintz (Detroit: Wayne State University Press, 1993), 105–28; and Shimon Frost, "Milestones in the Development of Hebrew Camping in North America: An Historical Overview" (in Hebrew with English summary), in *Kovetz Massad, Second Volume, Hebrew Camping in North America*, Shlomo Shulsinger-Shear Yashuv with Rivka Shulsinger-Shear Yashuv (Jerusalem: Alumni of Massad Camps, 1989), 17–79. See also, *Massad Reminiscences* (Jerusalem: Abraham Harman Institute of Contemporary Jewry, 1996); Shlomo Shulsinger, "Hebrew Camping—Five Years of Massad, 1941–1945," *Jewish Education* 17 (June 1946): 16–23; A. P. Gannes and Levi Soshuk, "The Kvutzah and Camp Achvah," *Jewish Education* 20 (Summer 1949): 61–109; Lisa Goodman, *Camp Yavneh—Then and Now* (New York: Jewish Theological Seminary of America, 1994); William B. Furie, "Yavneh," *Jewish Education* 17 (June 1946): 28–29; Shlomo Bardin, "The Brandeis Camp Institute," *Jewish Education* 17 (June 1946): 26–27; and Samuel M. Blumenfield, "Summer Camp Institute Sharon" *Jewish Education* 22 (Summer 1951): 37–40. Additional information on the Zionist camps can be found in the literature on Zionist movements such as Betar, B'nei Akiva, Hashomer Hatzair, Habonim, and others.

52. See Chaim Potok's introduction to Joselit and Mittelman's *Worthy Use of Summer*, 7, and also p. 26.

53. By the early 1940s there existed a noteworthy array of Zionist youth camps, including eleven Habonim camps, eleven Hashomer Hadati camps, seven Hashomer Hatzair camps, one Young Judea Camp (Tel Yehudah), and one Betar Camp (Brit Trumpeldor Organization of America). See Ben M. Edidin, "Zionist Youth Camps," in *Jewish Education* (June 1946): 24–25. On the beginnings of the Habonim camps, see J. J. Goldberg and Elliot King, *Builders and Dreamers: Habonim Labor Zionist Youth in North America* (New York: Herzl Press, 1993). See also, Joselit and Mittelman, *Worthy Use of Summer*, 26.

54. See Ells, *History of Organized Camping*, and Gibson, "History of Organized Camping"; see also Joselit, "Jewish Way of Play," 15.

55. Joselit, "Jewish Way of Play," 18.

56. For an example of individual synagogues acquiring camp sites, see Alfred Wolf, *Wilshire Boulevard Temple Camps: The First 25 Years, 1949–1974, A Personal History* (Los Angeles: Wilshire Boulevard Temple, 1975). Temple Israel of Minneapolis purchased Camp Teko in 1955.

57. Camp Morasha was established in 1964. Chabad Camp Emunah was established in the early 1950s. The National Conference of Synagogue Youth also sponsors camps.

58. See Sarna, "Crucial Decade of Camping," in the present text. For information on the beginnings of Conservative Judaism's Ramah camps, which were also established during this decade, see Burton I. Cohen, "A Brief History of the Ramah Movement,"

in *The Ramah Experience: Community and Commitment*, ed. Sylvia Ettenberg and Geraldine Rosenfield (New York: Jewish Theological Seminary/The National Ramah Commission, 1989), 3–18; Shuly Rubin Schwartz, "Camp Ramah: The Early Years, 1947–1952," *Conservative Judaism* 40 (Fall 1987): 12–41; and Michael Brown, "It's Off to Camp We Go: Ramah, LTF and the Seminary in the Finkelstein Era," in *Tradition Renewed: A History of the Jewish Theological Seminary of America*, ed. Jack Wertheimer, vol. 1 (New York: Jewish Theological Seminary of America, 1997), 821–54. On the Reconstructionist camp, see Jeffrey Eisenstat, "The First Reconstructionist Camp," *Contact: The Journal of Jewish Life Network* 4 (Summer 2002): 11.

59. Ramie Arian, "Jewish Camp for Adults-In-Training," *Contact: The Journal of Jewish Life Network* 5 (Summer 2003): 11. See also, Gary A. Tobin, "The Future of Jewish Camping," *Contact: The Journal of Jewish Life Network* 4 (Summer 2002): 6.

60. *Contact: The Journal of Jewish Life Network* 4 (Summer 2002), cover. Elisa Spungen Bildner, "Why I Support Jewish Camping," *Contact: The Journal of Jewish Life Network* 4 (Summer 2002): 4. For examples of how American camping programs have been exported to Israel and the Former Soviet Union, see article on the Jewish Agency for Israel Web site, "$10 Million Dollars Allocated by UJC to Summer Camps in Israel," www.jafi.org.il/iefund/news_article.asp?id=34 (July 2003), and "FSU Summer Camps Held in Three Locations" on the World Union for Progressive Judaism's Web site, www.reform.org.il/English/Contact/news.asp (September 25, 2003). The Israel Movement for Progressive Judaism reported that in 2003, 412 Israeli children attended that movement's summer camp program. See "E-mail Newsletter of the Israel Movement for Progressive Judaism," www.reform.org.il/English/Contact/news.asp (September 2003).

61. On Eliot's quote, see Sarna, "Crucial Decade of Camping," in the present text. The quote is attributed to Gerson D. Cohen, the late chancellor of the Jewish Theological Seminary (in an interview taped by Shuly Rubin Schwartz). See Joselit, "Jewish Way of Play," note 1, p. 15. On the coalescence of Jewish and American culture, see Sylvia Barack Fishman, *Jewish Life and American Culture* (Albany: State University of New York Press, 2000), and especially Fishman, *Negotiating Both Sides of the Hyphen: Coalescence, Compartmentalization, and American-Jewish Values* (Cincinnati, OH: Judaic Studies Program University of Cincinnati, 1996).

2   The Crucial Decade in Jewish Camping

Jonathan D. Sarna

Editors' Note: Jonathan D. Sarna's essay provides readers with a general over-view of Jewish camping in America, and in doing so he places the nascence of Reform Jewish camping into a larger context. Sarna reminds us that the found-ing of Union Institute in 1952 was one chapter in the overall history of Jewish educational camping in America.

Some of those who participated in the founding of the camp in Oconomowoc sensed the historical significance of their efforts. Their personal reminiscences demonstrate that the process of creating educational camps for Reform Judaism in America was both a personal and a communal achievement:

The opportunity to work on the development of a permanent camp came when the late Rabbi Eisendrath asked me to become the director of the Chicago and Midwest Federations. Mr. [Johann S.] Ackerman, one of our lay leaders, was so convinced of the value of the idea of a Jewish Reform Camp that he spent time with me to visit area sites, all of which we had to reject as unsuitable for our camp. Then we found an advertisement about Briar Lodge, a camp in Oconomowoc, Wisconsin, which was being offered for sale. We concluded rather quickly that this was the best site that we had found. The property cost us $63,000. We decided on a four-fold summer program. We declared that we would study and pray, work and play. From such simple pioneering undertakings developed rather soon the need for a permanent director. (Rabbi Herman Schaalman, June 13, 2000)

Once the property on Lac La Belle was acquired, the physical plant re-quired a lot of repair and cleaning which, along with the actual designing and construction of the first camp chapel, was largely undertaken by the rabbinic faculty and the staff. Camp life as we knew it in the early years had a very intimate feeling. The summer day revolved around the porches of the big house (Bayit), where, in between discussion groups, ping-pong games and impromptu song sessions seemed to always be going on. Tennis was played on cracked cement courts outside the Bayit. At the bottom of Bayit Hill stood a dramatic totem pole remaining from the previous occupants, out of place and yet memorable. The lake and chapel were the only other focal points of the scheduled activities. These were the modest beginnings of OSRUI. In those days, we called it Union Institute, or more informally and endearingly, simply "Oconomowoc." (Eudice G. Lorge, May 5, 2001)

As humble and unsteady as its beginnings may have been, Sarna asserts that Union Institute's founders were active participants in a new and important developmental phase of American Jewish camping.

The founding in 1952 of the first Union of American Hebrew Congregations (UAHC) camp, in Oconomowoc, Wisconsin, concluded the most portentous decade in the history of Jewish camping. Brandeis Camp Institute (1941), Camp Massad (1941), Camp Ramah in Wisconsin (1947), Camp Ramah in the Poconos (1950), and what later became known as Olin-Sang-Ruby Union Institute (1952) were all founded between 1941 and 1952, and so were a range of lesser-known but still influential camps, including Camps Aguda (1941), Avodah (1943), Yavneh (1944), Galil (1944), Lown (1946), and Sharon (1946). The decade also marked a turning point in the character of the whole Jewish camping movement. Before 1940, according to Daniel Isaacman's admittedly imprecise figures, some two-thirds of all new Jewish camps were either philanthropic, geared to the children of immigrants and the urban Jewish poor, or community-based camps founded by Jewish federations and community centers. By contrast, in the two decades following 1940 less than a quarter of all new camps fell into these categories, while almost 40 percent of them trumpeted educational and religious aims; they were sponsored either by a major Jewish religious movement, a Hebrew teachers' college, or a Hebrew cultural institution. Revealingly, fewer than 5 percent of all new Jewish camps had fallen into these categories before 1940. Indeed, until the 1940s, Hebrew-language camps (with one brief and minor exception) and the so-called denominational Jewish camps did not exist at all.[1]

Understanding the transformation that took place during the crucial decade of Jewish camping, when "intensive Jewish educational camps" developed, first requires a look back at the early history of Jewish camping in America.[2] The original Jewish summer camps were founded around the turn of the century, just at the time that the American camping movement as a whole began to develop. Although one enthusiastic writer dates the history of camping back to "the 40 year wilderness trek of the Children of Israel led by Moses,"[3] the organized camping movement as we know it usually traces its roots back to the school camp created by Frederick William Gunn and his wife in 1861. Camping spread slowly, but by the end of the nineteenth century, the first Protestant (1880) and Catholic (1892) camps commenced operations; Sumner F. Dudley started the first YMCA camp (1885); a few private camps for wealthier youngsters began, notably in New England (where Ernest Balch established his influential Camp Chocorua [New Hampshire] in 1881); the first "Fresh Air" funds designed to bring the uplifting benefits of country air to the urban and immigrant poor originated (1887); and the first family camp (1888) and girls' camp (1892) opened.[4]

The first known Jewish camps also came into existence at this time: Camp Lehman, founded in 1893 by the Jewish Working Girls' Vacation Society, on the site of what would later become Camp Isabella Freedman; and the Educational Alliance Camp, established in 1901 in Cold Springs, New York, and later incorporated as Surprise Lake Camp.[5] Thereafter, and until the Great Depression, camping developed rapidly in both the general and Jewish communities. Over one hundred summer camps of various types existed in the United States in 1910, and almost thirty-five hundred in 1933.[6] Although no parallel figures exist for Jewish camps, a *Directory of Summer Camps Under the Auspices of Jewish Communal Organizations,* published by the Jewish Welfare Board in 1936, listed eighty-eight camps in the United States and Canada, without taking account of the many privately run summer camps that American Jews had by then established.[7] Isaacman, in his study, enumerated seven varieties of Jewish camps that occupied the summers of young people before 1940, including private camps, federation-sponsored camps, Jewish community center camps, educational camps, Yiddish camps, Zionist camps, and philanthropic camps.[8] Jewish camps (like their non-Jewish counterparts) might also be divided into different class levels: (1) private camps that aimed to turn a profit and courted the well-to-do; (2) philanthropic camps that focused on immigrants, the poor, and the needy; and (3) communal and ideologically based camps, which originated later and tended to be more heterogeneous, that served those whose immigrant parents had risen into the middle class. In many ways camps thus reflected and extended the class structure already familiar to Jews from home.[9]

Several factors underlay the rapid growth of Jewish camps in the early decades of the twentieth century. For one thing, Jews, like other Americans, were swept up in "the cult of the strenuous life, whose most vigorous exemplar and prophet was Theodore Roosevelt."[10] Camping's primary goals in the early years, like those of the cult as a whole, were thoroughly antimodernist: they sought "to *restore* those values of life which come from living in the great outdoors," to "find joy in the *simplicity* of living," and to "develop a love of nature and a study of all that God created for our enjoyment."[11] Camp Kennebec, a private camp founded in Maine in 1907 by four young Philadelphia-area Jews, explicitly advocated Roosevelt's "strenuous life" goals. Jewish camping enthusiasts also believed that their programs effectively countered anti-Semitic stereotypes concerning Jewish weakness and also promoted the great goal of Americanization. Campers were thus supposed to breathe in the "pure sweet air of American mountains, lakes and forests" and to exhale any residual foreign traits. As the summer progressed, they were likewise supposed to imbibe the manners and mores of America, and to become (as one camper recalled in his old age) "stalwart, healthy American adults."[12] Even Jewish philanthropic camps, which, like their "Fresh Air" cousins, offered shorter vacations, less staff, and fewer amenities, promoted these goals. Besides restoring poor, malnourished, and ghetto-ridden Jews to renewed health and vigor, they also sought to build up the character of their charges and to do what they could to Americanize them.[13]

Initially, then, camps represented something of a counter-life for American Jews: the rural camp setting, the antimodernist values that camps championed, and the strenuous activities that filled the camp day ran counter to everything the vast majority of Jews experienced in their urban homes. Symbolically, the transition from home to camp was a move away from the workaday Jewish world and into the rural world of American gentiles. Small wonder that at most of these early camps Judaism was reduced to a whisper. For example, at Kennebec, according to its perceptive historian (herself the wife of a prominent rabbi and scholar): "The founders' policy of balancing an all Jewish enrollment with a non-Jewish staff, aimed at enriching everyone's experience, seemed to claim that religious observances, if any, should lean in the direction of neither faith. Thus the Quiet Hour (not a service) has always been held on Sunday (not Friday) night. From this has followed a tacit avoiding of anything Jewish except in the realm of humor or self-satire."[14] At Winslow, "cultivation of the child's Jewish interests and loyalties was not a paramount objective. . . . There were simple Friday evening services . . . and that was all."[15] At most Jewish Center and communal camps, as late as the 1930s, according to Isaacman, the situation was the same: they "were almost completely devoid of any meaningful Jewish programming or consciousness."[16]

To be sure, there were exceptions. Noted educator and bibliophile George Alexander Kohut, the son of Rabbi Alexander Kohut, founded Camp Kohut in Maine in 1907. According to his stepmother, he

> remembered always that he was a rabbi sworn to a special mission so far as these boys were concerned. He had to hold up to them the light that is Israel; he had to make them mindful of the dignity of the Jewish people

and the glory of the Jewish religion. In his Sabbath services conducted in a grove of apple trees, "God's temple," he frankly discussed with the boys the problems of the Jew in the modern world, the special problems of the first generation of American-born, the necessity for worshiping God and taking one's own part. He spoke to them of things that worried them, things that were generally never mentioned in their own homes.[17]

Rabbi Bernard C. Ehrenreich, ordained at the Jewish Theological Seminary and related by marriage to Rabbi Stephen S. Wise, knew Kohut and seems to have consciously followed in his footsteps. At Camp Kawaga in Wisconsin, which he founded in 1915, Ehrenreich, according to his biographer, "pursue[d] his life-long goal of bringing youth to God, of building a new and vital generation of American Jewish youth." His camp was reputedly "a laboratory for religious education," and he served as his campers' "spiritual guide."[18] Ehrenreich, Kohut, and a few other farsighted directors of private Jewish camps seem to have intuited camping's educational and religious potential long before most of their contemporaries did, although the extent of their camps' Jewishness should not be exaggerated.[19] Subsequently, during the interwar years, these pioneers were joined by professional educators—both secular and Jewish—who likewise gained new appreciation for what camping could accomplish. In turn, as we shall see, they set the stage for Jewish camping's "crucial decade."

The First Efforts at Jewish Educational Camping

Progressive educators worked out a new theory of camping during the interwar years. Focusing on camp as an educational setting, they emphasized its role in shaping the character and personality development of campers, both individually and as part of a group. "The organized summer camp is the most important step in education that America has given the world," Charles B. Eliot, former president of Harvard University, famously declared in 1922. Fear of summertime idleness and delinquency as well as anxieties concerning the fate of "latchkey children" further encouraged camping's development. In 1929 a volume titled *Camping and Character,* by Hedley S. Dimock and Charles E. Hendry (with a laudatory introduction by the renowned philosopher of education William H. Kilpatrick), brought together the central ideas of a new educational theory of camping. Based on extensive field research, it described how camps could foster the development of socially desirable ideals, attitudes, and habits.[20]

Progressive Jewish educators, notably Albert P. Schoolman, one of the worshipful disciples of the "father" of American Jewish education, Samson Benderly, had heard all of this as a student long before Dimock and Hendry's book.[21] Back in 1919 (when he was all of twenty-five years old), Schoolman began to apply these ideas at the Central Jewish Institute (CJI) that he directed.[22] Perhaps at the suggestion of his associate Leah Konovitz, CJI inaugurated a Jewish school camp, soon known as Cejwin, to overcome the problem of students' forgetting during the summer what they had learned at the institute's Talmud Torah school during the year.[23] A three-year experiment proved "auspicious," and the camp—"operated on the same standards as well-conducted private camps" and aimed at "a clientele of lower-middle-class families who send their children to the more progressive Jewish schools in the community"—then established permanent quarters near Port Jervis, New York. It became the first Jewish educational camp in the United States, and was dedicated to what its founder called "the art of Jewish living."[24]

Informal Jewish education became the hallmark of Cejwin; it promoted what Schoolman's successor described as "daily living activities and experiences . . . which fortify the knowledge, the feelings and attitudes of youth and make Jewish living worthwhile."[25] "The camp environment," Miriam Ephraim, Cejwin's assistant director, explained in 1936, "gives [Jewish boys and girls] an opportunity to socialize their knowledge, to make their information work" while also fostering "an at-homeness with their Jewish cultural background."[26] Schoolman himself at one point described the camp as an "educational paradise for the camp director," "an effective instrument for Jewish culture," and "an indispensable aid to the Jewish teacher for the education of his pupils."[27] Although after the first few years there were no formal classes at Camp Cejwin, and its standard of Hebrew fell far below what some of the more intensive Jewish camps would later demand, the camp proved highly influential. The founders of Camp Ramah, one of whom had attended Cejwin, drew directly on Schoolman's experience, and others, whether they admitted it or not, learned much from his success.[28]

The most immediate beneficiary of Cejwin's success, however, was a camp that Schoolman himself had a hand in establishing. In 1922 he and his gifted wife, Bertha, joined with two other pioneering American Jewish educator couples—Isaac and Libbie Berkson and Alexander and Julia Dushkin—to found a "private, self-paying experimental Jewish summer camp for the middle-upper-class Jewish families, which were then struggling with the Jewish education of their children."[29] Modeled on Cejwin but aimed at a different and wealthier clientele, Camp Modin in Maine advertised itself as "The Summer Camp with a Jewish Idea." "We sought to create a living synthesis of the classic Jewish traditions in home and synagogue with the new folkways of the *yishuv* [settlement] in Palestine, the American love of the outdoors and sports, with a sense of Jewish community living," Dushkin later explained. While formal Jewish education was optional at the camp, "each day periods were set aside for study." The camp also encouraged the speaking of modern Hebrew and the singing of modern Hebrew songs.[30]

Three features of Camp Modin are especially significant for historians of Jewish camping. First, the Schoolmans, Dushkins, and Berksons established Modin with the conscious aim of becoming financially independent; "it would be psychologically important for us as community workers, struggling for our ideas with and against communal *baale batim* [community leaders], to have independent financial income." The plan succeeded, and Dushkin reveals that he was later able to accept positions at the Hebrew University "at salaries below subsistence level," because he had this additional source of income.[31] In fact, economics played a role in all of Jewish camping, and private camps, when properly managed, proved to be very good businesses indeed. For example, one of the first private camps in Maine, Tripp Lake Camp for Girls, founded at the turn of the century by two sisters of Rebekah Kohut (Cyd and Eva Bettelheim), yielded a "splendid livelihood," according to Rebekah's recollections. George Alexander Kohut's Camp Kohut was likewise successful, she reports, and brought him "financial security."[32] The profit motive also helps to explain why the educational component of Jewish camping developed so slowly. Owner-investors feared that if camp were too much like school, then campers would not want to return, and their investment would be lost.[33] The success of Camps Modin and Cejwin demonstrated that this fear was exaggerated, but as we shall see, it was not totally groundless.

Second, women played a highly important role in running Camp Modin. According to Alexander Dushkin, "the three ladies, Libbie Berkson, Bertha Schoolman, and Julia Dushkin, were responsible at various times for the Girls' Camp and for 'opening and closing the camps.'"[34] Subsequently, Mrs. Berkson essentially ran the camp. Women played central roles at other camps too, especially, of course, at girls' camps, as the early example of Tripp Lake Camp and the charity camps of the Jewish Board of Guardians demonstrate. In 1916 two Jewish Sunday School teachers, Carrie Kuhn and Estelle Goldsmith, founded Camp Woodmere.[35] Later, during the "crucial decade" of Jewish educational camps, Rivka Shulsinger worked closely with her husband at Massad, Leah Konovitz Hurwich oversaw day-to-day operations at Camp Yavneh, and in 1947 Sylvia Ettenberg played a pioneering role in the founding of Camp Ramah. "Throughout the century," historian Nancy Mykoff observes, "Jewish women justified their camping activities in terms of extending their child-rearing duties to a more public sphere. This enabled them to journey to summer camp without crossing traditional gender boundaries. . . . But women's less traditional camping activities suggest that they challenged as well as confirmed contemporary ideas about male and female behavior." Through camps like Modin, they helped to transform "pieces of the 'great outdoors' into prototypes of the American home."[36]

Finally, Camp Modin prided itself on being a pluralistic Jewish camp. Although Dushkin subsequently described it as "religiously Conservative with leanings toward Liberal Reconstruction," it attracted youngsters of various religious backgrounds, including, Dushkin proudly reports, the children of such Orthodox leaders as Rabbis Meir Berlin and Leo Jung.[37] Into the 1950s many Jewish camps, like their counterparts the Jewish community schools, believed they could simultaneously meet the religious needs of a wide range of Jews by maintaining a "traditional" Jewish environment, complete with kosher food and Sabbath observance, but without strict allegiance to any particular religious movement. In the early years of Camp Massad, for example, Shimon Frost reports that the camp was the very "embodiment of the idea of *klal yisrael* [community of Israel; the reference for the totality of the Jewish people]. Children from Orthodox Zionist homes and children from the socio-cultural elite of Conservative and Reform Judaism lived together with children from secular Zionist homes. The cement that unified them all was Hebrew and Zionism."[38] Camp Yavneh in New Hampshire, an offshoot of the Boston Hebrew Teachers College, similarly sought to attract children from a range of religious backgrounds; in its case, the unifying cement was a shared commitment to Hebrew and Jewish study. This tradition of pluralism within Jewish camping, hearkening back to the idea that the community rather than the synagogue should oversee Jewish education, assumed that culture (and especially the Hebrew language) unified Jews, even as religion divided them. The ideology helps to explain the relatively late development of denominational Jewish camps, like those of the Conservative and Reform movements. They faced opposition from those who charged that they "fragment the Jewish community away from the ideal of *Klal Yisrael.*"[39]

Even as Camps Modin and Cejwin proved successful, the third prewar attempt at creating a Jewish educational camp failed. Camp Achvah, founded in 1927 by the "father" of modern Jewish education in America, Samson Benderly, was initially the summertime portion of an ambitious year-round program in leadership training. Called by the name *kvutzah* (cooperative group), and presumably influenced by the cooperative ideals of the Israeli kibbutz, it involved during the course of its existence a total of fifty outstanding New York Hebrew high school students whom Benderly sought to train for careers in Jewish educational leadership.[40] Those who were chosen—on the basis of scholarship, leadership potential, and personality—studied year-round both independently and in classes and then came together in summer for what became, in 1928, a full-scale study camp, conducted entirely in Hebrew. Like so many of Benderly's educational ventures, this small, elitist camp, conducted on a democratic basis without formal counselors, was far ahead of its time. Two participants in the program discovered years later that it had been remarkably successful: a third of their fellow campers went on to careers in Jewish communal life, and over half claimed to be very active in Jewish organizations.[41] But, probably for economic reasons, the *kvutzah* experiment ended after the summer of

1932; it was a casualty of the Great Depression. Camp Achvah itself labored on, filling a one-hundred-acre estate in Godeffroy, New York, that Benderly had purchased in the hope of furthering his vision of what a Jewish educational summer camp could accomplish. In its reorganized state, operating as a commercial enterprise, Achvah, like Cejwin and Modin, came to focus on informal Jewish education, with an emphasis on singing, dancing, and pageantry, as well as on impressive Sabbath celebrations and a memorable commemoration of *Tisha B'Av* (the Fast of the Ninth of Av). Even so, according to Alexander Dushkin, by 1941 the camp was deeply in debt—so much so that the fiasco nearly cost Benderly his pension. The experience serves as a reminder that the success of Jewish educational camping was by no means a forgone conclusion.[42]

Many of the underlying ideas and activities later associated with Jewish educational camping took shape at Camps Cejwin, Modin, and Achvah. Yet, during the interwar years, Jewish educational camping remained a small and high-risk venture. Educators, both general and Jewish alike, recognized camping's vast cultural and educative potential. The "total environment" of the summer camp, they understood, offered what one historian calls "an unparalleled venue for the transmission of values."[43] Meanwhile, Yiddishists, Zionists, and others demonstrated how camps could shape the "total environment" available to them to offer campers a taste of utopia, a seemingly realizable vision of an alternative communist, socialist, or Zionist way of life, complete with some educational content.[44] Still, camping remained out of reach for most American Jews, particularly in the dark days of the Depression, and most of those camps that did attract Jews promoted recreation and Americanization above all other goals. It was only afterward, between 1941 and 1952, in what we have dubbed the "crucial decade," that the core of camping's educational potential would more fully be realized, and Jewish educational camping finally took off.

The Crucial Decade for the Growth of Jewish Educational Camping

The large-scale emergence of Jewish educational camping, including the founding of Union Institute, forms part of a dramatic expansion in all aspects of American Jewish education that began in the late 1930s. In 1937 three significant Orthodox Jewish day schools were founded: HILI (Hebrew Institute of Long Island), Ramaz School in Manhattan, and Maimonides School in Boston. In the ten years between 1940 and 1950, ninety-seven different Jewish day schools were founded across the United States and Canada (as compared to twenty-eight that had been founded in the previous twenty-two years).[45] During the same period, adult Jewish education also experienced enormous growth. The Conservative movement's National Academy for Adult Jewish

Studies was founded in 1940, and according to Israel Goldman's survey, the adult Jewish education movement as a whole in America "began to emerge and develop." The Department of Continuing Education of the Union of American Hebrew Congregations was founded in 1948, the same year that B'nai B'rith began its adult Institutes of Judaism.[46] The Jewish Publication Society, which promoted Jewish education and culture through books rather than classroom instruction, also roared back to life with the waning of the Depression. Its total income increased fivefold between 1935 and 1945, and the number of books it distributed tripled.[47] Other publishers of Judaica, including university presses, experienced similar increases in Jewish book sales.[48] Finally, Jewish organizational life as a whole surged during this period. In 1945 the *American Jewish Year Book* reported that "a larger number of new organizations . . . formed during the past five years than in any previous five-year period, forty-seven new organizations having been established since 1940." "Interest in Jewish affairs," it explained, "has undoubtedly been heightened as a result of the catastrophe which befell the Jews of Europe under the Nazi onslaught."[49]

The Holocaust, the waning of the Depression, and the explosive rise during the interwar years of domestic anti-Semitism all undoubtedly influenced the "increased community interest and support for Jewish education" that so many contemporaries noticed.[50] Jewish education represented both a defensive response to adversity and a form of cultural resistance, a resolve to maintain Judaism in the face of opposition and danger. It also promised to prepare the community for the new responsibilities that it faced in the wake of the European Jewish catastrophe. "American Jews," the *American Jewish Year Book* reported as early as 1941, "are realizing that they have been spared for a sacred task—to preserve Judaism and its cultural, social and moral values." That same year, Hebrew Union College historian Jacob Rader Marcus, who would soon shift the central focus of his own scholarship from Europe to America, also pointed to the American Jewish community's new historic role: "The burden is solely ours to carry," he declared. "Jewish culture and civilization and leadership are shifting rapidly to these shores."[51] The arrival of learned Jewish refugees from Europe underscored the significance of the "cultural transfer" that was taking place between the old world and the new. At the same time, America generally was placing new emphasis on education. Federal aid during the Depression brought about a "remarkable improvement" in general education, especially within the public schools. Catholic parochial schools also experienced significant growth during these years—a development, as the historian of one Jewish day school notes, that "invited imitation in the Jewish sphere."[52]

The growth of Jewish camping followed directly on the heels of all of these developments. Perhaps unsurprisingly, formal and informal Jewish education expanded at roughly the same time and for many of the same reasons. Yet Jewish educational camping also benefited from three additional factors peculiar to the 1940s era. First, camps came to serve an important childcare function. With fathers away at war and mothers working, overnight camps offered worried parents the security of knowing that their children were in a safe and protected environment. Second, land was still relatively cheap at this time, and summer camps sold for much less than they had cost to build. Many camps had never recovered from the hard times of the Depression; others could not find adequate male staff during the war years and closed down. The founders of Camp Yavneh in Northwood, New Hampshire, particularly benefited from this buyers' market: they purchased a sixty-acre camp site in 1943 that met all of their requirements and cost a mere $18,000. "The owner had to sell it," Louis Hurwich recalled, "because war conditions made it impossible to find counselors and suitable help."[53] Shlomo Shulsinger, the founder of Camp Massad, similarly recalled how "many camps were for sale at good prices" in the early 1940s, since "many camp directors had been drafted, and those who hadn't couldn't keep up their camps for lack of manpower and food supplies."[54] A decade later the market had improved and Union Institute in Oconomowoc, Wisconsin, cost more—$63,000.[55] But given the rapidly rising cost of land, it too proved to be an excellent investment. Finally, all Jewish educational camps enjoyed a special (and rarely mentioned) advantage during eras of conscription. Many of their best male staff members were rabbinical students, who were exempt from the draft. This gave them a distinct staffing advantage over other camps that had trouble, during wartime, finding sufficient male staff for their operation.[56]

Against this background, Jewish educational camping came into its own during the "crucial decade." Indeed, the slew of remarkable and influential camps that were founded between 1941 and 1952 changed the face of Jewish camping and transformed camps into important components of Jewish educational and religious life. Educators recognized this at the time. "Not long ago the summer was considered a complete liability to Jewish Education," the editor and educator Azriel Eisenberg admitted in a June 1946 lead editorial introducing a special issue of *Jewish Education* devoted to summer camping. Comparing the summer to the Psalmist's "stone that the builders rejected," he predicted that, thanks to the advent of Jewish educational camps, the summer might in time "become the cornerstone in the future structure of American Jewish education."[57]

Brandeis Camp Institute (BCI), which opened in 1941 in Amherst, New Hampshire, embodied many of the strengths of this new "cornerstone." It began, much as Union Institute did, as an experimental summer leadership-training program. Founded by the charismatic Columbia Teachers College–trained Jewish educator Shlomo Bardin, then-director of the American Zionist Youth Commission, it evolved into a Los Angeles–based program for college-aged young adults (more than twice as many of them women than men) that combined recreation with experiential learning and placed a heavy emphasis on drama, music, and the celebration of Shabbat—"a distinctive form of Shabbat," historian Deborah Dash Moore observes, "that provided meaning, community and religious experience." Moore characterizes the BCI experience as "a form of spiritual recreation" and suggests that its real goals were "to inspire Jews to be Jews, to link them with Jewish peoplehood, to whet their appetite for more learning, and to encourage them to bring up their children as Jews."[58] These, of course, were precisely the goals that all of the Jewish educational summer camps espoused, however much their strategies for accomplishing these goals differed. Bardin especially emphasized the *transformative* power of camp, which is why (like the more recent Birthright Israel program) he focused on college students. In 1946 he published the following testimonial from a student at the University of Southern California, which, in his words, provided "a pertinent summary of the [camp's] imponderable values . . . in shaping Jewish personality." The testimonial (minus one or two details) might have been echoed by attendees or alumni of any one of the intensive Jewish educational camps established over the ensuing decades. Its message attesting to the transformative power of camp helps to explain why camping was so quickly and passionately embraced by innovative leaders within Conservative and Reform Judaism: "When I arrived at the Institute, I felt no particular attachment to the Jewish people. On leaving, however, I took much away with me. Pride in Jewishness; a desire to preserve the continuity of a brave people; a sense of belongingness in a well-defined group; a desire to create, as a Jew among Jews; a joy through my identification with a worthy cause—the establishment of a Jewish National Home in Palestine. All this is making life more meaningful. Youth all over the United States are crying for this. How I wish they could all share my experience."[59]

Similar testimonials emerged from the other significant Jewish educational camp that dates its origins to 1941: Shlomo Shulsinger's Camp Massad. Massad, which began as a day camp and became an overnight camp in 1942, was the first Jewish educational camp to place the Hebrew language at its core. When he was in his late twenties, Shulsinger, who was born in Jerusalem, recalled being part of a group that was "absolutely fanatic about Hebrew language and culture . . . as a basis for Jewish life." The camp's name, from the Hebrew word meaning "foundation," was inspired by a line from a poem by Hayim Nahman Bialik ("If you have not built the rafters but only the *massad* [foundation], be content, my brothers, your toil is not in vain"), and was supposed to symbolize the idea "that Hebrew camping would be the foundation for Hebrew education—and through it, for Jewish life."[60] Indeed, the camp sought "to give the Jewish child, during the months of summer vacation, a living and creative Hebrew environment,"[61] one that *molded* children from a young age, rather than *transforming* them in college. Thus, unlike BCI and Achvah, Massad did not focus chiefly on leadership development. Nor did it offer formal classes. Instead, it sought to create what Shulsinger described as "a little Hebrew world," a kind of Hebrew utopia that was at once staunchly American in its activities and celebrations, profoundly Zionist in outlook, "positive" toward Jewish religious traditions, and fanatical (especially in the early years) about the Hebrew language.[62] Given its Hebrew emphasis, the camp proved especially attractive to Jewish day school students; they formed its primary clientele. The camp's influence, however, extended far more broadly. "Over the years," Walter Ackerman has observed, "Massad set the standards by which all other Hebrew speaking camps were judged."[63] It also attracted a number of future Reform rabbis, including Balfour Brickner, who served on its staff as a lifeguard.[64] Although Massad does not seem to have directly influenced the founding of Union Institute, its rapid growth attracted notice from all Jewish educators. Its impressive rise from 47 campers in 1942 to 210 in 1945, and from over 600 campers in 1956 to over 900 in 1966, demonstrated that full-scale intensive Jewish educational camps could succeed both culturally and commercially.[65]

Both Massad and BCI were initially established by Jewish organizations (the Histadrut Ivrit and the American Zionist Organization) to further broad ideological aims: Hebraism and Zionism. By the 1946 special issue of *Jewish Education* devoted to summer camping, however, it was already clear that more limited, locally based Jewish educational camps were also starting up. In 1944, for example, the Boston Hebrew College established Camp Yavneh as an extension of its supplementary educational program. Not only was the camp committed to Hebrew (though not quite as single-mindedly as Massad), but it also featured ten to fifteen hours a week of formal classes—complete with tests. One former director recalls that "it was not at all uncommon for youngsters to awake at five in the morning, or earlier, to prepare."[66] The same year witnessed the founding in Cleveland of Camp Galil, an educational camp established by the director of that city's Bureau of Jewish Education. A year later, Chicago's College of Jewish Studies, in cooperation with the Chicago Bureau of Jewish Education, inaugurated plans for Sharon Camp, a small "summer camp institute" of "intensive Jewish studies" for college-aged students who were interested in becoming Jewish educators. This was the second camp that Chicago Jewish educators founded in the "crucial decade" of Jewish educational camping; the first, Camp Avodah (1943), had combined farmwork and Jewish living.[67] While neither of these camps were particularly significant, they helped to build local community support for the institution of Jewish camping. The next two ventures in Jewish educational camping that began in Chicago—Ramah and Union Institute—would change the face of Jewish educational camping forever.

The Advent of Educational Camping in the Reform
and Conservative Movements

Both Camp Ramah and Union Institute developed from the same concern for safeguarding America's Jewish future that animated the educational revival of the late 1930s and 1940s. Reform and Conservative Jews alike developed significant new youth groups at this time: the National Federation of Temple Youth (NFTY) in 1939 and Leaders Training Fellowship (LTF) in 1945. The former, originally focused on young adults in their early twenties, proved an immediate success and subsequently expanded its coverage to embrace teenagers.[68] The latter, established as part of the Jewish Theological Seminary's "Ten Year Plan to Reclaim Jewish Youth to Religious and Ethical Life," was much more elitist than NFTY; it aimed "to identify and cultivate the best young people within Conservative synagogues and lead them into Jewish public service."[69] Both organizations looked upon camping—a total immersion program in Judaism—as a central component of their program, and both entered the camping field in 1947.

Camp Ramah in Wisconsin, which opened in 1947, was by far the more ambitious of these undertakings. It also represented the first significant foray into intensive educational camping by an American Jewish religious movement. Earlier camps, as we have seen, were established by institutions (like the Central Jewish Institute), movements (Hebraism, Zionism), or individuals (Dushkin, Benderly). They professed to be Jewishly pluralistic, embodying the *klal yisrael* ideal. Camp Ramah, by contrast, was founded by and for the Conservative movement. Those who established it, concludes Shuly Rubin Schwartz in her history of the camp's early years, "saw camping as one vehicle to further the goals of the Conservative movement as a whole." Along with LTF, which was overseen by the same people who were in charge of Camp Ramah, these youth-oriented institutions aimed to create an indigenous Conservative leadership—both lay and rabbinic—that would perpetuate the movement into the next generation.[70]

Camp Massad, Schwartz shows, "had a profound effect on the development of Ramah on all its levels." Yet even as it emulated Massad, Camp Ramah also deviated from it in significant ways, partly because most of its campers were less well-equipped for a Hebrew-speaking camp—they attended supplementary afternoon Hebrew schools rather than Jewish day schools—and partly because Ramah's program responded to many of the criticisms leveled at Camp Massad: that it was too authoritarian, too Zionist, too focused on Hebrew, and somewhat hypocritical in its approach to religious practices. Many of Ramah's founders, Schwartz suggests, "constructively channeled their discontent with Massad by founding and working in Ramah." They also sought to adapt the Massad model to suit the needs of the Conservative movement.[71]

While the central ideas and educational philosophy underlying Camp Ramah took shape at the Jewish Theological Seminary in New York, where LTF was also housed, the camp itself opened in Wisconsin, thanks to the tireless efforts of Chicago-area Conservative rabbis and lay leaders, notably Rabbi Ralph Simon and Reuben Kaufman, chair of the Chicago Council of Conservative Synagogues. Simon, whose own children had attended Camp Massad, was reputedly "the pivotal figure who introduced the idea of such a camp to the Chicago area and then closely supervised its development."[72] Local lay leaders of the Conservative movement, responding to the widespread call to intensify educational programming for Jewish youth, endorsed the idea and agreed to support the camp, with the following significant stipulation: "This camp will be for children of parents affiliated with a Conservative Congregation and will be sponsored by the Council only; that is not in connection with the Board of Jewish Education."[73] Camp Ramah thus represented a declaration of independence on the part of local area Conservative Jewish leaders. They pointedly broke with the prewar pattern of pluralism in Jewish education overseen by a community-wide (if somewhat Orthodox leaning) Board of Jewish Education. Instead, they insisted that their new camp, like a growing number of their suburban synagogue schools, would now be avowedly Conservative—both in its philosophy and in its constituency.[74] The Reform Jewish camping movement, in time, followed much the same course.

In three other ways too, the new Conservative camp distinguished itself from its predecessors in Jewish educational camping, but, revealingly, in these cases the Reform movement camps did not subsequently follow its lead; instead, all three features remained unique to Ramah. First, Camp Ramah was directly overseen by the Jewish Theological Seminary, the training ground of the Conservative movement, rather than by its synagogue movement, the United Synagogue of America. The seminary's Teachers Institute assumed responsibility for the educational supervision of the camp (it also supervised LTF), and before long the seminary assumed financial responsibility for Ramah as well. Camp Ramah thus operated on the top-down model historically preferred by the Conservative movement: the seminary ruled. Second, Camp Ramah believed in formal study for *everybody*. The staff too was supposed to regularly attend classes in camp. The aim was to underscore the idea that for young and old alike, "living a full Jewish life meant studying every day"— nobody was exempt.[75] Finally, every Ramah camp had a professor-in-residence, most often from the Jewish Theological Seminary. "Originally," according to Michael Brown, "the professor had no formal duties but was to serve as a role model for campers and staff 'of a Jew who continues to study.' He would also act as 'a buddy of the director in times of crisis.' Over the years, the professor came to be the guarantor at Ramah 'of the principles of Conservative Judaism.' . . . The professor became the representative and the symbol of the Seminary in camp."[76]

By the early 1950s Ramah was a movement. A (short-lived) Ramah in Maine had opened in 1948. A (still-flourishing) Ramah in the Poconos opened in 1950. And more camps were in the planning stages. Camping had become one of the most successful of all of the Conservative movement's postwar initiatives.

Reform Jewish camping, meanwhile, was developing in a quite different direction. Beginning in 1947, and probably at the instigation of the new and highly creative director of the youth department at the Union of American Hebrew Congregations, Rabbi Samuel Cook,[77] NFTY initiated a series of short conclaves and Leadership Institutes that it held at various camp sites (Camp Henry Horner in Painesville, Ohio; at Camp Lake of the Woods in Decatur, Michigan; etc.). The program of the 1948 Leadership Institute featured "classes," "services," and "study" in addition to "sports," "dramatics," "campfires," "dancing," and "fellowship," and it aimed to "create a strengthened movement for Reform Judaism." The program was described as a "huge success," and Rabbi Ernst M. Lorge, one of those who directed the program, expressed the conviction "that conclaves and other camping programs are essential to Jewish education."[78]

Lorge was no stranger to Jewish camping. He and Rabbi Herman Schaalman, then-director of the Chicago Federation of the Union of American Hebrew Congregations, along with several other German-born Reform rabbis, had experienced Jewish camping in Germany, where, according to Lorge, it had an "incredible effect . . . on Jewish education and living."[79] Rabbi Alfred Wolf, who played a central role in the establishment of Camp Hess Kramer (1952) and other Reform Jewish camps that operated under the auspices of Wilshire Boulevard Temple in Los Angeles, similarly credited his German experience with stimulating his interest in camp: "You might say that Camp Hess Kramer began when, in my teens, I was called upon to organize Jewish youth groups in Heidelberg, in a Germany just shaken to its roots by the Nazi take-over. It was then that I realized how much of Jewish values I could get across to young people as we were hiking or camping together under the open sky."[80] These rabbis subsequently witnessed the impact of both Jewish and Christian camping in America, and their resolve to create a movement of Reform Jewish camping was reinforced. But though the German experience was an important underlying factor in the development of Reform Jewish camping, it was not (as some claim) determinative. As early as 1946, the American-born Sam Cook had attempted, unsuccessfully, to acquire a permanent camp site for the Reform movement.[81] That same year, Rabbi Joseph L. Baron of Milwaukee (born in Vilna), who thought he had actually found a camp donor, described in a letter, "how anxious we have all been to develop a stimulating religious educational program for our youth during the summer months, how particularly important such a program is in this post-war era, and how much the success and growth of our summer activities depend on a suitable site in the country."[82] In the immediate postwar years, the development of a Reform Jewish camp was thus on the agenda of a wide range of Reform Jewish leaders, natives and immigrants alike. In the end, though, no project made real headway until 1951, and then the project took shape at the local level, spearheaded by rabbis and lay leaders in Chicago.

On March 29, 1951, the UAHC Chicago Federation, headed by Rabbi Schaalman, unanimously approved "the project of building a camp for our youth." The Chicago lay leader who headed up the project, Johann S. Ackerman, knew that the national body was already "exploring the field for a camp" so that NFTY conclaves would not continually have to wander, but he argued that "the Chicago Federation does not need to wait, it could be first." The example of Camp Ramah, which had so recently been purchased for the seminary by Conservative Jewish lay people in Chicago, was presumably a factor here, but the minutes are (probably purposefully) vague.[83] They disclose only that "Rabbi Lorge explained other camp programs for Jewish youth in which he had participated" and that Rabbi Arnold Wolf "explained that other Jewish camps combined study and sports." Whatever the case, the meeting was a resounding success, "with all present enthusiastically endorsing the project."[84] The executive board of the UAHC agreed, and by July 1951 an appropriate site had been identified for possible purchase: a private Jewish camp known as Briar Lodge in Oconomowoc, Wisconsin. The details of the purchase and the proposed use of the camp had been ironed out by November, and what UAHC president Maurice Eisendrath enthusiastically described as "the first 'Union Institute of the U.A.H.C.' ever to be officially and actually established" was announced to Midwestern area rabbis on February 26, 1952. It was to be known, simply, as Union Institute.[85]

The new camp differed markedly from Ramah, Massad, and in fact from all of the other Jewish educational camps that had been established in the "crucial decade" of Jewish camping. First of all, Hebrew played little role in the camp. There was no Hebrew in the camp's name and hardly any Hebrew in its curriculum; and, for that matter, there was no emphasis on Zionism at first.[86]

Second, most campers attended the camp for two weeks or less. In the initial year, there were "2 two-week Institutes . . . primarily for young people from Chicago and the Midwest," a one-week Adult Institute, two ten-day Leadership Institutes sponsored by NFTY, and a three-day Labor Day Conclave of the Chicago Federation of Temple Youth. Some 442 people participated in camp activities during that first year, but none of them devoted their full summer to Jewish living and learning.[87] This same pattern of short "institutes" rather than a full summer of "immersion" became a feature of Union Institute. Its program, like Reform Jewish education as a whole, was essentially supplementary; it left a great many summer weeks open for secular pursuits.

Third, Union Institute served a different age range than the other camps;

the bulk of its campers were teenagers or adults. An "experimental one-week's session for 11 and 12-year-olds" was only initiated in 1954 (later in the 1950s, a "junior session" was created for children aged 9 to 11).[88] Like Brandeis Camp Institute, which, as we have seen, focused on the college-aged, Union Institute initially sought to *transform* its campers. Massad and Ramah, by contrast, sought to *mold* them.

Fourth, more than at any other Jewish camp, Union Institute emphasized direct contact with rabbis as a central feature of its program. Visiting rabbis were treated as celebrities, akin to the "professor-in-residence" at Camp Ramah. They taught the ninety-minute study sessions, led regular "bull sessions" with participants, and were the camps' dominant personalities. Each summer more rabbis offered to come to Union Institute, some of them sacrificing a portion of their vacations in order to do so. Union Institute thus promoted closer relations between rabbis and young Reform Jews. Over time, it also stimulated many young people to enter the rabbinate.[89]

Finally, and perhaps as a consequence of the deep rabbinic involvement in the program, Union Institute placed a much heavier emphasis than any other Jewish educational camp on promoting spirituality. Indeed, during the opening summer of 1952, religious activities were described in a report to the board as "probably the most successful single facet" of the camp. In addition to regular morning and evening prayers, which were "creatively developed by a committee of young people," there were "cabin prayers at night, and a recitation of prayers before and after each meal." "Very frequently," according to this same report, "a genuine mood of religious devotion was generated at these occasions, and many of the participants were deeply moved by them."[90] Later these creative services and the whole informal mode of camp worship would have a major impact on the Reform movement as a whole.

Within a few years, Union Institute, like Ramah, became a full-scale camping movement. Camp Saratoga (later Swig) opened in California, and three more camps opened by 1958, all of them guided by the Youth Division of the Union of American Hebrew Congregations. Unlike the Ramah camps, however, which were centrally directed from New York, the Union camps operated under a considerable degree of local autonomy.[91] Just as individual congregations enjoyed a great deal of latitude under the UAHC structure, so too did the individual camps. In this respect, as in so many others, the camps reflected the character of the movement that sponsored them.

The Lasting Influence of Educational Jewish Camping

The establishment of Union Institute rang down the curtain on the most creative and influential decade in the whole history of the American Jewish camping movement. Between the early 1940s and the early 1950s a wide range of exciting and innovative camps opened their doors, including, as we have seen, Brandeis Camp Institute, Camp Massad, Camp Ramah, and Union Institute. This unprecedented proliferation of Jewish educational camps reflected critical developments taking place within the larger American Jewish community, notably, (1) a dramatic expansion in all aspects of American Jewish education, (2) a new focus on young people and their leadership training, and (3) a perceptible shift over time from the "ideological" emphases of the early 1940s, seen in the Zionist, Yiddishist, and Hebraist camps, to the "denominational" identities of the 1950s, when Ramah and the Union camps expanded. Beyond merely reflecting critical developments, however, the new camps also came to have a shaping influence upon them. A whole generation of young, impressionable American Jews came under the spell of these camps—some young people were "molded" by them, others "transformed"—and from their ranks the next generation of rabbis, scholars, and lay leaders emerged. This was the return on the crucial decade's investment in Jewish educational camping, and during the second half of the twentieth century the investment continued to pay rich dividends across the spectrum of American Jewish life.

Notes

1. Recalculated from figures in Daniel Isaacman, *Jewish Summer Camps in the United States and Canada, 1900–1969* (Philadelphia, PA: Dropsie University, 1970), 118. For a critique of Isaacman's methodology and biases, see Baila Round Shargel, "The Literature of Ramah," *Conservative Judaism* 40 (Fall 1987): 56–57.

2. The term "intensive Jewish educational camp" is borrowed from Burton Cohen; see his "The Jewish Educational Summer Camp," in *Judaism and Education: Essays in Honor of Walter I. Ackerman*, ed. Hayim Marantz (Beer Sheva: Ben Gurion University, 1998), 245–52.

3. Eugene A. Turner Jr., *100 Years of YMCA Camping* (Chicago: YMCA, 1985), 25.

4. The standard "History of Organized Camping" was published by Henry William Gibson in various issues of *Camping* magazine, beginning in 1936, which, conveniently, have now been brought together on microfilm. See also Frank L. Irwin, *The Theory of Camping* (New York: A. S. Barnes, 1950), 3–7, and Daniel Cohen, "Outdoor Sojourn: A Brief History of Summer Camp in the United States," in *A Worthy Use of Summer: Jewish Summer Camping in America*, ed. Jenna Weissman Joselit and Karen S. Mittelman (Philadelphia: National Museum of American Jewish History, 1993), 10–13.

5. For the history of Jewish camping, see especially Daniel Isaacman, "The Development of Jewish Camping in the United States," *Gratz College Annual of Jewish Studies* 5 (1976): 111–20, and Shimon Frost, "Milestones in the Development of Hebrew Camping in North America: An Historical Overview" (in Hebrew with English summary),

in *Kovetz Massad*, vol. 2, *Hebrew Camping in North America*, ed. Shlomo Shulsinger-Shear Yashuv with Rivka Shulsinger-Shear Yashuv (Jerusalem: Alumni of Massad Camps, 1989), 17–79.

6. Gibson, "History of Organized Camping," presents these figures in his fourth chapter (unpaginated.)

7. *1936 Directory of Summer Camps Under the Auspices of Jewish Communal Organizations* (New York: Jewish Welfare Board, 1936); Isaacman, *Jewish Summer Camps*, surveyed only half as many camps from this period (see p. 118).

8. Isaacman, *Jewish Summer Camps*, 118.

9. Jenna Joselit argues that "Unlike other youth-oriented institutions like the Boy Scouts or the YMCA which offered an alternative, competing perspective, Jewish summer camp co-existed amicably with the same social sphere as the Jewish home and the afternoon school. Far from supplanting or vying with domestic and communal values, it sought instead to extend and deepen them." While this may exaggerate both the subversive nature of the scouting and YMCA movements, and the social conformity of Jewish camps, the hypothesis warrants investigation. See Jenna Weissman Joselit, "The Jewish Way of Play," in Joselit and Mittelman, *Worthy Use of Summer*.

10. Jackson Lears, *No Place of Grace: Antimodernism and the Transformation of American Culture, 1880–1920* (New York: Pantheon, 1981).

11. Gibson, "History of Organized Camping," unpaginated (italics added). There is, of course, a parallel here to the European youth movements of the time that similarly extolled the countryside over the city and promoted the value of communing with nature. The *Judischer Wanderbund Blau-Weiss* (Jewish Hikers Association Blue and White), founded in 1912, reflected this same back-to-nature ideology; see Steven Lowenstein in *German-Jewish History in Modern Times*, ed. Michael A. Meyer (New York: Columbia University Press, 1997), vol. 3, 148.

12. David Lyon Hurwitz, "How Lucky We Were," *American Jewish History* 87 (March 1999), esp. 34, 42.

13. Frances Fox Sandmel, *The History of Camp Kennebec* (North Belgrade, ME: n.p., 1973), 1; Herman D. Stein, "Jewish Social Work in the United States, 1654–1954," *American Jewish Year Book* 57 (1956): 74; Charles S. Bernheimer, "Camps as Character Builders," in *Half a Century in Community Service* (New York: Association Press, 1948), 112–16. For a famously critical portrait of the "vacations" offered to immigrants by Jewish charities, see Anzia Yezierska, "The Free Vacation House," in *Hungry Hearts and Other Stories* (1920; New York: Persea Press, 1985), 97–113.

14. Sandmel, *History of Camp Kennebec*, 17–18.

15. Hurwitz, "How Lucky We Were," 39.

16. Isaacman, *Jewish Summer Camps*, 133.

17. Rebekah Kohut, *His Father's House: The Story of George Alexander Kohut* (New Haven, CT: Yale University Press, 1938), 113. Rebekah was Kohut's stepmother.

18. Byron L. Sherwin, "Portrait of a Romantic Rebel, Bernard C. Ehrenreich (1876–1955)," in *Turn to the South*, ed. Nathan M. Kaganoff and Melvin I. Urofsky (Charlottes-

ville: University of Virginia Press, 1979), 10–11; Harold S. Wechsler, "Rabbi Bernard C. Ehrenreich: A Northern Progressive Goes South," in *Jews of the South*, ed. Samuel Proctor, et al. (Macon, GA: Mercer University Press, 1984), 62.

19. Albert P. Schoolman, writing in 1946, recalled that even "the very best Jewish camps" in 1920, even if they "served kosher food, had a Friday evening service and a 'Shabbat' meal with 'Kiddush,'" failed to observe the Sabbath thereafter. "Saturday, in preparation for Sunday visiting, became clean-up day for the camp." *Jewish Education* 17 (June 1946): 7.

20. Turner, *100 Years of YMCA Camping*, 46–50; Irwin, *Theory of Camping*, provides a later summary of educational theory concerning camping.

21. Alexander M. Dushkin, "A. P. Schoolman: The Story of a Blessed Life," *Jewish Education* 36 (Winter 1966): 72; see also the references to progressive educators in Alfred P. Schoolman, "Jewish Educational Camping: Its Potentialities and Realities," ibid., 77–86.

22. On the Central Jewish Institute, see David Kaufman, *Shul with a Pool: The "Synagogue-Center" in American Jewish History* (Hanover, NH: Brandeis University Press, 1999), 153–59.

23. The claim is made by her subsequent husband, Louis Hurwich; see his *Memoirs of a Jewish Educator,* trans. and ed. Aaron Darsa (Boston: Bureau of Jewish Education of Greater Boston, 1999), 233; Schoolman himself credits the "Women's Auxiliary" of CJI for the camp's beginning in his "The Jewish Educational Summer Camp: A Survey of Its Development and Implications," *Jewish Education* 17 (June 1946): 9.

24. In 1913 Samson Benderly briefly experimented with extension courses in religion and history for young people who spent summers with their parents in Arverne, Long Island, but his biographer's claim that he thereby "founded" Jewish educational camping is baseless. See Nathan H. Winter, *Jewish Education in a Pluralist Society: Samson Benderly and Jewish Education in the United States* (New York: New York University Press, 1966), 81, 185.

25. Abraham P. Gannes, "Camp—A Children's Community," *Jewish Education* 36 (Winter 1966): 91.

26. Quoted in Joselit, "Jewish Way of Play," 26.

27. Schoolman, "Jewish Educational Summer Camp," 12.

28. Shuly Rubin Schwartz, "Camp Ramah: The Early Years, 1947–1952," *Conservative Judaism* 40 (Fall 1987): 17; Dushkin, "A. P. Schoolman," 74. For Schoolman's influence on Massad, see *Massad Reminiscences* (Jerusalem: Abraham Harman Institute of Contemporary Jewry, 1996), 6–7, 11–12.

29. Alexander M. Dushkin, *Living Bridges: Memoirs of an Educator* (Jerusalem: Keter, 1975), 63. In an earlier telling, Dushkin described it as a plan to create a "private summer camp for children of well-to-do Jewish families"; see Dushkin, "A. P. Schoolman," 73.

30. Dushkin, *Living Bridges,* 64, 67.

31. Dushkin, "A. P. Schoolman," 74; Dushkin, *Living Bridges,* 63–64.

32. Rebekah Kohut, *More Yesterdays: An Autobiography* (New York: Bloch, 1950), 178; Kohut, *His Father's House*, 111.

33. See Schwartz, "Camp Ramah: The Early Years," 21, where Sylvia Ettenberg recalls that in 1947 some members of the Chicago Council of Conservative Synagogues suggested to her that she should not mention the study aspect of Camp Ramah when she went about recruiting potential campers.

34. Dushkin, *Living Bridges*, 65.

35. Kohut, *More Yesterdays*, 178; Bernheimer, *Half a Century in Community Service*, 17; Nancy Mykoff, "Summer Camping," *Jewish Women in America: An Historical Encyclopedia*, ed. Paula E. Hyman and Deborah Dash Moore (New York: Routledge, 1997), 1362.

36. Mykoff, "Summer Camping," 1363.

37. Dushkin, *Living Bridges*, 67–68.

38. Frost, "Milestones in the Development of Hebrew Camping in North America," 35 (translation mine). See also, *Massad Reminiscences*, 44, where Rabbi Ray Arzt recalls that at Massad, "Orthodox, Conservative, Reform, Hebraists, secularists—all were in that camp and I cannot remember any tension whatsoever among the groups. The camp was run on a more or less traditional basis, *t'fillot* [prayers] every morning. Those people among the counselors who had strong objections and did not like prayer did not go."

39. Isaacman, *Jewish Summer Camps*, 30.

40. A. P. Gannes and Levi Soshuk, "The Kvutzah and Camp Achvah," *Jewish Education* 20, no. 3 (1949): 61–69; Winter, *Jewish Education in a Pluralist Society*, 131–43; Frost, "Milestones in the Development of Hebrew Camping," 20–21.

41. Gannes and Soshuk, "Kvutzah and Camp Achvah," 68.

42. Dushkin, *Living Bridges*, 158.

43. Mykoff, "Summer Camping," 1361.

44. Fradle Freidenreich, reading an earlier version of this essay, has persuasively argued that Yiddish camps, of which there were about twenty-five before World War II, promoted an educational agenda as early as the 1920s and were therefore forerunners of Jewish educational camping. Zionist camps such as Moshava, sponsored by the Habonim movement, likewise promoted an educational agenda. In both cases, of course, the education was distinctly ideological, as were the camps. Full-scale studies of the Yiddishist and Zionist camping movements remain to be written.

45. Alvin I. Schiff, *The Jewish Day School in America* (New York: Jewish Education Committee of New York, 1966), 37, 42, 44, 49.

46. Israel M. Goldman, *Lifelong Learning among Jews* (New York: Ktav, 1975), 308; Deborah Dash Moore, *B'nai B'rith and the Challenge of Ethnic Leadership* (Albany: SUNY Press, 1981), 230–33. B'nai Brith's Committee on Adult Jewish Education was founded in 1950.

47. Jonathan D. Sarna, *JPS: The Americanization of Jewish Culture* (Philadelphia: Jewish Publication Society, 1989), 183–84.

48. Charles A. Madison, "The Rise of the Jewish Book in American Publishing,"

Jewish Book Annual 25 (1967–1968): 81–86; Amnon Zipin, "Judaica from American University Presses," *Jewish Book Annual* 42 (1984–1985): 172–82.

49. *American Jewish Year Book* 47 (1945–1946): 559.

50. Ibid., 234.

51. *American Jewish Year Book* 43 (1941–1942): 28, 780, 789.

52. Judah Pilch, ed., *A History of Jewish Education in the United States* (New York: American Association for Jewish Education, 1969); Diane Ravitch, *The Great School Wars* (New York: Basic, 1964), 239; Lawrence Cremin, *A History of Education in American Culture* (New York: Henry Holt, 1953), 568–69; Shaul Farber, "Community, Schooling, and Leadership: Rabbi Joseph B. Soloveitchik's Maimonides School and the Development of Boston's Orthodox Community" (PhD dissertation, Hebrew University, 2000), 105–06, 108.

53. Hurwich, *Memoirs of a Jewish Educator*, 235.

54. *Massad Reminiscences*, 17.

55. J. S. Ackerman to Phineas Smoller, July 7, 1952, OSRUI Papers, American Jewish Archives.

56. See Hurwich, *Memoirs of a Jewish Educator*, 236.

57. Azriel Eisenberg, "The Stone Which the Builders Rejected," *Jewish Education* 17 (June 1946): 2.

58. Deborah Dash Moore, "Inventing Jewish Identity in California: Shlomo Bardin, Zionism, and the Brandeis Camp Institute, in *National Variations in Jewish Identity: Implications for Jewish Education*, ed. Steven M. Cohen and Gabriel Horenczyk (Albany: SUNY Press, 1999), 201–21.

59. Shlomo Bardin, "The Brandeis Camp Institute," *Jewish Education* 17 (June 1946): 27.

60. Shlomo Shulsinger, "*Massad Memoirs: How It All Began*," and *Massad Reminiscences*, 9, 11; see also Bardin, "Brandeis Camp Institute," in *Kovetz Massad*, vol. 2, 83–96.

61. Shlomo Shulsinger, "Hebrew Camping: Five Years of Massad (1941–1945)," *Jewish Education* 17 (June 1946): 16.

62. Shulsinger, "Massad Memoirs," 10; Shulsinger, "Hebrew Camping," 18; cf. *Kovetz Massad*, vol. 2, 86.

63. Walter Ackerman, "A World Apart: Hebrew Teachers Colleges and Hebrew-Speaking Camps," in *Hebrew in America: Perspectives and Prospects*, ed. Alan Mintz (Detroit: Wayne State University Press, 1993), 115–17.

64. See Haskel Lookstein, "What I Learned from Massad," in *Kovetz Massad*, vol. 2, 334 [in Hebrew].

65. *Massad Reminiscences*, 15; *Kovetz Massad*, vol. 2, 31, 93–94; Shulsinger, "Hebrew Camping: Five Years of Massad," 23.

66. William B. Furie, "Yavneh," *Jewish Education* 17 (June 1946): 28–29; Hurwich, *Memoirs of a Jewish Educator*, 233–47; Ackerman, "World Apart," 116; and Frost, "Milestones," 68–73.

67. Samuel M. Blumenfield, "Summer Camp Institute Sharon," *Jewish Education* 22

(Summer 1951): 37–40; Isaacman, "Development of Jewish Camping," 116. It is not clear when Sharon actually opened. Blumenfield dates the initial organizational meeting to 1945, but the camp was not mentioned in the 1946 issue of *Jewish Education*. It likely began in 1946.

68. Michael A. Meyer, *Response to Modernity: A History of the Reform Movement in Judaism* (New York: Oxford, 1988), 307; "NFTY after Fifty Years: A Symposium," *Journal of Reform Judaism* 36 (Fall 1989): 1–38; Eve S. Rudin, "The Development of Reform Jewish Youth Programs," senior honors thesis, Brandeis University, 1992.

69. Michael Brown, "It's Off to Camp We Go: Ramah, LTF, and the Seminary in the Finkelstein Era," in *Tradition Renewed: A History of the Jewish Theological Seminary of America*, ed. Jack Wertheimer (New York: Jewish Theological Seminary of America, 1997), vol. 1, 826–27. The United Synagogue had created a "Young People's League" for eighteen-to-thirty-five-year-olds in 1921. It was abandoned in 1951 in favor of a new more broadly based United Synagogue Youth (USY) program aimed at Conservative youngsters between the ages of thirteen and seventeen. See Pamela S. Nadell, *Conservative Judaism in America: A Biographical Dictionary and SourceBook* (New York: Greenwood Press, 1988), 347.

70. Shuly Rubin Schwartz, "Camp Ramah: The Early Years, 1947–1952," *Conservative Judaism* 40 (Fall 1987): 17, 22.

71. Ibid., 18–20.

72. Ibid., 20.

73. Ibid., 21.

74. Burton I. Cohen, "A Brief History of the Ramah Movement," in *The Ramah Experience: Community and Commitment*, ed. Sylvia C. Ettenberg and Geraldine Rosenfield (New York: Jewish Theological Seminary/National Ramah Commission, 1989), 5–6; see also, Seymour Fox with William Novak, *Vision at the Heart: Lessons from Camp Ramah on the Power of Ideas in Shaping Educational Institutions* (Jerusalem: Mandel Institute and the Council for Initiatives in Jewish Education, 1997).

75. Schwartz, "Camp Ramah," 24.

76. Brown, "It's Off to Camp We Go," 831–32.

77. On Cook's significance, with the assistance of Eleanor Schwartz, see Rudin, "Development of Reform Jewish Youth Programs," 20.

78. *Chicago Councilor* (1948); NFTY "First Annual Leadership Institutes" brochure (1948); and Ernst Lorge to Sidney I. Cole (October 22, 1948), all in OSRUI Papers, American Jewish Archives (hereafter, AJA).

79. Lorge to Cole (October 22, 1948); Edwin Cole Goldberg, "The Beginnings of Educational Camping in the Reform Movement," *Journal of Reform Judaism* 36 (Fall 1989): 6–7. See also, Steven Lowenstein's discussion of German-Jewish youth organizations in M. Meyer, ed., *German-Jewish History in Modern Times* III, 147–50; and Michael Brenner, "Turning Inward: Jewish Youth in Weimar Germany," in *In Search of Jewish Community: Jewish Identities in Germany and Austria, 1918–1933*, ed. Michael Brenner and Derek J. Penslar (Bloomington: Indiana University Press, 1998), 56–73.

80. Alfred Wolf, *Wilshire Boulevard Temple Camps. The First 25 Years, 1949–1974: A Personal History* (Los Angeles: n.p., 1975), 5 [Jacob Rader Marcus's copy of this privately printed memoir is found in the rare book room of the Brandeis University library].

81. Rudin, "Development of Reform Jewish Youth Programs," 21.

82. Letter from Joseph L. Baron to Maurice Eisendrath, June 30, 1946, Joseph L. Baron Papers, in the possession of AJA.

83. Goldberg, "Beginnings of Educational Camping," 8, is less tentative on this point, but cites no sources. "Another factor that helped convince lay people of the need for a camp," he reports, "was the establishment of Camp Ramah. If the Conservative movement had a camp, then the Reform movement needed to acquire one too."

84. "[Minutes of the] Combined Committee for Camp Project Meeting, Thursday, March 29, 1951," OSRUI Papers, AJA.

85. Memo from Herman E. Schaalman to J. S. Ackerman, July 9, 1951; "Memorandum on Camp Institute," November 29, 1951; memo from J. S. Ackerman to Mae O. Garland and Sherman Pearlstein, December 27, 1951; memo from Herman Schaalman to "All Rabbis in the Midwestern, Rocky Mountain & Great Lakes Regions of the Union including all the Rabbis in Chicago," February 26, 1952; memo from Maurice N. Eisendrath to J. S. Ackerman, February 29, 1952; J. S. Ackerman, "History and Purpose of Union Institute," January 23, 1955; Dedication invitation, December 24, 1952; all in OSRUI Papers, AJA; Goldberg, "Beginnings of Educational Camping," 8.

86. An undated fact sheet, probably from 1952, in the OSRUI Papers reports that "No politics of any sort will be discussed (Zionism, communism, etc.). The American Flag will be the only flag raised and lowered."

87. "Preliminary Report of Summer Operation of Oconomowoc" [1952], OSRUI Papers, AJA.

88. "Report on Union Institute Program to Chicago Federation, U.A.H.C.," May 27, 1954; 1959 Union Institute Brochure, OSRUI Papers, AJA.

89. "Report of the Union Institute Program to Chicago Federation, U.A.H.C.," May 27, 1954; undated fact sheet (probably 1952); Goldberg, "Beginnings of Educational Camping," 8–9.

90. "Preliminary Report of Summer Operation of Oconomowoc" [1952], OSRUI Papers, AJA.

91. Goldberg, "Beginnings of Educational Camping," 9.

3 The Beginnings of Union Institute in Oconomowoc, Wisconsin, 1952–1970

Creation and Coalescence of the First UAHC Camp

Michael M. Lorge and Gary P. Zola

It is impossible to discuss the beginnings of Reform Jewish camping in America without reconstructing the history of Union Institute. The early history of Union Institute embodies the story of Reform Jewish camping's first stirrings. The content of this chapter emerges from the rich collection of camp records and supplementary primary source documents.[1] Oral histories provided by some of the camp's founders augment the archival data. Collectively, these sources reveal the factors that motivated and enthused a relatively small group of rabbis and lay leaders to join forces in a successful effort to establish American Reform Judaism's first camp.

Creation: A Plan for a Permanent Camp

By the late 1940s, Jewish camping in the United States was hardly a novel idea. In fact, the roots of Jewish camping in America can be traced back to the 1880s, when organized camping in the United States, as we know it, first took shape.[2] Union Institute was the official name of the first camp of American Reform Judaism. Since then it has been affectionately called, simply, "Oconomowoc" or "Camp" by its campers, staff, and faculty. In 1967 the camp adopted the name Olin-Sang Union Institute to acknowledge the philanthropic support of these two families. The name changed again in 1972 when "Ruby," a third major donor, was added to "Olin-Sang," and as a result the initials OSRUI are also used to refer to the camp. In this essay the authors refer to the camp as "Union Institute," which was the camp's name for the majority of the period discussed here. Union Institute opened in 1952. On the basis of oral tradition, some have traced its beginnings to the summer of 1951. Nevertheless, the camp's own records and our research leave no doubt that the camp was purchased and welcomed its first campers in 1952. In July 1951, the property is mentioned for the first time, when an architectural firm was sent to determine the feasibility of the property for use as a summer camp. The report stated, "the property is at present being used exclusively as a boys' camp." Union Institute was purchased on February 2, 1952, and formally dedicated on Sunday, August 24, 1952.[3]

Union Institute's birth can be traced to several key factors. First, the national leadership of the Union of American Hebrew Congregations (UAHC) began to focus the Reform movement on the importance of youth programming and educational camping.[4] This effort was spearheaded through the work of its national youth organization: the National Federation of Temple Youth (NFTY).[5] The interest shown by many in the UAHC's national administration fostered an atmosphere that was receptive to the efforts of a relatively small group of camp visionaries who ultimately succeeded in the establishment of Reform Jewish camps in different regions of the country.[6]

However, the imprimatur of the national movement in and of itself may not have given rise to a Reform Jewish camp. Although the UAHC's interest in establishing a camp for the movement reaches back to the early 1940s, the efforts to found a Reform Jewish camp bore fruit in the early 1950s only when the project garnered significant local support.[7] This second factor explains why the Reform movement's first camp was located in the Chicago region. The serendipitous presence there of a dedicated group of people who understood the value of camping as an educational and community-building tool served as a catalyst for the effort. Their commitment to this idea grew out of their own personal experiences with camping in other settings.[8] Curiously, during Union Institute's embryonic stage, these various catalysts largely operated independent of each other, but both were crucial to the successful establishment of American Reform Judaism's first official camp.

The UAHC's Precursory Initiatives to Establish a Camp

The UAHC had been sponsoring regional youth conclaves for more than a decade before the establishment of Union Institute. In the summer of 1941, two years after the establishment of the National Federation of Temple Youth in 1939, four local regions of NFTY sponsored Labor Day weekend conclaves at camp sites in the East and the Midwest. After attending a 1944 NFTY conclave in Waukegan, Illinois, Rabbi Arthur J. Lelyveld published a report in which he reflected upon the experience, concluding that the Reform movement "must have more conclaves. . . . We must put to work without delay the earmarked funds which our UAHC has set aside for the establishment of a permanent camp site which will be the home of an all-summer program of youth leadership training."[9]

Lelyveld's call for the movement to intensify its conclave and camping program for youth was answered in part by the efforts of Rabbi Sam Cook. Cook was a pioneer of Reform Jewish youth programming. Shortly after NFTY's official establishment, he organized what may have been the first regional Labor Day Conclave for the UAHC's Pennsylvania State Federation, held at Camp Pinemere in the Pocono Mountains. After Cook became director of the NFTY in June 1946, he began to encourage the creation of Labor Day weekend conclaves in various regions of the country. By the late 1940s, 725 Reform Jewish youth delegates had attended institutes and conclaves at rented facilities in six different states from coast to coast.[10]

Before Union Institute's founding in 1952, the UAHC had made other attempts to acquire a permanent camp facility. Prior to World War II, five thousand dollars had been "earmarked" by the national board for this very purpose, but no action was taken. Later, in the spring of 1946, three camp sites in the eastern United States were considered for purchase, but these efforts ended in failure because of either the unsuitability of the camp site or the lack of adequate funding.[11]

A private effort to establish a UAHC camp facility also emerged in June 1946. A friend of Rabbi Joseph L. Baron of Temple Emanuel-El in Milwaukee, L. M. Kesselman, owned land on Pelican Lake in northern Wisconsin. Kesselman was willing to donate this property if a camp that featured a "religious educational youth program" was built on it. Baron, who seems to have been part of larger conversations about the need and desire to acquire camp property, wrote in a letter to Rabbi Maurice Eisendrath, president of the UAHC, "we have all been anxious to develop a stimulating religious educational program for our youth during the summer months [and] how particularly important such a program is in this post-war era, and how much the success and growth of our summer activities depend on a suitable site in the country." Unfortunately, Kesselman placed terms on the offer that the UAHC could not accept.[12] The hunt for a suitable UAHC camp site continued.

Chicago Reform Rabbis, Summer Youth Programming, and the Establishment of Union Institute

In 1947, Chicago—like other regions of the country influenced by Rabbi Sam Cook's initiatives—began to offer regional Labor Day Conclaves wherein Reform Jewish teenagers and local rabbis gathered for recreation and study. In form and content these programs were precursors to the summer camping programs that ultimately took root in Chicago and other parts of the country. The Chicago-based conclaves were held at private camps in Michigan and, on occasion, at Jewish camps such as Camp Henry Horner in Ingleside, Illinois. Such events brought a cadre of rabbis together with more than one hundred young people to study in an informal outdoor setting that fostered an ideal atmosphere for learning.[13] Reflecting on these conditions years later, Rabbi Ernst M. Lorge, an organizer of the Chicago conclaves, said, "We foresaw that the educational experience in a summer camp for two or three weeks would equal or surpass what we could give a Jewish kid during a whole year at Sunday School."[14]

In 1948 the First Annual NFTY Leadership Institute was organized at Camp Lake of the Woods, in Decatur, Michigan. These NFTY Institutes focused on youth leadership and promised to "provide a meeting ground for the first conference of leaders, future leaders, and directors of the Reform Temple Youth Groups . . . to discuss common objectives, concerns, techniques, and philosophies." Leadership Institute participants chose between two five-day sessions: August 23–28 or August 28–September 2. The program's educational theme focused on the newly established State of Israel and included classes in beginning Hebrew. The event was planned and organized primarily by rabbis from the Midwest region, including Ernst M. Lorge and Arnold J. Wolf of Chicago; Leon Fram of Detroit, Michigan; Jerome Folkman of Columbus, Ohio; Harry Essrig of Grand Rapids, Michigan; and Rabbi Eugene Borowitz of St. Louis, Missouri. The faculty also included professors from the Hebrew Union College (HUC) in Cincinnati: Abraham Cronbach and Robert L. Katz. Speakers from the Joint Distribution Committee and the Garrett Biblical Institute in Evanston, Illinois, also participated in these events. The Institute's organizers asserted that the program would "shape the future of our local temple groups and create a strengthened Movement for Reform Judaism."[15] After the 1948 conclave, Ernst Lorge wrote an enthusiastic letter to his friend and HUC classmate Rabbi Leo Lichtenberg: "We have seen repeatedly for the past few summers that we can accomplish so much with our young future leaders in a camp setting. When they leave the conclaves it is not just what they have learned, but what they have experienced and how they feel about current matters impacting our lives as Jews. We must find a way to create our own summer camp program as other Jewish institutions have done."[16]

The notable success of the regional Labor Day Conclaves and the NFTY Leadership Institutes prompted some Reform Jewish leaders around the country to make the establishment of a permanent camp facility a priority for the movement. This effort was intensified by the appointment of Harry L. Lawner of Dayton, Ohio, to chair the UAHC National Camp Institute Committee. This committee was dedicated to acquiring a permanent summer camp.

The Chicago rabbis who organized the regional Labor Day Conclaves and had participated in summer programs for Reform Jewish youth also hoped to obtain a permanent summer-camp site for the Chicago Federation of the UAHC: "Camp was born out of previous retreats that were on Labor Day week-ends, such as our Labor Day weekend at Camp of the Woods in Michigan. Those were great functions where really all the Temple groups of the Chicago area got together . . . , but every year it got bigger. Then finally, some of us thought that we should have a permanent camp for the summer."[17]

To act on this vision the region needed to gain the approval of the UAHC's president, Rabbi Maurice Eisendrath, and its executive board. Previous failed attempts by the UAHC to establish a camp for the Reform movement had likely convinced Eisendrath and the UAHC's lay leadership that if the UAHC were to acquire its own camp, the endeavor would require solid evidence of local financing. This in turn would gauge the community's level of interest in such a project.[18] Eisendrath made it clear that before he would approve the purchase of a camp by one of the UAHC's regions, he would need to be convinced that the facility would be supported locally. Lawner wrote to Jacob Logan Fox (the attorney for the Oconomowoc transaction) and informed him that Eisendrath had approved the camp's purchase on the condition it "be self-sustaining and would require no financial outlay on the part of the Union, either with regard to capital expenditure or maintenance."[19] Despite overwhelming documentary evidence to the contrary, many of those who worked to establish Union Institute later insisted that the primary reason the Chicago region had to raise money for a UAHC camp locally was the national leadership's ambivalence about the purchase of a camp facility.

In addition to the flurry of activity in Chicago, the western regional office of the UAHC undertook efforts to establish a UAHC camp in that part of the country. Rabbi Phineas Smoller, then serving as the UAHC's regional director in Los Angeles, spearheaded an effort to acquire a local camp for the UAHC. Interestingly, Smoller had been the director of the UAHC's Chicago Federation until Herman Schaalman arrived in 1949. During his tenure in Chicago, Smoller worked with the cadre of local rabbis who had been actively involved in the development of the NFTY Institutes. Thereafter, rabbis and lay leaders in California worked toward establishing a UAHC camp as well. In September 1951, Lawner had written to J. S. Ackerman (who at the time was president of the Chicago Federation of the UAHC) to ask if the Chicago group had "taken an option on the Briar Lodge camp yet." (Briar Lodge was the Oconomowoc site and is further described below.) Lawner, who had been in communication with Smoller, told Ackerman that "Mr. Ben Swig of San Francisco has offered to contribute $5,000 and to raise $50,000 for the establishment of a camp in California. . . . he shares your personal enthusiasm for this type of development." In this letter he also states, "we will have to follow some of the mandates from the Executive Board in obtaining approval from the Committee, the President of the Union, and from you, as president of the Chicago Federation."[20] This statement foreshadows some of the tension between the national UAHC leadership and local Reform movement leadership that evolved (and continues today) concerning the financial needs and programming decisions for UAHC camps.

By 1950 Eisendrath knew that at least two local regions, the Chicago region and the California region, were raising funds for the purchase of a suitable camp site that would benefit both the region and the movement as a whole.[21]

Advocates for Reform Jewish Camping in Chicago: A Leadership Profile

A number of young rabbis in the greater Chicago area who were involved in the movement's youth programs had become convinced that Reform Judaism needed to develop a permanent camp of its own. Among those most active in the drive to acquire a camp for the Chicago region were Rabbi Herman E. Schaalman, who was the new regional director of the UAHC, and local rabbis Joseph Buchler, Ernst M. Lorge, Karl Weiner, and Arnold J. Wolf.[22]

Schaalman, Lorge, and Weiner had a keen interest in Jewish youth activities that stemmed from their involvement in various Jewish youth movements in Germany before fleeing Nazi Germany to settle in the United States in the 1930s. Schaalman, a student at the *Hochshule für die Wissenshaft des Judenthums,* was one of several rabbinical students whom Rabbi Leo Baeck sent to Cincinnati, Ohio, to study at Hebrew Union College in 1936. Upon his ordination in 1941, Schaalman assumed the pulpit of Temple Judah in Cedar Rapids, Iowa. There he began teaching young people in informal settings under the auspices of the Jewish Chautauqua Society's institute programs. In 1943 Schaalman served as a chaplain at a summer camp sponsored by the Methodist Church. In later years he attributed his own interest in establishing a camp for Reform Jewish youth to the time he spent at the Methodist camp: "On the invitation of the Jewish Chautauqua Society I participated in the Methodist summer camp in Clear Lake, Iowa. The impact of over 800 young people and 120 pastors interacting with each other in an informal setting was powerful. I decided then and there that we ought to have something like this for our own teenagers."[23]

Ernst Lorge came to Cincinnati from Mainz, Germany, in 1936 on a scholarship that had been awarded to him by the Sigma Alpha Mu fraternity. Lorge had been a youth leader in the Jewish scouting movement of Germany. Once in Cincinnati, he finished his undergraduate degree at the University of Cincinnati and enrolled in HUC's rabbinical program. While studying at HUC, Lorge served as a *Habonim* youth group adviser and worked at Camp Caravan in Twinsburg, Ohio, and also at a camp sponsored by the New York Section of the National Council of Jewish Women. As a young rabbi, Lorge also became associated with the Boy Scouts of America. He served as a chaplain/rabbi at various Boy Scout camps. Years later he credited all of these experiences as crucial to the beginning of Union Institute: "This particular idea [Union Institute] was an outgrowth mostly of these [youth] retreats, but also an outgrowth of [the fact that] some of us . . . had gone to Zionist camps. And the third ingredient [was that] some of us . . . , under the auspices of the Jewish Chautauqua Society, had become resource persons in Christian camps. The Protestants were way ahead of us. Out of these three ideas . . . we finally said this is what the Reform Movement needs more than anything else."[24]

Karl Weiner, too, was interested in youth activities. Weiner, a rabbinic ordainee of the Jewish Theological Seminary in Berlin, fled to America in 1939 and settled in Chicago in the late 1940s. Weiner, along with Lorge, was one of the local rabbis who organized and served as faculty for the region's Labor Day Conclaves and NFTY Institutes in the late 1940s. This experience fueled his interest in the drive to establish a camp for the Reform movement.

A number of American-born rabbis working in the Chicago region also actively supported the establishment of a Reform Jewish camp. These rabbis had been influenced by their experiences in various American camping programs. Joseph Buchler, for example, had considerable camp experience and campcraft skills. Arnold J. Wolf, a 1948 HUC graduate serving as an assistant rabbi at Congregation Emanuel, had been actively involved in Reform Judaism's youth activities. He also served as a faculty member for the recently initiated NFTY Institutes. All of these rabbis attested to the importance of the movement's youth programs, and they recruited lay leaders to join them in supporting the purchasing of a camp for the Reform movement of Chicago.

The success of Chicago's Reform Jewish community in establishing the movement's first camp can be credited to the emergence of a remarkable collaboration between the region's rabbinate and lay leadership, who shared a common enthusiasm for the camping project. When Schaalman became the new director of the Chicago Federation of the UAHC, he played a pivotal role in galvanizing the rabbinic and lay parties who had been championing the importance of youth and camping in Chicago for a number of years. Many lay leaders in the region had been actively involved in the UAHC on the national level. One of the most prominent was Chicago optometrist Samuel Sylvan Hollender. In addition to the role he played in creating the Chicago Federation of the UAHC, Hollender served as the organization's national chairman from 1946 to 1951. Another Chicago lay leader involved nationally in the UAHC was the engineer and industrial manufacturer Sidney I. Cole, a lifelong enthusiast of the Reform movement's youth and camping initiatives. Cole became chair of the board of Union Institute and the national chairman of the UAHC in 1971. Other lay proponents of Reform Jewish camping in Chicago included Jacob Logan Fox, Sidney Robinson, and Robert J. Cooper.[25]

One of the most ardent lay champions of Reform Jewish camping in the Chicago region was Johann S. Ackerman. Ackerman, an auto accessories manufacturer, was also active in Chicago politics and made two unsuccessful runs for the state House of Representatives, in 1956 and 1958. During the late 1940s he was serving on the board of the Chicago Federation of the UAHC when the drive to purchase a camp for the region began to take shape. He supported the camp project enthusiastically. Once Union Institute was purchased, Ackerman became the first chair of the camp's board of governors.[26] On March 29, 1951, he spoke to a group composed of Chicago Federation board members who were interested in the region's youth activities. Lay leaders of various Chicago area congregations were also invited. He reported on the plans to develop a camp and urged those in attendance to move ahead, stating, "the National Federation is now exploring the field for a camp, but the Chicago Federation does not need to wait, it could be the first."[27]

These lay leaders proved to be as firmly dedicated to the creation of a camp for the region as were many of the local rabbis. It was this cadre of local rabbis and lay leaders who worked collaboratively and successfully to establish the first permanent camp of the Reform movement.

The "Chicago Group" and the Purchase of Union Institute, Oconomowoc

A formal plan to pursue the development of a camp project in the Chicago region took shape at a special meeting of the UAHC's Chicago Federation on March 29, 1951. Nearly thirty-five people attended this meeting to discuss plans for purchasing a camp. Delegations from ten Reform congregations were in attendance, five of which were led by the congregation's rabbi. Schaalman, director of the Chicago Federation of the UAHC, led the discussion, urging the attendees to purchase a great property in Racine, Wisconsin, that was available.[28] Those in attendance heard impassioned presentations on the value of Jewish camping by Rabbis Ernst Lorge, Arnold Wolf, and Joseph Buchler. The minutes of the meeting testify to the fact that the rabbinic speeches enthused the laity about the camp project. Ackerman "urged everyone's cooperation in making this camp a reality for our youth." At the meeting's end, the chair, G. H. Emin, pleaded with the group "to help put this camp project across." The meeting concluded with a unanimous vote "enthusiastically endorsing the project of building a camp for our youth," and a "Special Committee" composed of rabbis and laity was charged with the responsibility of developing a plan of action.[29]

In the aftermath of the meeting a warm collaboration between the region's rabbis and lay leaders clearly emerged. In a letter written to Lorge a few weeks after the meeting, Sidney I. Cole noted that "many people who will support the camp effort will do so because of your words . . . there are many of us . . . supporting the camp, but when you or Herman [Schaalman] or the others speak, the cause is won." Shortly thereafter, news of the region's exuberance had reached the desk of the UAHC's national Camp Committee chair, Harry Lawner. Writing to Lorge, Lawner effused, "I have remarked that with leaders like Herman [Schaalman], Joe [Buchler], Sid [Cole], Logan [Fox], and you, the Chicago Federation camp project is certain to grow."[30]

The "Special Committee" (repeatedly referred to as the "Chicago group" in UAHC correspondence) continued its search for a suitable camp site. A few months after the March 29 meeting, the committee inspected a private boys' camp named Briar Lodge in Oconomowoc, Wisconsin. Briar Lodge Camp had originally been built as a private residence in 1903. In 1934 the estate was converted into a private camp facility for Jewish boys.[31]

A team of architects surveyed the site and appraised its value and suitability as a camp for the Chicago region. Convinced that this property was the one they had been searching for, the Special Committee, working with Schaalman, spent the next several months raising funds for the down payment of sixteen thousand dollars and mustering the support it needed to close the deal. Schaalman raised the funds from lay leaders, including Ackerman and Sidney Robinson. Money was also needed to fund repairs and upkeep.[32]

To ensure the financial viability of the camp project, the regional leadership immediately appealed to the local temple Sisterhoods, asking them to support the effort.[33] At the pivotal organizing meeting, which took place on March 29, 1951, Ackerman requested that the regional Sisterhoods raise a minimum of thirty-five thousand dollars for the project. Although the Sisterhoods did not commit themselves to the sum Ackerman solicited, they did pledge to contribute a significant portion of the funds that were needed.[34]

Moreover, on November 29, 1951, in a "Memorandum on Camp Institute," it is reported that the Sisterhoods of the Chicago area and the state of Illinois had pledged to raise the money needed to pay the camp's mortgage on an ongoing basis. In a letter containing the "First Interim Report" on the operations and conditions of Union Institute, the critical fund-raising role of the local Sisterhoods was underscored: "The major [fund-raising] effort . . . is being made by the Illinois Federation of Temple Sisterhoods, which is energetically active in raising funds for our capital requirements." In addition to the role of the Sisterhoods, this letter also mentions that "a Lac La Belle Cotillion" for teenage youth was being planned in an effort to raise funds.[35]

By the end of 1951 all of the necessary components had come together: leadership, organization, and fund-raising. That December a Camp Project Committee executed a letter of understanding with the owners of Briar Lodge stating its intention to purchase the camp. The deed for the camp was recorded on February 22, 1952, and subsequently conveyed to the UAHC president, Rabbi Eisendrath, by J. S. Ackerman.[36]

A Coalescence of Energy

The requisite permission to proceed with the purchase came on January 18, 1952, when the Chicago Camp Committee received word that Eisendrath and the UAHC's chairman of the board, Samuel S. Hollender, had approved its request to consummate the Briar Lodge deal. Eisendrath enthusiastically thanked Ackerman and the Chicago group in writing for their efforts, stating: "I cannot tell you what a tremendous thrill I received when . . . I held in my hand the actual certificate of ownership, for the first 'Union Institute' of the UAHC ever to be officially and actually established. This is indeed an historic document which I am going to have photostated [*sic*] and forwarded to the American [Jewish] Archives. It is undoubtedly the very first such accomplishment in our long annals; and everyone knows just how personally responsible you have been for this significant and marvelous achievement."[37]

Eisendrath's jubilance did not alter the fact that the relationship between the Chicago group and the UAHC had not yet been adequately defined. When the UAHC gave the Chicago region permission to proceed with the purchase, it did so by adopting a resolution insisting that any camp purchased by the Chicago region would have to be "under the Union's sponsorship." In a memorandum to Ackerman, Schaalman explained the UAHC's official stance vis-à-vis the region's desire to purchase a camp. He told Ackerman that if the region acquired a camp, then the "details of programming and operations were to be worked out in constant consultation with the Executive Board of the Union and the members of the Union's staff." Not surprisingly, the Union's executive board insisted that a movement camp purchased with regional funds must still be under the direction of UAHC. The local lay and rabbinic leadership ultimately maintained complete decision making over programming and operations, and the national organization's role was limited to a few seats on the camp board.[38]

Initially, the new corporation—and not the UAHC—held the deed of property. The camp's attorneys advised that it was necessary for the camp to have a legal presence in Wisconsin for real estate tax purposes. However, the national leadership of the UAHC was not satisfied with this arrangement. Writing to Ackerman in March 1952, Harry Lawner asked pointedly how the Union could be expected to direct the camp's policies and programs if it did not hold the deed of property. Lawner insisted that the Chicago region transfer ownership of the corporation that held the land to the UAHC: "if the Union is to control the policies of the camp, it seems to me that the Union should control the corporation and the title."[39] The issue of ownership was resolved by placing a number of UAHC National board members on the board of Union Institute and, simultaneously, making the UAHC the sole stockholder of the Wisconsin corporation. Some years later, the deed of property was indeed transferred to the UAHC.[40]

The camp was officially incorporated on May 22, 1952, in the state of Wisconsin as the Union Institute of the UAHC. Although the camp's records do not preserve the deliberations on how the first Reform Jewish camp's name was chosen, it is quite likely the word "Union" refers to the camp's association with the UAHC. The term "Institute" is probably a reference to the highly successful NFTY Leadership Institutes that began in 1948 as a direct outgrowth of the regional camp conclaves. So long as the Reform movement had no camp of its own, these "Leadership Institutes" were housed at rented camp facilities. Once the movement had purchased its own camp site, it was the expectation of the Chicago Camp Committee that such events would now be held at the region's camp in Oconomowoc, Wisconsin—hence the name Union Institute. It is interesting to note that other UAHC camps would pick up on the first camp's name and incorporate the term "Institute" into their names (e.g., the Goldman Union Camp Institute and the Kutz Camp Institute). Both entities communicated with Chicago leadership on this and other organizational matters.[41]

In an appendix to the document of incorporation, the camp's founders formulated a noteworthy "Statement of Purpose": "The Union Institute, Inc., a nonprofit organization, has been established in order to provide facilities for the young people and adults of our Reform Congregations for the purpose of worship, study, and fellowship. It is our hope that it will thus serve as a means towards the intensification of their Jewish experience based upon the Liberal-Reform interpretation of the Jewish past and present. It shall thus become an instrument towards the creation and continued development of a Living Judaism."[42]

A document that was produced after the Oconomowoc site was purchased but before the first summer opened explained, "the purpose of the Union Institute, UAHC, is to teach our young people Judaism, its culture and background and to train spiritual leaders. It's an exciting experience in living Reform Judaism." Another memorandum written in November 1951 proposed a similar vision: "The purpose of the program is to provide for our youth and adults an intensive religious Jewish experience, to develop leadership for our congregations and to train young people in their responsibilities as Americans and Jews."[43]

Various slogans attempted to summarize the goals of the camp. The terms "Living Judaism" and "Living Reform Judaism" echo in all of the camp's materials throughout the early years. In other promotional materials that attempt to summarize Union Institute's mission, the camp is described as a place "where thinking youth share ideas and ideals in the happy fellowship of a country camp." The first printed brochure uses the phrase "experiences in Jewish living." A later brochure declares that the camp in Oconomowoc was "a woodland setting for study, worship, work and play."[44]

Notwithstanding the resolution of the ownership of the camp, there were ongoing disagreements over the UAHC's financial responsibility for the cost of operation and the annual losses that occurred during the camp's early years of existence. The local camp leadership understood its obligation to fund the purchase of the land and the requisite mortgage, but had never considered or discussed other financial burdens. In fact, the minutes of the meetings to formulate the camp project recorded no conversation that even anticipated the possibility that the camp might lose money![45]

Though the UAHC Camp Committee chair, Harry Lawner, wanted the UAHC to own the newly acquired camp in Wisconsin, the national body continued to disclaim any financial obligation to the camp project. Local leaders reminded the Union that if it wanted to control the camp, it would have to provide some sort of monetary support. In a letter to the UAHC's board chair, Samuel Hollender, Ackerman—now chair of the camp's board—noted that if the Union wanted to oversee the camp, it would need to contribute funds to the effort:

> I want to clarify the oft repeated reference to the fact that the Union assumes no financial obligation either in connection with the capital expenditure for the camp or for the maintenance of the camp. The fact of the matter is that neither I nor others who have made substantial contributions to the Camp Institute would have done so if it were not for the fact that the Union of American Hebrew Congregations is sponsoring these Institutes and will be the sole owner of them. Ownership implies responsibility for an enterprise and, while it is true the officers and directors of the Union Institute which we have organized plan to raise all of our capital requirements . . . we cannot take the position that the Union has no responsibility in the matter.[46]

Despite Ackerman's appeal, the UAHC never agreed to cover the camp's operating expenses and budgetary shortfalls. Still, throughout the first decade of the camp's existence, Union Institute's board repeatedly turned to the UAHC in search of financial support. By and large the UAHC did not accede to these periodic appeals (although it did provide the camp with considerable funding on a number of occasions, including retiring the original mortgage and providing funds for a subsequent land purchase). Over time, the UAHC's national board recognized the programmatic success of the camp and became increasingly responsive to its appeal for operational support, eventually providing funds for all of the camp's staff and other needs.[47]

The Evolution of Administration and Programming: An Overview

Years 1952–1955

Now that the first Union Institute had become a reality, it was necessary to begin the work of directing its program. Schaalman found he had expanded his own job description as regional director to include camp director of Union Institute. He served in this role for the camp's first summer.

There can be little doubt that Schaalman's tireless work as both the regional director of the UAHC and camp director contributed to the success of Union Institute during its fledgling years. Even before the camp held its first summer session in 1952, J. S. Ackerman expressed his concern that the responsibilities of directing both the regional office and the camp would "result in either overtaxing [Schaalman's] physical capacity or some breakdown in [the work of the regional office]." The camp needed a director who had the time and wherewithal to tangle with the needs of the physical plant, raise funds, and hire staff. The UAHC agreed.[48]

At the conclusion of the camp's first summer of operation, the board began to look for a director who would relieve Schaalman of these additional responsibilities. Initially they relied on a series of young, recently ordained rabbis to direct Union Institute. In January 1953, Rabbi Gerald Raiskin had just returned from spending a year in Israel after his ordination from HUC. Rabbi Sam Cook, NFTY's director, learned of Raiskin's return and recommended him to become the director of Union Institute and a part-time director of the Chicago Federation of Temple Youth (CFTY). Raiskin served in that role through the end of the 1953 camping season, reporting to Schaalman with regard to the camp and to Cook with regard to youth work. Raiskin recalled, "Programming at the camp was secondary to the idea that we were building a camp. This was a new idea. Therefore, everyone spent time working at physical chores. If you didn't know how to build a chapel when you came to camp, you did when you left." According to Raiskin, during Union Institute's early years new terminology arose to describe those rabbis who spent time with young people at camp, referring to them as "youth rabbis." It is interesting to note that a few HUC professors served on the camp's faculty during this time, including Dr. Abraham Cronbach. Cronbach, who taught sociology at HUC, always dressed in a suit and vest. "He ate alone in his room on the second floor of the big house but when he came to teach the kids you could hear a pin drop."[49]

In the summer of 1953, Ben Swig came to Union Institute in Oconomowoc with an exploratory committee interested in creating a Reform Jewish camp in California. Aside from observing the operation, the committee asked Raiskin to consider coming to California to be the director of the UAHC's second camp, to be located in Saratoga. Raiskin declined, but he did not remain at Union Institute in Oconomowoc.

Raiskin was succeeded by another HUC ordainee, Rabbi Daniel E. Kerman, who arrived in Chicago in the early fall of 1953. Kerman ran the camp during the summer of 1954 and continued to function as the camp's director through December of that year.[50]

Kerman was replaced by the camp's first full-time director, Rabbi Irwin Schor. Ordained by HUC in 1952, Schor had served as a military chaplain during the Korean War. Before becoming the director of Union Institute he had been serving as the assistant rabbi at Temple Sholom in Chicago. In addition to his work as Union Institute's director, Schor, like his predecessors, served as youth director for the Chicago Federation of the UAHC and the Chicago Federation of Temple Youth.[51]

The brochure for the first summer at Union Institute expressed the excitement and anticipation that had grown around the search for a permanent camp site. "At last, it's come true! The Federation [Chicago Federation of UAHC] has finally bought its own 'summer home. . . . ' No more sojourning as strangers on other peoples [sic] territory. Chicago, pioneering for the whole country, has finally come into its own 'stamping grounds' [sic]."[52]

Those who were involved with the new camp continually enthused about Union Institute's ability to inspire youth to become actively involved in Jewish life. From its earliest days, the camp involved rabbis in every aspect of the program—not just as teachers, but also as storytellers and baseball pitchers. The early summers ran a daily schedule that included hymns and services at flag raising, study sessions with faculty, "bull sessions," evening services led by the campers, and more typical camp fare. These activities bore a remarkable resemblance to the programmatic content of the Labor Day Conclaves and NFTY Institutes.[53] It is clear that the educational activities associated with these youth conclaves and weekend institutes in the late 1940s served as a model for the informal educational program that developed at Union Institute.

The rabbis who had been active in the establishment of the camp initially functioned as an unofficial program committee during the first several years of the camp's existence. This rabbinic group met periodically to evaluate and develop the content and the methodology of the camp's educational program. The minutes of these meetings reflect detailed and energetic discussions on the educational goals of the camp. Eventually these conversations led to the development of the informal education format that characterizes the camp's program to the present day.[54]

These educational techniques were summarized in the minutes of a Program Committee meeting attended by Rabbis Karl Weiner and Ernst Lorge as well as lay leaders Robert Cooper, David Gottlieb, and Phillip L. Brin, director of Union Institute in 1955. In addition to evaluating and restating the "purposes and goals of Union Institute," these minutes state:

It was generally agreed that a controlled environment was essential to the educational processes at Union Institute and that this controlled environment was dependent on staff direction. Mention was made of attitudes and activities in the dining room, cabins, sleeping, etc., and that more emphasis should be placed on group living in the cabins. The problem of clarity of what we wish to accomplish was raised and it was pointed out that only when we know what we wish to accomplish in detail can we utilize the techniques of education to their fullest. Rabbi Weiner raised the question of creativity as a problem and pointed out that to him this is a means. Rabbi Lorge expressed the view that creativity is both to him a means and a goal and that the ulpan technique [intensive classroom instruction employing creative teaching methods, usually for Hebrew language immersion], which emphasizes creativity, was very suitable to special groups, but not necessarily to Instituters.

As the discussion ensued, it became apparent that it was necessary to evaluate the effect that the Institute sessions in the past have had upon our youth. Various problems were brought forth, e.g., as a result of writing their own prayers they felt that they could not have "living Judaism" through the Union Prayerbook and thru the services conducted by their own rabbi; often their sense of values back in the city was distorted and caused confusion in their lives at home, school and temples; the rabbi's role at the Institute was minimized to the point where the youth almost rejected rabbinic authority in the areas of worship. It was felt that we must constantly evaluate the program of the past and use the evaluation for building future programs that will meet the needs of youth in the reform movement.[55]

Clearly, the approach to Jewish education at Union Institute would be based on a collaborative relationship between faculty and staff stressing a combination of creativity and content.

During the first few summers of its existence, Union Institute ran two camping sessions per summer: "1st Period" and "2nd Period." Each period was limited to eighty people, and evincing concern that the camp might not be able to accommodate all of those who were interested in attending, camp brochures warned that campers may be able to enroll in only one of the summer's two sessions. These summer sessions (which would later be called Junior and Intermediate Sessions) were originally designed for "all boys and girls presently of confirmation age" and CFTY members.[56] The campers and counselors were to be screened by a committee. It was decided that as a matter of policy Union Institute should be open to those teenagers who came from "any Jewish home whether they belonged to a Temple or not."[57]

The camp also offered a weeklong session for adults during its first summer.

The brochure provides little evidence as to the specific nature of these adult sessions, but the camp continued to offer such programs during the first years of its existence. Beginning with the summer of 1953, the camp also offered a special session for those who belonged to the CFTY.[58]

Eventually the adult session began to attract Sunday School teachers from Reform temples in the region. By the summer of 1955 the camp began offering "Teacher Training Institutes." These programs quickly attracted wide appeal, and during the summer of 1958 the "Teacher Training Institute" hosted more than seventy teachers of religious schools, who traveled to camp from Toronto, Dallas, Omaha, Cincinnati, and Chicago. These institutes were organized and directed by Rabbi David I. Cedarbaum, then serving as director of the Department of Religious Education for the Chicago Federation, UAHC.[59]

For the first several years of the camp's existence, NFTY ran its National Institutes at Union Institute. Directed by Rabbi Sam Cook, the NFTY Institutes took place in August at the conclusion of the camp's summer program. Cook also attended camp board meetings during the years that NFTY Institutes were held in Oconomowoc.[60]

Years 1955 to 1963

Evidently, during the summer of 1955 there was some significant tension between the camp's staff and administration. Phil Brin, Schor's successor, recalled that he was hired to establish strict rules governing relationships between staff and older campers.[61] At a special meeting held in Chicago on October 3, 1955, the board's chair, Robert Cooper, expressed his view that steps needed to be taken "to correct certain difficulties and errors that had occurred both at camp and in the general relationship between the director and others." Deliberations at this meeting focused on issues of authority between the rabbinic leadership, the camp administration, and the staff. Rabbi Schaalman urged "that the relationship between the faculty and general staff be clarified," and Rabbi Lorge proposed "that the young adult staff be carefully screened."[62]

It is evident that the board was concerned that these conflicts might affect the recruitment of new campers and staff members. The result of these deliberations was the departure of Rabbi Schor. In parting ways with the camp's director, the board informed the rabbi "of the decision . . . to ask that a trained youth worker instead of a rabbi be employed." The exact reason for the board's decision to allow Schor's departure is unclear. There is an indication that the "difficulty" noted in the minutes may have been connected to Schor's unsuccessful attempt to reconcile his role as a rabbi and as a director of the new camp. His perspective on the tensions appeared in his parting thoughts to the camp board, wherein he urged that there be boundaries on the faculty's role at camp. He told the board that the summer camp staff was "ingrown" and therefore "cannot be held responsible for their actions, since they often feel it is their camp, and not that they are a staff of a camp." This attitude, which often can have a positive impact as well as being problematic, continues with current staffs. OSRUI and the other UAHC camps encourage and benefit from staff members who grew up as campers. Schor's recommendation aside, it is clear that the cadre of rabbis who were so involved in the creation of Union Institute—now functioning as a Rabbinic Program Committee—continued to play an influential role in the camp's affairs. Upon Schor's departure, the camp's board established a decisive new policy: Union Institute would hence-forth be directed by a non-rabbinical, professional youth director—a policy that is still in effect today.[63]

In 1957 the Rabbinic Program Committee changed its name to the Rabbinic Advisory Committee (RAC). The RAC continued to give the camp educational and religious counsel. It is interesting to note that the significant role played by the rabbis at Union Institute was never formally authorized either by the camp's board of governors or the UAHC. Undoubtedly, the rabbis' influence over the camp's educational and religious program derived from the pivotal role that many of the region's rabbis played at the camp's inception.[64]

At this same time, another debate arose. The rabbis and the board of governors struggled over who had final authority over the content of the camp's educational program. In contrast to the rabbis, the board of governors was authorized by the UAHC to establish camp policy and to raise funds for capital improvements. The lay leaders who helped to establish the camp continued to be actively involved in Union Institute's affairs through their presence on the camp's board of governors. An effort was made to have lay representatives from every Reform congregation in the greater Chicago area serve on the camp's board.

The board of governors routinely discussed the status of the camp's physical plant. In the late 1950s the board undertook a capital improvement campaign to raise one hundred thousand dollars "for the purposes of paying off the mortgage and rehabilitating the site." The board also purchased additional property on two separate occasions during the 1950s, including a piece of land that was dedicated as the Froehlich Campus.[65]

From time to time, the work of the board and the rabbis overlapped. For instance, before the first summer session in 1952 the board determined that "no politics will be discussed, ([such as] Zionism or Communism.)" Most notably, the American flag was the only flag to be raised and lowered at camp. These policy statements did not seem to faze the rabbis, who organized curricula on Israel, Zionism, and Jewish immigration for the summers of 1952 and 1953. The board's policy directives on the matter of educational content were promptly overlooked. In fact, the rabbis who pioneered the Chicago youth conclaves had already focused on Israel at a conclave in 1948. In regard to education, the board's strictures on these matters had little influence after the camp's first summer.[66]

From 1954, when Rabbi Irwin Schor became the camp's first full-time director, to the present day, Union Institute has had five full-time directors.[67] Several directors served the camp for considerable periods of time, and the camp's overall development has been shaped understandably by each director's interests and instincts.

Phillip L. Brin assumed the directorship in December 1955, following the departure of Rabbi Schor. Brin was the first director with experience in youth work. Before coming to Union Institute, he had served on the professional staff of the Deborah Boys Club in Chicago's Albany Park. He was a member of Temple Beth Israel in Chicago, and Rabbi Lorge—the congregation's rabbi—recommended him for the position. Brin made many changes to the structure of the sessions. He considered everything to be experimental. In accordance with the camp board's newly established policy, he concentrated largely on administrative matters. Brin focused his energies on increasing camper enrollment, hiring a quality staff, maintaining good relationships with the staff, developing a plan for physical growth of Union Institute's plant, and securing the camp operation financially. Nevertheless, he was responsible for an important educational innovation. During the summer of 1958, he hired Dr. Oscar Miller, a professor at the University of Illinois at Chicago and Temple Beth Israel's religious school principal, to serve as the camp's first program director.[68]

Brin began his directorship at the very time board members were becoming increasingly aware of the camp's shortcomings, including its operational and physical limitations. The camp was small—only nine acres in size—and the structures were dilapidated. Only a few months after Brin took over, a meeting was held at which one of the camp's founders, Rabbi Schaalman, suggested the board consider purchasing an alternate property in Antioch, which was owned by the state of Illinois. Schaalman informed the board that the Antioch property was "most desirable because of the splendid condition of the buildings which, without cabins, would accommodate 80 or 90 campers, as well as its better accessibility to Chicagoans." Three months later, after the summer of 1956, the subject of selling the property in Oconomowoc and purchasing a new camp site came up again at an executive committee meeting. Rabbi Richard Hirsch, Schaalman's successor as director of the Chicago Federation of the UAHC, told the executive committee that a new site would offer the camp "greater opportunity for growth." Nevertheless, after considerable discussion, a decision was made to retain and refurbish the property in Oconomowoc while simultaneously undertaking a successful effort to purchase an additional forty-one acres of land adjacent to the camp's original nine acres.[69]

Brin's tenure as director was dominated by the drive to fortify the camp's finances and renovate its facilities. Several of his administrative initiatives proved to be extremely farsighted. In 1959, for example, he succeeded in developing a master plan for ongoing expansion of the camp's physical plant. This plan included architectural renderings of cabin units, staff lodging, and even a cultural center. Some of these ideas were eventually put into place. Brin also conceived of bringing highly motivated high school age boys to camp. These teenagers were too young to be counselors and too old to be campers, but they wanted to spend their summers at Union Institute. So Brin developed a program in which these boys spent part of their days doing work for the camp (i.e., kitchen work, grounds maintenance, driving, etc.) and also spent time in worship and study experiences. This program was essentially a "work-study" program, and participants were called "kitchen boys." In subsequent summers these "kitchen boys" became members of the camp's counseling staff, and some of them went on to Jewish professional careers. Today, work-study programs for high school students abound in the UAHC camping movement.[70]

After the summer of 1960, five years after becoming the director of Union Institute, Brin resigned in order to work for Temple Sinai in Chicago. It is clear that his years as Union Institute's director were of tremendous personal import. Brin observed that he had gained much from his experience at Union Institute and that he would forever be indebted to the camp. Perhaps alluding to his frustration with the fact that his work as director had been primarily administrative, Brin wrote: "I realize that the material things of the Union Institute gave me nothing, but rather the experiences of living and learning with children and adults is what helped me to grow and develop a great admiration for my religion."[71]

Brin's successor, Norman Buckner, began work in December 1960. As noted, by this time Union Institute had grown considerably. As of 1957 an estimated five thousand young people from congregations across the United States and Canada had participated in a summer session at Union Institute. The camp's annual operating budget now exceeded fifty thousand dollars. Buckner immediately began to upgrade the camp's athletic program by instituting a horseback riding program, canoeing, riflery, and a wide range of track and field sports. During Buckner's tenure, Union Institute even installed a small putting green (complete with a sand trap) for the camp's young golfers. Buckner also took steps to build some of the structures projected on the master plan that had been developed during Phil Brin's tenure as director.[72]

Buckner directed Union Institute for two years. Difficult relationships with the staff seem to have been a factor in his departure. In a letter to former staff members written just months before leaving his post, Buckner admitted, "although my actions may not have demonstrated my intensive interest, you may be sure that I have often thought of you." Paradoxically, at the very same meeting at which the camp's board approved the budget and construction of a new faculty lodge—a major building project that Buckner had shepherded through the camp's board—his successor, Irving B. Kaplan, was introduced.[73]

One measure of the camp's success during the first decades of its existence can be gauged by the expanding number of young people who chose to spend their summers in Oconomowoc. In 1954 eighty-three campers attended Union Institute. By 1960, only six years later, the camp served more than five hundred children each summer![74] Similarly, Union Institute's weekend study programs and retreats introduced an ever increasing number of adults to the camp. The camp's weekend programs served nearly one thousand adults in 1956 alone.[75] By the late 1950s Union Institute ran five different sessions for children aged nine to eighteen each summer. In addition, the camp hosted special programs for NFTY and CFTY at the summer's end. Toward the end of that first decade, the camp's rabbinic and lay leadership began planning for the camp's future. They wanted to expand Union Institute's physical plant and further develop its educative potential.

Every meeting of the camp board dealt with fund-raising matters and new moneymaking initiatives. A series of fund-raising pamphlets and brochures was developed.[76] A capital campaign was launched in 1955 that continued throughout the latter part of the 1950s. At the same time, however, the region's Sisterhoods continued to support the camp. In 1956 they sought to collect a dollar a year from every Sisterhood member to support Union Institute. That effort brought more than six thousand dollars to the camp's coffers in 1958.[77] The Sisterhoods also resolved to raise funds needed to construct a new infirmary at the camp.[78] In addition, money came to the camp from many philanthropic individuals, including a special challenge grant of fifteen thousand dollars from board member Samuel Froehlich.[79] Individual synagogues also contributed to the camp's fiscal campaign, including Temple Beth Israel of Chicago (Rabbi Ernst M. Lorge), Temple Judea of Skokie (Rabbi Karl Weiner), Sinai Temple of Michigan City (Rabbi Karl Richter), Congregation Emanu-El B'ne Jeshurun of Milwaukee (Rabbi Joseph L. Baron), and Temple Sholom of Chicago (Rabbi Louis Binstock). In a letter to temple presidents, Harry M. Brostoff wrote that the board of Temple Beth Israel decided to "assume a partial responsibility for the financial upkeep of Union Institute."[80]

In 1956 and 1957 campers paid $99 tuition for a two-week session at camp. By 1960 the fees had gone up to $120 for a two-week session.[81] During this same time period, loans from the UAHC supplemented the camp's budget.

Years 1963 to 1970

During the first decade of its existence, Union Institute matured both programmatically and operationally. Within a remarkably brief period of time, the basic components of the camp's educational program congealed. A functional administrative structure was in place, and the camp's day-to-day financial needs were being met. Most importantly, the vision of the camp's rabbinic and lay founders was validated; Union Institute was established as an educational experiment, but it quickly gained widespread acceptance as a valuable educational resource for the Reform movement both regionally and nationally. The other camps of the movement looked to Union Institute for programmatic and educational content—particularly because of its active rabbinic faculty.

As Union Institute evolved, so too did the UAHC's overall camping program. By 1956 the Union had already acquired four additional camps: one in Saratoga, California; one in Kunkletown, Pennsylvania; one in Zionsville, Indiana; and one in Warwick, New York. The expanding number of UAHC camps underscored the need to further define the fiscal and administrative duties of the individual camps in relation to the camps' corporate owner, the UAHC. The relationship between the UAHC and its first camp in Oconomowoc naturally charted a course that would guide the Union as the owner of a family of camps. Furthermore, as described earlier, many of Union Institute's pioneering lay leaders went on to assume positions of leadership in the UAHC's Camp Committee. Ackerman became the committee's chair and, based on his experience with Union Institute, assured the national committee that the movement's camps would serve as a stimulant to the development of future leadership for American Reform Judaism.[82] By 1962 the UAHC decided to engage a national director of camping. Sidney Cole reported that a national camp director's salary would be paid by income to be derived—on a pro rata basis—by each of the UAHC camps.[83]

Bernard Sang's life illustrates how local leadership that developed from within Union Institute eventually influenced the UAHC nationally. As a youth, Sang was involved in the founding of NFTY, served as its second national president, and attended Union Institute. Later, he practiced law in Chicago and served on the national UAHC board, remaining involved in its youth and camping programs. Sang and his family were instrumental in the physical development of Union Institute, making several significant purchases of land for the camp. He also established the Community Development Foundation for Reform Judaism in 1965 to support Union Institute financially. Notwithstanding his involvement nationally, Sang created the foundation to assure that any money raised locally would be used solely for Union Institute.

The idea of developing innovative program units tailored to specific age groups and extracurricular interests began early in Union Institute's history.[84] For example, in 1961 Rabbi Richard Hirsch addressed the camp board on future programmatic initiatives at a two-day retreat held at Union Institute to consider the theme "Union Institute's Role in New Frontiers for Jewish Education: Philosophy and Program."[85]

In 1960, after experimenting for a few years with junior, intermediate, and high school sessions, the camp developed a one-week session for high school students called Torah Session. Its mission was to provide "an intense study experience for motivated campers over 15 years old." Torah Session developed a unique esprit de corps by assembling a distinguished faculty that included local rabbis, faculty from Hebrew Union College, and faculty from other parts of the country. The topic in its first season was "The Study of Torah Is the Most Important Commitment."[86]

It was during the early 1960s that Union Institute initiated a novel program for American Reform Judaism: an intensive Hebrew-speaking unit. Many of the rabbis who worked at Union Institute during its early years were interested in strengthening the camp's Hebrew program. Rabbi Mark Shapiro, of B'nai Jehoshua Beth Elohim in Glenview, Illinois, served as a song leader at Union Institute during the early years of its existence. He noted that the "growth of Hebrew was first in the songs and then in the prayers. In the early days of camp there seemed to be an assumption that if a song had more than five Hebrew words, don't try and teach it, because American kids cannot read or remember more Hebrew than that."[87] In 1957 Rabbi Victor Weissberg, of Temple Beth El in Chicago, noted that Union Institute succeeded in interesting its campers in Hebrew, but it did not teach the language. He urged the camp to consider a more ambitious program of Hebrew education.[88] The camp's first program director, Oscar Miller, continued to agitate for the expansion of Hebrew instruction, especially conversational Hebrew. Some of the camp's staff were already spending time in Israel through the UAHC's International Exchange Program.[89] In addition, visiting Israeli staff members strengthened the camp's ties with Israel and the Hebrew language.

By 1962 the Rabbinic Advisory Committee began discussing the implementation of a new Hebrew-speaking program to be called "Pioneer Camp," a four-week-long program running concurrently with the two intermediate sessions (each of which was two weeks in length). Significantly, the rabbis hoped to recruit an all Hebrew-speaking staff to lead the unit. They also recommended the hiring of one staff member who would be responsible for directing the unit's program.[90]

When Union Institute advertised its programmatic offerings for the summer of 1963, a Pioneer Camp was listed in the brochure. A news release promoted the new program: "Pioneer Camp, a new and exciting program, is now being offered to 11, 12, and 13 year olds who have completed at least three years of Hebrew study. This session will be limited to 35 campers, who will live in tents, on a pioneer farm camp. It is designed to teach the Hebrew language as a living tongue, and the language of our tradition. A trained staff of Hebrew speaking counselors will live with campers, for one month. Pioneer camp is designed for the honor students of our affiliated congregations."[91]

However, disagreement arose among the rabbis as they argued whether Pioneer Camp should be for pre-confirmation or post-confirmation students (i.e., 8th and 9th graders, or 10th and 11th graders). The proponents of the younger, pre-confirmation group argued that Pioneer Camp would encourage these young people to return to their temples with a heightened enthusiasm that would benefit the synagogue's programs. Those who thought the program should be for older students argued that a Pioneer Camp would encourage students to continue their Hebrew education throughout their high school years. Rabbi Karl Weiner, then chair of the Rabbinic Advisory Committee, convened a special meeting of ten rabbis to resolve the conflict. For the first time in Union Institute's history it was decided that all Reform rabbis in the Chicago region should be polled by mail to garner their views on the matter.[92] The poll was conducted, though the results were not preserved.

Nevertheless, because of this debate and the arrival of the camp's newest director, Pioneer Camp did not begin in 1963 as originally announced. Instead, its inaugural summer was 1964, with Donald M. Splansky as its first unit head. Writing to the campers a few weeks before the onset of the summer, Splansky (today a rabbi in Boston) outlined Pioneer Camp's educational objectives while stressing the program's overall uniqueness: "We will be pioneering in many ways, both in the work at the camp farm and the cabin life away from the main camp area. We will be pioneering in studying Hebrew intensively and in learning to speak Hebrew in everything we do. Finally, the whole program will be a pioneer project, the first time at Union Institute and the first time in all the Reform Jewish camps."[93] By the late 1960s Pioneer Camp began to be known as "Chalutzim" (Pioneers).[94]

In February 1963 Irving B. Kaplan became the director of Union Institute. Though Kaplan had not been affiliated with Reform Judaism before assuming the camp's directorship (he was raised in a Conservative synagogue), he came to Union Institute with youth and camping experience. Kaplan possessed many personal qualities that appealed to the camp's rabbinic and lay leadership. He was an ardent Zionist with a strong love of the Jewish people, and he had a dynamic, colorful, and charismatic personality. By the end of his first summer, he had reinvigorated the camp and galvanized the support of rabbis, lay leaders, staff, and campers alike.[95]

Kaplan's magnetism, vigor, and creativity were evident from his first days on the job. Within weeks of becoming the director of Union Institute, Kaplan participated in a television broadcast titled "In This World" that aired on NBC's Chicago affiliate the morning of March 31, 1963. Kaplan wrote and directed this TV program with Ralph Garber, a Union Institute staff member. The broadcast was one of Kaplan's marketing initiatives designed to increase the camp's enrollment. It tried to capture a sense of the excitement that Union Institute fostered among its campers and highlighted its educational innovations.[96]

A few years later Kaplan exploited his theatrical interests once again when he became a familiar weekend personality on a local television show called "The Magic Door." In this weekly broadcast, Kaplan played the role of an imaginary character named "Tiny Tov," who traveled on a magic feather to experience various aspects of Jewish life and history. Children of all religions throughout the Chicago area watched "The Magic Door," and the show bolstered Kaplan's personal reputation along with that of the camp he directed. Though he never donned his "Tiny Tov" costume at camp, the character was part of Kaplan's camp persona, and the director's overall wit and charm enabled him to become the focal point of the camp's overall spirit.

Kaplan inaugurated a number of new programs during his tenure as director of Union Institute. In his first summer he transformed the junior counselor program into the camp's first Counselor-In-Training (CIT) program, designed for students who had completed "half or all of their high school senior year." Before this, such high school students were called "junior counselors," but there was no formal training for them. The CITs would be required to attend special preparatory classes and workshops at camp before becoming junior counselors later in the summer.[97]

During the months leading up to Kaplan's first summer as director, the camp experienced its first significant new construction since its founding in 1952. After years of struggling with limited and inadequate facilities, the camp's board succeeded in raising the funds needed to build a separate campus for girls, with six redwood cabins and a "rather luxurious washhouse."[98] Simultaneously, work began on a faculty lodge, which was completed in the spring of 1964. The lodge, which housed the rabbinic faculty, became one of the most handsome structures at camp.

In addition to the physical growth that occurred during Kaplan's tenure, Union Institute expanded its program and enrollment. Kaplan recognized that these two objectives were interrelated: more campers meant more tuition and more funds for operations. Two months after he became director, he told the camp's board that registration was his "largest concern." However, in order to attract and accommodate more campers, the facilities needed to be enlarged and improved. Kaplan set out to achieve both objectives simultaneously.

Though money had been raised to complete a new campus for girls, there were no resources to build a new campus for the experimental Pioneer Camp when it opened in 1964. This Hebrew-speaking unit lived in military surplus tents until the camp could afford to build cabins. Similarly, in 1968, when Kaplan realized that Union Institute did not have enough beds to accommodate the growing number of applications for his intermediate sessions (called the Kallah Unit from 1967 on[99]), he turned this shortage to his advantage by establishing another tent unit called Kibbutz HaTzofim (Scouts). The program patterned itself after an Israeli kibbutz. In announcing the new unit, the camp's brochure explained: "Our newest innovation, the Tzofim camp . . . utilizes the same program objectives with the same caliber of staff specialists and rabbinic faculty as in the Kallah sessions, with the added feature of outdoor living."[100] The camp's growth spurt prompted the acquisition of more acreage and the building of new cabin units and camp facilities. By the end of Kaplan's tenure in 1968, Union Institute had grown significantly.

The programmatic changes that occurred during Kaplan's tenure were a direct result of the strong staff he recruited. Working with the faculty that by then included several former campers and staff who had been inspired by the camp in its earlier years, Kaplan hired a number of program directors and unit heads who teamed up with Oscar Miller, who had become the camp's overall education director. The camp's programmatic offerings were broadened with the introduction of educational sessions that featured simulation games and sociodrama. Its program of arts and crafts and athletic offerings were also expanded.

Israel and Zionism received increased attention during Kaplan's tenure as director. In addition to his role as champion of the Chalutzim Unit, Kaplan also sought to make the teaching of modern Hebrew a regular feature in every aspect of the camp's daily program. He engaged the services of Hebrew language specialists, who developed innovative strategies for integrating Hebrew learning into the camp's daily program. Kaplan brought the Jewish educator Fradle Freidenreich to Union Institute to serve as a Hebrew specialist to work with all of the units. Drawing on her background and experience in Yiddish camping, Freidenreich developed an integrated Hebrew program using games and an intensive vocabulary in informal Hebrew classes for the general camp. Many of the rabbis—such as Splansky, Sheldon Gordon, Hillel Gamoran, and Leo Wolkow—who served on the camp faculty played a crucial role in bolstering Hebrew learning at Union Institute during this period.

In 1968 Kaplan and the camp's faculty organized a group trip to Israel. Many of those who participated in this new initiative were former Chalutzim campers. The program was called *Tiyul La'Aretz* (A Trip to Israel). It was during this same summer that Kaplan announced his intention to permanently move to Israel. His decision to make aliyah affected the camp community in that for many campers and staff members, Kaplan became the first personal acquaintance who chose to settle in Israel. Campers, staff members, and faculty liked Kaplan, and his unexpected departure suddenly made Zionism and Israel more personal and familiar. In subsequent years a number of former Union Institute campers and staff members would also settle in Israel.

As the summer of 1968 came to a close, Union Institute began searching for a new director. The following summer, Rabbi Allan Smith, who later went on to serve as the director of the UAHC's youth division, served as interim director at Oconomowoc. In 1970 Gerard W. Kaye was appointed director. Like Kaplan, Kaye was a young man (only twenty-four years old when he was named director) who had spent a number of years doing youth work on the staff of the American Zionist Youth Foundation. Kaye arrived at camp with a firm background in Jewish learning, experience in youth work, and a creative approach to Jewish education. At the time of this writing, thirty-five years later, Jerry Kaye continues to serve as the director of Union Institute and is known as an innovator and builder within the world of American Jewish educational camping.

Conclusion

Historically speaking, the first half century of Union Institute's existence may be divided into two distinct periods: the beginning and early years, and the era of Jerry Kaye. In light of the fact that Jerry Kaye has directed Union Institute for more than half of the camp's fifty-plus years, an additional historical assessment of his tenure will need to be written at some point in the future. It is necessary to point out, however, that since 1970 a remarkable array of important programmatic innovations has occurred. Under Kaye's leadership, Union Institute has experienced unprecedented growth, both in its physical plant and in the number of campers it serves annually. Kaye's influence on the programmatic character and general development of the Reform movement's first camp is, without exaggeration, significant and reaches well beyond the boundaries of the camp.

This review of the camp's early history reveals several noteworthy points. Union Institute in Oconomowoc, Wisconsin, was the first UAHC camp. As such, it occupies a unique place in the history of Reform Jewish camping in America. Although the camp's founding was clearly a project of Chicago's Reform Jewish community, for the first few years of its existence Union Institute became, de facto, the UAHC's national camp. Simultaneously, it is important to bear in mind that the effort to establish the camp in Oconomowoc was certainly not the first attempt by the UAHC to found a camp for America's Reform Jewish community. While these efforts ultimately bore first fruit in the Chicago region of the UAHC—due to the vision and drive of a unique collaboration of rabbinic and lay leadership—long before the establishment of Union Institute, the UAHC had created a national camp committee that sought to encourage such efforts throughout the country. Initially the UAHC's interest in Reform Jewish summer camping did not include a budgetary commitment. The Union maintained that its first camp would need to secure local financial support for all aspects of its operation.

Moreover, the birth of Union Institute in that place and at that time occurred because of a timely coalescence of UAHC regional leadership and an assortment of local rabbis who were camping enthusiasts and youth rabbis. These rabbis acquired their interest in Reform Jewish camping through their own personal experiences. Some, like Herman Schaalman, had witnessed the effect that camping had on church denominations. Others, like Ernst Lorge and Karl Weiner, understood camping's potential from their involvement with Zionist youth organizations before immigrating to the United States and later in other Jewish camps in America. There were also those, like Joseph Buchler and Arnold Wolf, who had been influenced by American camping. All of these rabbis were interested in youth work, and three of them had organized the youth conclave programs that were held in the late 1940s. It is also noteworthy that the educational vision these young rabbis advocated was quickly and enthusiastically embraced by a cadre of local Reform Jewish lay leaders, some of whom were coincidently national leaders in the UAHC.

The initial success of Union Institute stems largely from the unique Reform infrastructure that its founders unabashedly applied to the fabric of camp. This Reform Jewish character expressed itself in (1) the prominent role of the rabbinic faculty at camp, (2) the rapid development of a community of committed Reform Jewish staff members, (3) the camp's firm commitment to liturgical innovation and creative expression, and (4) Union Institute's official status as an auxiliary of the Reform movement's congregational union, the UAHC.

Finally, the fact that Union Institute was founded *after* the establishment of the State of Israel in 1948 is of tremendous significance. The program of the Reform movement's first camp was shaped largely by younger rabbis who were not attracted to the ideological and liturgical conventions typically associated with Classical Reform Judaism. The Reform Jewish atmosphere of the new camp was created by those who associated themselves with what Dr. Michael A. Meyer has termed the "reorientation" of American Reform Judaism. The few restrictions recommended by lay leaders in the camp's founding documents were simply ignored by those who created the institute's program and curriculum.[101] This fact enabled Union Institute to pursue educational and religious programming that was, to a significant degree, independent of the conventional approach to Reform Judaism as it was practiced in many of the region's synagogues during the 1950s and early 1960s.

Since Union Institute was established in 1952, literally thousands of Reform Jewish youth experienced the impact of Jewish summer camping on their lives. These campers returned to their congregations with an unshakeable devotion to a Reform Jewish practice they experienced at Union Institute. Some of these campers would go on to become the rabbis, cantors, and Jewish educators of a new generation. Others became prominent lay leaders who sought to foster elements of their Reform Jewish camping experiences in their congregational communities and, indeed, into the work of the UAHC itself. In this way, Union Institute in particular and Reform Jewish camping in general have had a progressively significant impact on the development of American Reform Judaism in the last half of the twentieth century. Just as the camp's founders repeatedly promised in advocating for the creation of Union Institute in Oconomowoc, Wisconsin, Reform Jewish camping became a vital catalyst in the ongoing development of Reform Jewish life in America.

Notes

1. Unless noted otherwise, all correspondence and primary source documents cited in this essay can be found in the Rabbi Ernst M. Lorge Collection, the Jacob Rader Marcus Center of the American Jewish Archives (AJA), Cincinnati, Ohio. Union Institute's papers and programmatic materials are also deposited at the AJA.

2. See chapters by Gary Zola, Jonathan Sarna, and Hillel Gamoran in this volume.

3. See "Warranty Deed" for the purchase of "Union Institute of the UAHC"; "Report from Harry R. Nortman of Loebl, Schlossman and Bennett to the Chicago Federation," July 31, 1951; "Program" for the camp's dedication ceremonies; and Rabbi Herman E. Schaalman's "Report from the Minutes of Union Institute's Annual Meeting," January 23, 1955.

4. The Union of American Hebrew Congregations (UAHC) officially changed its name to the Union for Reform Judaism (URJ) in November 2003. For consistency and historical accuracy, the URJ will be referred to in this essay as the UAHC.

5. The National Federation of Temple Youth (NFTY) was founded in 1939. It is known today as the North American Federation of Temple Youth.

6. See Richard J. Goldman, "The History of the Reform Jewish Youth Movement in America and Europe since 1880," term paper, Hebrew Union College-Jewish Institute of Religion, 1968, at the Jacob Rader Marcus Center of the American Jewish Archives (AJA), Cincinnati, Ohio, especially, pp. 3–12. After the establishment of Union Institute in Oconomowoc, Wisconsin, Reform Jewish camps were inaugurated in Saratoga, California; Kunkletown, Pennsylvania; and Zionsville, Indiana, during the 1950s.

7. Goldman, "History of the Reform Jewish Youth Movement," 17–18.

8. Edwin Cole-Goldberg, "The Beginnings of Educational Camping in the Reform Movement," *Journal of Reform Judaism* (Fall 1989): 7. See also, Alan Cook, "Towards a History of Olin-Sang-Ruby Union Institute: A Documentary Study," term paper, Hebrew Union College-Jewish Institute of Religion, 2000, 2–3 (AJA).

9. Goldman, "History of the Reform Jewish Youth Movement," 14–16.

10. Ibid., 13, 17–19; see also, "President's Report," in "Minutes of the UAHC Executive Board Meeting," December 3, 1949, 200–01.

11. On the UAHC's unsuccessful attempts to purchase its own camp, see Goldman, "History of the Reform Jewish Youth Movement," 17–18.

12. Letter from Rabbi Joseph L. Baron to Rabbi Maurice Eisendrath, June 30, 1946 (AJA).

13. See *Chicago Councilor* (Fall 1947): 3–4. The *Chicago Councilor* is a publication of the Chicago Council of NFTY Affiliates.

14. Taped interview of Ernst Lorge, May 1972 (Lorge Papers, AJA).

15. See program brochure for NFTY's First Annual Leadership Institutes (Lorge Papers, AJA).

16. See letter from Rabbi Ernst M. Lorge to Rabbi Leo Lichtenburg, October 5, 1948 (Lorge Papers, AJA).

17. Ernst Lorge interview, May 1972.

18. Goldman, "History of the Reform Jewish Youth Movement," 17–18.

19. See letter from Harry L. Lawner to J. Logan Fox, January 18, 1952; see also, letter from J. S. Ackerman to Dr. S. S. Hollender (UAHC's national chairman of the board), March 12, 1952 (Lorge Papers, AJA).

20. Letter from Harry L. Lawner to J. S. Ackerman, September 28, 1951 (Lorge Papers, AJA).

21. Ibid. See also, "Minutes of the UAHC's Executive Board Meeting," September 6, 1951, Appendix A, 78–79 (Lorge Papers, AJA).

22. See "Minutes of the Combined Committee for Camp Project," March 29, 1951 (Lorge Papers, AJA).

23. Herman E. Schaalman, *Chicago Jewish News*, July 21–27, 2000, 11.

24. Ernst M. Lorge letters to Joseph Brown at Careran Camp and taped interview of Ernst M. Lorge, May 1982 (Lorge Papers, AJA).

25. On Hollender, see *Who's Who in American Jewry, 1938–1939*, and the Samuel S. Hollender Nearprint file (AJA); on Cole, see Obituary, *New York Times*, October 30, 1972, and Sidney I. Cole Nearprint file (AJA). On Fox, Robinson, and Cooper, see Nearprint files (AJA).

26. On Ackerman, see Johann S. Ackerman Nearprint file (AJA).

27. See "Minutes of the Combined Committee for Camp Project," March 29, 1951.

28. Ibid.

29. The lay leaders who joined the rabbis on the "Special Committee" were Ackerman, Frank Kohn, J. Logan Fox, Sidney I. Cole, and Max Robert Schrayer. See also, "Minutes of the Combined Committee for Camp Project Meeting," March 29, 1951.

30. Letter from Sidney I. Cole to Rabbi Ernst M. Lorge, May 4, 1951 (Lorge Papers, AJA); see also, letter from Harry L. Lawner to Rabbi Ernst M. Lorge, undated.

31. See original Briar Lodge Camp brochure (Lorge Papers, AJA).

32. "Report of the Architect," July 31, 1951; see also, letter from Rabbi Herman E. Schaalman to Rabbi Ernst M. Lorge, October 11, 1951 (both in Lorge Papers, AJA).

33. "Sisterhoods" here refers to the regional association of the National Association of Temple Sisterhoods (NFTS), known today as Women of Reform Judaism (WRJ).

34. "Minutes of the Combined Committee for Camp Project Meeting," March 29, 1951.

35. "Memorandum on Camp Institute," November 29, 1951; see also, "Dear Friend Letter," October 9, 1952 (Lorge Papers, AJA).

36. See "Letter of Offer to Purchase" from Johann S. Ackerman to Mrs. Mae O. Garland and Mr. Sherman Perlstein, December 27, 1951; see also, "Warranty Deed," February 22, 1952.

37. Letter from Maurice N. Eisendrath to Johann S. Ackerman, February 29, 1952 (Lorge Papers, AJA).

38. Note from Rabbi Herman Schaalman to J. S. Ackerman, July 9, 1951; Reports of Nominating Committees and Presidents' Reports (Lorge Papers, AJA).

39. Note from Rabbi Herman Schaalman to J. S. Ackerman, July 9, 1951; letter from Howard Brown to J. Logan Fox, February 15, 1952; and letter from Harry Lawner to J. S. Ackerman, March 25, 1952 (all in Lorge Papers, AJA).

40. See "Directors and Officers of Union Institute, 1952"; letter from Howard G. Brown to Jacob Logan Fox, October 31, 1951.

41. On the history of NFTY and the NFTY Leadership Institutes, see Goldman, "History of the Reform Jewish Youth Movement," especially, p. 19. See also, brochure for the "First Annual Leadership Institutes," held at Camp Lake of the Woods in Decatur, Michigan, August 23–28, 1948, and August 28–September 2, 1948.

42. Document titled "Union Institute, UAHC—Appendix 'A'" (Lorge Papers, AJA).

43. See Proposal for Union Institute titled "Union Institute, UAHC owned by the Chicago Federation of the Union of American Hebrew Congregations," undated, circa 1952; see also, Union Institute brochures for the years 1952–1956; "Memorandum on Camp Institute," November 29, 1951 (Lorge Papers, AJA).

44. See Union Institute printed brochures for the years 1952–1956; see also, proposal for Union Institute titled "Union Institute, UAHC owned by the Chicago Federation of the Union of American Hebrew Congregations," undated, circa 1952, and "Proposed Summer Program for Union Institute," undated but predating the summer of 1953 (Lorge Papers, AJA). The term "living Judaism" is not unique to Union Institute. See Gary P. Zola, "Jewish Camping and Its Relationship to the Organized Camping Movement in America," in this volume.

45. See Report of the "Finance And Budget Committee," February 24, 1955; "Report by President of Union Institute," Fall 1955; "Minutes of the Executive Meeting," March 22, 1956; and "Asset Statement," July 23, 1957.

46. See letter from J. S. Ackerman to Dr. S. S. Hollender, March 12, 1952.

47. For examples of instances when the UAHC helped the camp financially during these early years, see letter from Rabbi Richard G. Hirsch to Rabbi Maurice N. Eisendrath, November 28, 1956; "Report of Camp Committee Meeting," July 29, 1960; letter from Mollie Motch to Dr. Arthur T. Jacobs, December 9, 1960; and letter from Rabbi Richard G. Hirsch to Mrs. Mae O. Garland, December 15, 1960.

48. See letter from J. S. Ackerman to Dr. S. S. Hollender, March 12, 1952.

49. Michael M. Lorge's telephone interview with Gerald Raiskin and Neesa Sweet's follow-up interview, August 20, 2002, and January 5, 2004.

50. Ibid. See also, "Minutes of Executive Committee," August 12, 1953; and Rabbi Herman E. Schaalman's "Report to the Annual Meeting of Union Institute," January 23, 1956 (misdated in original as 1955).

51. Nearprint file (AJA).

52. See also, Mimeographed Preliminary Pamphlet Announcing the First Summer Offerings for Union Institute, Spring 1952.

53. Camp-printed brochures for the years 1952–1955 and Ernst M. Lorge interview (May 1972) (Lorge Papers, AJA).

54. "Minutes of the [Rabbinic] Program Committee," November 9, 1955, and March 20, 1956.

55. Ibid.

56. See Mimeographed Preliminary Pamphlet Announcing the First Summer Offerings for Union Institute, Spring 1952; see also, Union Institute's printed brochure for the summer of 1952 and camp brochures for the summers of 1953, 1954, and 1955 (Lorge Papers, AJA).

57. See proposal for Union Institute titled "Union Institute, UAHC owned by the Chicago Federation of the Union of American Hebrew Congregations," circa 1952 (Lorge Papers, AJA).

58. Union Institute's printed brochure for the summer of 1952. See also, camp brochures for the summers of 1953, 1954, and 1955 (Lorge Papers, AJA).

59. See Rabbi David I. Cedarbaum to Temple Educators (mimeographed letter), November 15, 1962. See also, Phillip Brin to Board of Governors (mimeographed letter), July 1958.

60. See "Meeting of the Executive Committee of Union Institute," August 12, 1953, and May 24, 1956. Camp brochures indicate that after the summer of 1958, NFTY ceased holding its NFTY Institutes at Union Institute in Oconomowoc.

61. Interview with Phil Brin by Neesa Sweet, January 2004.

62. "Report of Meeting of the Evaluation Committee of Union Institute," October 3, 1955. For references to earlier staff problems, see "Minutes of the Executive Committee of Union Institute," November 9, 1953, and Robert Cooper's "Report to the Annual Meeting of Union Institute," January 23, 1956 (misdated in original as 1955).

63. See "Director's Report at the Annual Meeting of Union Institute," January 23, 1956. See also, "Minutes of the Meeting of the Evaluation Committee of Union Institute," October 10, 1955 (Lorge Papers, AJA).

64. "Minutes of the Meeting of Rabbinical Advisory Committee," January 24, 1957 (Lorge Papers, AJA).

65. President's Report for 1954 and 1955 (Lorge Papers, AJA). Letter from Robert J. Cooper to Union Institute Board Members, April 23, 1956; see also, "Quick Facts" (fundraising publicity), 1956 (Lorge Papers, AJA).

66. Proposal for Union Institute, Oconomowoc, Wisconsin, circa January 1952; docu-

ments from 1952 and 1953 titled "Class Schedules for the Junior Session at the Union Institute."

67. See appendix in this volume.

68. For the director's job description at the time of Brin's employment, see "Confidential Director's Report on Summer Program," September 14, 1955. Also see interview of Brin by Neesa Sweet, January 2004. On the acquisition of new property for the camp, see letter from Phillip L. Brin to J. Logan Fox, December 4, 1956 (and accompanying mimeographed map); Rabbi Richard G. Hirsch to Rabbi Maurice N. Eisendrath, November 28, 1956; Phillip L. Brin to A. C. Oosterhuis, January 8, 1956; and Phillip Brin to Special Committee of Union Institute Board of Governors, December 7, 1956 (all in Lorge Papers, AJA).

69. See "Minutes of the Executive Committee of Union Institute," May 24, 1956, and "Minutes of the Executive Committee of Union Institute," August 19, 1956 (Lorge Papers, AJA).

70. See "Master Plan," November 5, 1959 (Lorge Papers, AJA). On the "kitchen boy" project, see oral interview with Donald M. Splansky, November 7, 2003. Splansky went on to become a rabbi as did another "kitchen boy," Stephen Arnold.

71. Letter from Phillip L. Brin to Rabbi Ernst M. Lorge, December 7, 1960 (Lorge Papers, AJA).

72. Phillip L. Brin to Summer Staff (mimeographed memorandum), August 20, 1957, and "Minutes of Union Institute's Annual Meeting of the Board of Governors," January 23, 1956. With regard to activating the master plan, see "Minutes of the Special Committee of Union Institute," July 29, 1960 (Lorge Papers, AJA).

73. Norman Buckner to Camp Staff (mimeographed memorandum) November 21, 1962. See also, "Camp Committee Meeting—Union Institute," April 24, 1963 (Lorge Papers, AJA).

74. Sidney I. Cole to Board of Governors (mimeographed memorandum), July 26, 1959. See also, "Director's Report to the Board of Governors," August 23, 1958 (Lorge Papers, AJA).

75. See "Quick Facts" (fund-raising publicity), 1956.

76. See "Minutes of the Finance and Budget Committee and Fund Raising Committee," February 24, 1955. See also, fund-raising pamphlet titled "One of the Finest Projects of Reform Judaism Needs your HELP" (Lorge Papers, AJA).

77. "Minutes of the Executive Committee," April 15, 1958.

78. "Meeting of the Development Committee," November 2, 1959.

79. "Minutes of the Meeting of the Executive Committee," July 26, 1960.

80. See mimeographed letter from Harry M. Brostoff to temple presidents, December 6, 1957; see also, "Minutes of Meeting of Board of Governors," July 25, 1959 (Lorge Papers, AJA).

81. Union Institute press release, to general media in Chicago area, October 26, 1962 (Lorge Papers, AJA).

82. See "Meeting of Board of Governors," July 26, 1959.

83. "President's Report to the Union Institute Board," August 15, 1956 (Lorge Papers, AJA). On the national camp director's salary, see "Minutes of Camp Committee Meeting," April 24, 1963, p. 3.

84. Note from Phillip L. Brin to Fundraising Committee, October 14, 1959 (Lorge Papers, AJA).

85. Pamphlet advertising the forthcoming Annual Board of Governors Meeting on April 15–16, 1961. (Pamphlet was mailed with accompanying letter from board chair Sidney I. Cole on March 9, 1961 [Lorge Papers, AJA].)

86. 1960 Camp Brochure (Lorge Papers, AJA).

87. Interview with Rabbi Mark Shapiro, May 1987 (Lorge Papers, AJA).

88. See handwritten letter from Rabbi Victor H. Weissberg to Rabbi Richard G. Hirsch and Phillip Brin, 1957.

89. By example, Sue Ellen Lorge Schwartz returned from the UAHC's International Exchange in 1964 and went directly to the Pioneer program that summer, and Laura Schwartz Harari participated in both programs a few years later.

90. See "Minutes of Rabbinic Advisory Meeting," October 18, 1962 (Lorge Papers, AJA).

91. Union Institute press release, October 26, 1962, and Norman Buckner to Rabbis (mimeographed letter), October 31, 1962.

92. Letter from Rabbi Karl Weiner to Rabbis Joseph Buchler, Joseph Strauss, Mark S. Shapiro, David Cedarbaum, Herman Schaalman, Ernst Lorge, Arnold Wolf, Hayim Perelmuter, and Robert Marx, November 7, 1962; and Rabbi Karl Weiner to Chicagoland Rabbis (mimeographed letter), November 17, 1962.

93. See "Union Institute Campers News," December 1963, and Donald Splansky's letter to the first group of Pioneer campers (Lorge Papers, AJA).

94. See Camp Brochures, 1968 and 1969 (Lorge Collection, AJA). See also, Hillel Gamoran's "The Road to Chalutzim" in this volume.

95. "Minutes of Camp Committee Meeting," April 24, 1963.

96. See "News Bulletin—Union Institute UAHC is Featured on NBC-TV," March 25, 1963.

97. Memorandum from Irving B. Kaplan to Rabbis, Temple Youth Advisors, and Temple Youth Chairmen, February 21, 1963.

98. Memorandum from Irving B. Kaplan to Camp Committee of Union Institute, July 2, 1963.

99. The term *Kallah* refers to a convention of teachers and students that occurred in the rabbinic academies of Babylonia.

100. With regard to registration, see "Minutes of Camp Committee Meeting," April 24, 1963, p. 2. With regard to the expansion of program units, see camp brochures for the summers of 1964–1968 in the Olin-Sang-Ruby Union Institute Collection (AJA).

101. Michael A. Meyer, *Response to Modernity* (New York: Oxford University Press, 1988).

4 Making the Magic in Reform Jewish Summer Camps

Michael Zeldin

Editors' Note: Michael Zeldin provides readers with an analysis of informal education—the learning methodology that is often implemented at Jewish camps. He argues that at least since the 1980s, sharp distinctions between the use of informal education techniques in summer camps and formal education techniques in day schools and religious schools have increasingly become blurred.

Zeldin begins his discussion by acknowledging that as the first UAHC summer camp, Union Institute played a central role in the development of informal education for the entire Reform movement. In the 1950s the founding faculty at Union Institute were keenly aware of the fact that they were employing a distinctive, and in many respects new, approach to Jewish education. Although the pioneering educators in Oconomowoc did not refer to their methodology as "informal education," it is evident from their own reminiscences that the rabbis who developed the camp's approach to Jewish learning recognized that they were participating in a new experiment in Jewish education:

> *The question was raised whether a topical rather than a text approach is better for camp. It was generally agreed that a controlled environment was essential to the educational processes at Union Institute . . . it was pointed out that only when we know what we wish to accomplish in detail can we utilize the techniques of education to their fullest. One rabbi raised the question of creativity and pointed out that to him this is a means. Another rabbi expressed the view that creativity is both a means and a goal. (Program Committee Meeting of Union Institute Faculty, November 9, 1955)*

As Zeldin points out, part of the magic of a camp experience is tied to charismatic individuals and intense identification. Union Institute's founding faculty understood how the camp provided such encounters. To them every part of the day at Union Institute was a teaching opportunity, even sports and meal-times:

> I happily acknowledge that one of the most important influences on me was my experience as a Union Institute camper growing up in the 50s and early 60s. I was inspired by a host of wonderful rabbinic teachers whom I came to know during my annual two-week stays at camp. We would sit around under a tree or some other landmark on the gracious expanse of lawn in front of the Bayit and talk about life and Torah with wonderful rabbis. And if later a plump, bookish youngster wanted to ask a question or add an observation between ping-pong games on the porch, the resident rabbis were available. (Rabbi Ralph D. Mecklenburger, July 5, 2000)

Zeldin notes that community and social intimacy are essential compo-nents of the informal education experience, and he underscores the fact that camp's social and physical environments help educators to communicate Jewish values. When the staff and faculty at Union Institute were at their best, these elements were intuitive and foundational: "In this setting of privilege and crea-tive Judaism a communal experience has been developed allowing for the possi-bility of Jewish culture and teaching to join in shaping the moral and physical character of young people" (Rabbi Michael Perelmuter, August 10, 2000).

At Union Institute there has always been a drive to compel campers to expe-rience the past in an effort to have them "relive" specific historical events or imbibe Jewish values. Zeldin emphasizes that there are multiple ways of learn-ing and, therefore, different ways to reach different campers: "It was always incredible, fascinating to go into a planning session at camp. Once the topic was established the conversation began and it would build on itself, really grow with one faculty member or counselor adding to the idea of the previous, until a challenging program emerged. Then sometimes the challenge was if we could really make it happen" (Rabbi Hayim Goren Perelmuter, April 2000).

These approaches to informal education triggered the use of sociodrama and simulation that became legendary at Union Institute: "The rabbinic staff that came to Union Institute almost uniformly were dedicated to learning about the unique qualities of Judaism. They discussed themes and the educational value and then proposed techniques for implementation. I suggested the shiur-sicha format.[1] Some of the rabbis encouraged the use of this format and carefully outlined techniques that occasionally involved socio-dramas" (Oscar Miller, April 8, 2000).

As the following chapter emphasizes, the Reform movement's educational camps have significantly influenced Jewish education in America. It was at

Union Institute that these educational innovations and experimentations first began to affect the character of Reform Jewish learning.

For more than fifty years, the sign at the entrance to the Disneyland parking lot has read "The Happiest Place on Earth." Disneyland is a Magic Kingdom that creates happy experiences and lasting memories for its visitors. But as any adult visitor realizes, none of the "magic" of Disneyland happens by accident; everything is carefully planned and orchestrated down to the smallest detail.

The comparison of Reform Jewish camping to the Disneyland experience is at once both complimentary and disparaging. A visit to Disneyland and a summer at a Reform Jewish summer camp can both be intense, engrossing, and exhilarating. The memories can last a lifetime. But Disneyland is, ultimately, artificial. Nothing is real; the experience has no connection to life outside the park. For Reform Jewish camping the challenge is to make the magic, but to make it real and keep it connected to life beyond camp.

For me, like for so many others, the years spent at a UAHC camp were indeed magical. They were the most formative years of my life. For ten summers and almost as many winters, I worked at Camp Swig in Saratoga, California. Working with children helped me understand who I was becoming as a young adult. Creating powerful Jewish programming alongside my fellow staff members helped me discover my potential for leadership, for vision, and for understanding complex systems. Devoting endless hours to dreaming and debating and planning helped me form friendships that have lasted a lifetime. And immersing myself each summer in a Reform Jewish environment shaped the vision of Jewish life and Jewish living that I have carried with me into my family life, my community life, and my professional life. In two deeply personal ways, my years at Swig set the course of my future: I met the teenage girl who grew up to be the woman who became my wife, and I discovered the calling that would become my profession.

Throughout those years at Camp Swig, even as those of us on staff developed immense pride in the pioneering camp programming we were creating on the West Coast, Oconomowoc shone to us as a beacon from the Midwest. Tales of the first Reform Jewish summer camp entered our consciousness through the lore that traveled the Reform Jewish grapevine. Occasionally a camper would come to California after summers in Wisconsin and would tell tales of camaraderie, *ruach* (spirit), and great programming. From time to time, a counselor from Oconomowoc would find his or her way to the redwoods of Saratoga and regale us with inspiring accounts of Reform camping in the Midwest. And as we were building the Solel (Pathfinders) Hebrew program from a handful of younger campers lost in a sea of teenagers to the pride of Swig, we constantly looked to Chalutzim (Pioneers), Oconomowoc's Hebrew program, as our inspiration.

The pride of youth and the chauvinism that camp people feel for their own camp prevented me from thanking the pioneers of Oconomowoc for showing the way. My contribution in honoring the fiftieth anniversary of Olin-Sang-Ruby Union Institute is, in some small measure, a belated expression of gratitude to the campers and counselors, the unit heads and specialists, the educators and rabbis who helped Oconomowoc become the quintessential Reform Jewish summer camp and who developed its program into a model of Jewish education.

In this chapter I hope to contribute to the ongoing development of Reform Jewish camping by examining camping through educational—and in particular, curricular—lenses. Curriculum can be understood as a "course to be run," and in this sense it applies to schools, with their prerequisites and requirements, more than it applies to camps. But curriculum can more aptly be understood as all the experiences that participants have under the auspices of an institution. This holistic view of curriculum applies to camps as well as it does to schools. Curriculum thus involves conceptualizing, creating, molding, and implementing all of the activities and environments camps offer, from the moment campers first see a promotional video or pick up a camp brochure, to the last tear they shed as they drive away from camp, and even as they carry memories back to their homes and communities. Curricular thinking involves the programs and activities along with the human dynamics among campers and between campers and staff; it includes the policies and procedures the camp invokes, the culture the camp creates, and the traditions and rituals that are such an important part of camp life.

My goal is to help readers become "connoisseurs" of camp programming, with sophisticated perceptions about what happens at camp, how it happens, and why it happens.[2] Just as a wine connoisseur appreciates the subtleties of wine, understands what goes into winemaking, and has a sophisticated understanding of the qualities of fine wines as well as a vocabulary to express that understanding, I hope that readers of this chapter will become "camp connoisseurs" who appreciate the subtleties and complexities of Jewish education at Reform Jewish summer camps. As I was preparing a camp program several years ago, someone asked me why I was working so hard to shape every detail of the program. "Why worry?" she asked. "You can't lose. You have everything going for you at camp. You don't even have to do much planning and the program will be a success." I reacted by saying that it was precisely *because* we had "everything going for us at camp" that we had a choice: we could build on the foundation we were given to create incredibly powerful experiences, or we could squander the opportunity. "Good enough," I told her, "is not good enough when it comes to planning for camp." That is the premise of this chapter: sophisticated program planning based on connoisseurship can make Reform Jewish summer camps even more powerful forces in the lives of those who participate in them.

The Magic of Camp

Camp is magic. Children who go to camp escape the pressures of the school year, leave the city behind, and enter an entirely different reality. A 1998 National Public Radio broadcast of the series *This American Life* called "Notes on Camp" set out to explain why "people who love camp say that non-camp people simply don't understand what's so amazing about camp."[3] The broadcast illustrated the enchantment of camp by presenting some of the magical moments children experience and by interviewing present and former campers about their camp experiences. For one former camper, who then went on to be a counselor, "all the best moments of [my] life have either been at camp or with camp people." This counselor explains that camp "changes people's lives. Like people live their life around camp. Like I would not be who I am if it wasn't for camp." Several campers reflect on their camp experience: "I'm so secure here. It's such a haven for me." "My friends at home are so different from my friends here." "It's not really 'living' at home."

It would be easy to imagine a similar broadcast on Jewish camping that described children's reactions to camp in similar terms: experiences at Jewish camps differ significantly from the common experiences children have in other parts of their lives. Indeed, several of the segments of "Notes on Camp" describe experiences of Jewish children in Jewish camps, one in a Zionist camp and one in a camp run by the Israeli army. What is striking is how similar these segments of the broadcast are to the segments taped at boys' and girls' camps that are nonideological and that do not serve any particular religious or ethnic clientele.

Ira Glass, producer and narrator of *This American Life*, attributes the magic of camp to three programmatic elements: charismatic people, intense identification with a group, and the reenactment of camp ritual. The camp counselor with a magnetic personality stands at the heart of the camp experience. Campers look up to, and often idolize, their counselors. Counselors have "high status," and their influence comes from both their words and their actions. They help shape the camp environment, create the social atmosphere that embraces campers, and provide examples of what campers can become in a few short years. What is so powerful about counselors' influence is that it is not limited to any single area or sphere of activity. Counselors provide guidance and modeling on questions as diverse as relationships, sports, Jewish living, and how to dance. "Notes on Camp" even relates how a particularly charismatic counselor coached one of his campers through his first kiss!

A second powerful element in camp magic is identification with the group. "Notes on Camp" describes the intensity of the "color wars" experience in terms that are transcendent: campers lose themselves in the group experience and "spend most of [the time] crying and screaming. It's thrilling being part of a team at this level of intensity." This sense of belonging makes camps psychologically fulfilling for most participants. At the same time, campers experience being part of something that is bigger than a conglomeration of individuals. Campers who have attended Jewish summer camps often speak of the Shabbat experience in similar terms. Even years later they remember the power of being surrounded by hundreds of others dressed in white to welcome Shabbat.

The third element that contributes to the magic is the enactment of camp rituals. "Traditions are part of every camp, and not just because they're fun. These traditions bring kids back year after year.... It's part of what makes camp thrilling. It is using all of the stagecraft that all the worlds' religions have always used . . . to thrill children, to make them feel part of something big and special." Perhaps because summer camp represents a special time in a special place, campers invest special meaning in how things are done and identify the traditions with the place, and the place with the experience. Any change in the rituals sparks intense opposition. One camper explained the power of camp rituals by saying, "I come back for the traditions. I expect everything to be here the way it was last year 'cause that's the reason I come back. I guess if everything changed I wouldn't like it anymore."

The challenge for Reform Jewish camps is how to utilize these three powerful elements—charismatic counselors, intense identification with the group, and enactment of rituals and traditions—to further the Jewish goals of the camp. One experience illustrates how all three elements can be combined. "Box 66," a promotional slide show used to recruit campers to Camp Swig in the late 1960s, includes a recording of the final night's ritual.[4] The camp director, Rabbi Joseph B. Glaser (known in camp as "Rabbi Joe"), gathers the entire camp community on the central lawn on the last night of camp. Shabbat is ending and so is the camp session; the campers are packed to go home the next morning. They gather in a circle around a large wooden Star of David. Spaced around the star are dozens of candles, providing the only light other than the single Havdalah candle Rabbi Joe is holding. Havdalah becomes the metaphor for going home: "We are standing on holy ground," Rabbi Joe says, referring to camp and implying that leaving camp in the morning will be a separation from this holy space and a return to the mundane. One by one, the most beloved counselors and specialists are called to approach the Star of David and blow out a candle, until Rabbi Joe himself extinguishes the last candle. The implication is not lost on the campers: they will yearn to return to camp just as Jews long for Shabbat to return. The enactment of this ritual, session after session, summer after summer, encapsulates the elements Glass identifies and inter-twines them with Jewish rituals and metaphors of holiness, separation, and Shabbat. Camp magic and Jewish majesty become one.

Formal and Informal Jewish Education

The magical power of Jewish summer camps is often attributed to their being the quintessential example of informal education. Education—both formal and informal—encompasses all the modes a society has at its disposal to trans-mit its culture to the next generation and to help young people develop the knowledge, skills, and capacities they need to reach their individual potential. The former aim seeks to meet the needs of societies to perpetuate themselves, and the latter focuses on the needs of individuals to prepare to live "the good life" however it is defined in different social contexts. Schools are the major institutions created by societies to fulfill these functions. They look different from one another because the cultural heritages they seek to pass on are differ-ent and because they serve societies that define "the good life" differently.

The creation of national systems of universal, free public education in the nineteenth century focused attention on schools as *the* institutions of educa-tion. A broader view of education in modern societies developed in the latter part of the twentieth century, building on the work of historians Bernard Bailyn and Lawrence Cremin.[5] Bailyn and Cremin emphasize the role that other institutions play in achieving both the cultural transmission and indi-vidual development aims of education. Each of these institutions perform edu-cational functions even though their primary purpose is something other than education.

Historically, the home and the synagogue were the main educational insti-tutions of the Jewish community, but in the nineteenth and twentieth centuries the Jewish community, too, focused its energy on schools and invested them with the responsibility for educating youth. As the Jewish community has broadened its view of education, the Jewish summer camp is one of many institutions other than schools that have taken on educational roles. These non-school forms of education—including family education, adult education, Jewish community centers, youth movements, campus programs, Jewish mu-seums, and Israel trips—are usually lumped together with camping under the banner of "informal education."

Despite their prime position in the pantheon of institutions of informal education, Jewish camps share many features with the *most formal* institutions of Jewish education, Jewish day schools. In conventional terms, camping sits on the informal end of a spectrum, day school on the formal end, and supple-mentary religious school somewhere in the middle. Religious schools are placed between camps and day schools because they look like schools (they have classrooms in which children learn a predetermined curriculum from teachers), but they frequently use a variety of informal educational approaches. But placing religious schools between camps and day schools obscures the significant similarities between the two.

Camps and day schools occupy similar places in the Reform Jewish community. Both are forms of Jewish education that are only a few generations old, Reform camping having begun in the late 1940s and Reform day schools a generation later, in the early 1970s. Today there are fewer than two dozen institutions of each type in North America (sixteen Reform camps, including camps sponsored by individual Reform temples, and twenty Reform day schools, several sponsored by individual congregations). Both camps and day schools are credited by their admirers with an extraordinary degree of success in educating Reform Jewish children. Indeed, they are both touted as "the answer" to the problem of Jewish continuity and the perceived failure of Jewish supplementary schools. As a result, both the camping movement and the day school movement are growing as new camps and schools are added at a slow but steady rate. Finally, both camps and day schools touch only a small percentage of Reform Jewish children each year, summer camps having about forty-five hundred beds,[6] and day schools enrolling about forty-five hundred students.[7] In sum, camps and day schools occupy similar places within the Reform movement: they educate a relatively small group of Reform Jewish children but are credited with being extraordinarily effective at shaping their Jewishness.

The educational similarities between camps and day schools are equally significant. First, both camps and day schools have a significant amount of time they can devote to Jewish education, especially as contrasted with the limited time available in supplementary schools. Campers attend camp from one to eight weeks a summer, with approximately fourteen waking hours per day that are available for camp-oriented activities. Students attend day school approximately seven hours per day, five days per week, for about thirty-six weeks during the year. (By contrast, students who attend religious schools usually meet between two and five hours per week for thirty weeks per year.)[8] Thus, camps and day schools do not have to deal with the most significant constraint facing supplementary schools: the severe limitations on the time available to address their educational goals.[9]

A second similarity between camp and day school is that in both environments Jewish life can be played out naturally in its rhythms within the time available. Daily *t'filla* (prayer) and the recitation of *brachot* (blessings) before and after meals can become natural parts of daily life at camp, and Shabbat can be a natural part of the week. In day school, *t'filla, brachot,* and the celebration of holidays can occur at the appropriate time in ways that feel genuine.

Third, both camp and day school offer the opportunity to connect Judaism to other areas of children's concerns and interests. At camp Judaism is not confined to a limited part of the day designated for Jewish programming, but can be related to manners at mealtime, sportsmanship during athletics, and personal prayer during a hike in the woods. Similarly, in day school Judaism is not limited to Judaica classes, but can be integrated into the study of other disciplines and connected to other activities in which children participate during the day. As a result, both camp and day school convey the message that Judaism can be a part of daily living and not something to be attended to only at temple or during a few afternoon or weekend hours each week.

Fourth, children and their parents choose to attend camp or day school for instrumental reasons that may or may not overlap with the more intrinsic goals of educators. Some parents send their children to camp for the recreational opportunities the camp offers, others for the social ties their children will develop, and still others for the educational and religious experiences the camp provides. One of the key questions parents ask is about the recreational facilities (Is there a lake? A tower? Ample athletic facilities?). The attractiveness of a camp to potential clients is largely a function of the excellence of its "secular" program, the "instrumental" activities it offers. Similarly, parents choose a day school education for their children for a variety of instrumental reasons, including safety and convenience; excellence of the school's program of secular studies; or the opportunities the school offers in art, music, computers, and other activities. Some parents, of course, choose day schools for the program of Jewish studies the school offers. In both camp and day school, despite the variety of parental motivations, and in spite of how high or low a priority parents may place on the Jewish component of the program, the camp or school has the potential to maintain and emphasize its commitment to the Jewish goals that are the raison d'être of the institution.

Fifth, both camp and day school provide for intensive interpersonal interactions, what Walter Ackerman refers to as "intimacy." This intimacy "serves as a backdrop for unparallel opportunities for self-discovery and interpersonal relationships." [10] By living together for weeks or months, campers have the opportunity to form strong and lasting bonds. The peer group assumes extraordinary power in the eyes of campers. In addition, the constant interaction with counselors provides campers the chance to learn from Jewish models. [11] The availability of artists, specialists, rabbis, cantors, and Jewish educators makes being at camp a potentially rich experience in which campers are exposed to a wide variety of adult models who possess a wide variety of skills and areas of expertise. Similarly, in day school a child's classmates become his or her primary peer group. Spending seven hours a day with a small group of classmates creates an intense peer experience, which in many cases leads to friendship patterns that persist over the seven years of elementary school and beyond. Day schools, too, have a wide array of adult models who are available to children for long periods of time: general studies teachers, Jewish studies teachers, assistants or co-teachers, specialists, psychologists or social workers, and coaches.

Finally, educators in camps and day schools make most curricular decisions locally. While UAHC camps are part of a system of camps stretching from coast to coast, from Canada to the South, each camp is free to make its own decisions about programs, themes, and activities. (Some Reform camps are even more autonomous in that they are sponsored by Reform temples and have no organizational ties with the UAHC.) Within the camp, unit heads and counselors have a fair degree of autonomy in determining the daily activities that make up the campers' curriculum. Similarly, although Reform day schools are members of PARDeS, the Progressive Association of Reform Day Schools, a UAHC affiliate, each school is free to determine its own curriculum, goals, programs, and course of study. And each classroom teacher makes the decisions about what activities will take place in the classroom each day. This curricular autonomy places great responsibility on the shoulders of educators in these two settings.

If day schools, the most formal educational institutions, share so many characteristics with camps, does it make sense to suggest that camps are "informal" and are therefore educationally different and unique? If day schools and camps are more like each other than like supplementary schools, is the distinction between formal and informal education meaningful and helpful in thinking about creating programs for camps? The mental set that views camps as fundamentally different from schools obscures educational thinking and planning for camps.

This view is supported by scholars and educators who have argued from different vantage points that the formal/informal distinction is not helpful. In a penetrating analysis of Jewish education, David Resnick provides a critique of the conventional distinction between formal and informal Jewish education. Resnick argues that supplementary schools, which are usually thought of as formal, are really informal.[12] He bases his argument on Barry Chazan's seminal paper, "What Is Informal Jewish Education?"[13] Chazan identifies eight characteristics of informal Jewish education:

1. Participation is voluntary.
2. Grades are not awarded; any evaluation that takes place is concerned with "feedback for today rather than prediction about tomorrow."
3. The orientation is intrinsic ("for its own sake") rather than instrumental (preparing people for something in the future).
4. The settings are highly interactive and participatory.
5. There is a plan, program and direction; that is, there is a curriculum,

which is usually developed locally, is highly flexible, and is usually not called a curriculum.

6. There is "an aura of fun and relaxation."
7. Educators are not called teachers and generally do not feel driven to cover material.
8. There is a "great emphasis on the group in the process of education."[14]

Chazan goes on to question "the popular wisdom" that claims, "Jewish schooling is responsible for teaching the basic building-blocks of Jewish literacy and knowledge and that informal education focuses on Jewish sociability and identification." He critiques the distinction between formal and informal education as "artificial and harmful." Both schools and camps transmit knowledge, and both schools and camps affect Jewish identity. He concludes that "they should be seen as alternative educational approaches to the overall goal of the development of knowledgeable and committed Jews."[15]

Resnick carries the argument even further by showing that "the kind of education done in almost all North American Jewish schools . . . meet[s] most of the criteria for informal education." Participation is voluntary; classroom education tries to focus on the meaning of modern-day Judaism (even if it often misses the mark); educators have tried to make Jewish classrooms interactive (although they are often not very successful); the curriculum is flexible and is not driven by external mandates; occasionally, in what Resnick calls "the best Jewish schools," learning is fun; and, as "several researchers have claimed . . . the major accomplishment of Jewish schools is their value as an agent of Jewish socialization."[16]

In sum, then, the distinction between formal and informal education, and in particular the notion that camps and schools lie on a continuum from informal to formal, is misleading. This conclusion is mirrored by Jack Wertheimer, who claims that since the 1980s the distinctions between formal and informal education have become blurred.[17] He cites examples collected by Bernard Reisman showing that settings usually thought of as formal have adopted informal methodologies, and educators in settings usually thought of as informal have increasingly placed greater emphasis on "formal Jewish content."[18]

Thus, it may not be helpful to think of Jewish education in "bifurcated" terms, with camps using informal approaches and schools utilizing formal ones. Rather, it may be more helpful to consider a "blended" view, in which camps and schools both reflect and utilize elements that are traditionally thought of as formal and informal.

According to the "bifurcated" view, formal education takes place in classrooms, while education at camp takes place outside of the classroom. Schools focus on cognitive learning; camp activities are experiential and focus on the emotional. Schools are highly structured; camp is structured informally. In schools, the teacher is the authority; in camp, counselors are more like older siblings than authority figures. Schools are designed to teach Jewish content; camp is designed to help campers develop a Jewish identity. In schools, social contact is a secondary concern; camps, on the other hand, are explicitly designed to facilitate social contact.

In contrast, a "blended" view combines formal and informal elements and recognizes that both forms of education take place in both schools and camps. Religious schools often conduct field trips, hikes, or retreats outside of the classroom, while classroom-style learning, even if it takes place outdoors, is often part of a camp program. Schools often include affective components, and a camp program may include a study session that is largely if not entirely cognitive. Religious schools can be informal places: children can dress informally, call teachers by their first names, and feel relaxed in carpeted classrooms with couches. Camps can be quite formally structured, with hierarchies of administration and with ladders of advancement from CIT to junior counselor to senior counselor. In some classrooms, teachers encourage shared inquiry as students and teachers learn together. While teachers may ultimately have authority over student behavior, some teachers disguise their authority behind friendliness, warmth, and an air of informality. But the supposed lack of authority in camp may be the same: some adult always has ultimate responsibility and authority over participants' behavior. Many religious schools no longer focus on the teaching content and instead try to develop students' Jewish identities, and many camp sessions have themes that are aimed at teaching Jewish content. Some schools make explicit attempts to facilitate socializing during breaks, social hours, out-of-class activities, and through the selection of specific teaching techniques. When camps become entirely social, one may wonder whether they have ceased to be educational. In sum, this "blended" view may help educators recognize that the distinctions between formal and informal education may not be all that significant when planning Jewish education for either setting.

Multidimensional Education

Rather than thinking of Jewish education in either-or terms (either informal or formal; either identity-based or content-focused; either experiential or cognitive), it is more useful to think about Jewish education in any setting, camp or school, along a continuum from a single dimension to multiple simultaneous dimensions. Regardless of where it takes place, Jewish education can be effective to the degree that it creates a rich tapestry of opportunities across a range of educational dimensions, including goals, human resources, environment, and modes of learning.

Goals

Goals focus the attention of educators on what they are seeking to accomplish in a program, course, lesson, or activity. They are therefore stated in terms of what the course or teacher should try to do rather than what students should work toward. It may be possible to identify a single goal or multiple goals for any given educational experience. For example, a camp specialist may identify the goal of introducing campers to a set of Israeli dance steps or helping them master certain Israeli dances. A classroom teacher may set the goal of teaching students to recite a specific prayer or understand the components of a life-cycle ritual. More often than not, in both camp and school, educators hold multiple goals simultaneously. The dance specialist may be introducing a new step, teaching a new dance, and helping campers master a new choreography all at the same time. The classroom teacher may be striving to reinforce word recognition skills while teaching a prayer, or may want students to understand the concept of ritual as they learn specific life-cycle rituals.

Yet even in these situations where the educator holds more than one goal, the goals themselves often fall into a narrow range. The broader the range of multiple goals, the more likely it is that the educational experience will be powerful. A dance specialist who hopes to engender a love of dance, an appreciation of the social experience of group and line dancing, and a commitment to the modern State of Israel at the same time he is teaching the steps holds multidimensional goals. The classroom teacher who seeks to help students understand the power of ritual to ease significant life passages, heighten their appreciation of the way Jewish community enhances individual experiences, and stimulate students' creative expression at intense moments while simultaneously teaching the concept of ritual and the skills associated with a particular ritual is working toward multiple goals.

It is possible to hold multiple types of goals, to write them in handbooks and in curriculum books, without actually addressing them. In this case, obviously, they do not serve to strengthen the educational experience. Schools often focus on the development of knowledge and skills and pay lip service to the development of Jewish identity. Camps sometimes pay so much attention to identity and socialization that they neglect Jewish content. A powerful educational experience in either camp or school will establish and address multiple layers simultaneously.

Human Resources

Elementary school classrooms typically operate with a single teacher who is in charge of orchestrating the entire educational experience for children. At times, an aide, co-teacher, or *madrich* (counselor; in this case, a teaching assistant) is also present. But in the words of the African proverb popularized by

Hillary Clinton, "it takes a village" to educate a child. Camps are often like villages in that many adults work with children during the course of each day: counselors and co-counselors; specialists, rabbis, cantors, and educators on faculty; kitchen and office personnel; and nurses and doctors. Schools often have many of these same resources available: teachers, specialists, rabbis, cantors, and educational leaders, as well as support staff. All the adults in the educational environment can see themselves first and foremost as educators, specifically *Jewish* educators. Whether they work in the kitchen or the office, in a cabin or in a classroom, after health and safety, everyone's first priority can be to serve as a "Jewish role model" and to teach, directly or indirectly, what it means to be an active, engaged Jew.

In summer camps it is not uncommon for a group of counselors who are only a few years older than their campers to work together to plan and execute a Jewish educational program. In order to work on the program, they themselves often have to learn the subject matter of the program, and so other staff members, often slightly older unit heads, become the educators of the educators. In schools these same young people are often sent to classrooms—either alone as teachers or as *madrichim*. Up to a point, the greater the number of such people who interact with students, the more likely the educational program will be effective. Having more people available to carry the educational messages, using them in concerted ways, and allowing them to be Jewish learners as well, creates the sense of "village" that can promote Jewish living and learning.

Environment

Jewish camps are, either consciously or unconsciously, based on Plato's idea that the community educates and John Dewey's notion that "all of life educates." [19] Dewey said that "above all, [educators] should know how to utilize the surroundings, physical and social, that exist so as to extract from them all that they have to contribute to building up experiences that are worthwhile." [20]

John Westerhoff explains the importance of the environment by distinguishing between schooling and socialization. [21] According to Westerhoff, socialization is much broader than schooling, because it includes all the formal and informal influences through which people acquire their understandings and ways of living. Isa Aron extends this line of thinking in writing about instruction as "furnishing someone with knowledge, usually by means of a systematic method" and enculturation as "holistic and more serendipitous," and neither segmented nor ordered. [22] Enculturation, as Westerhoff explains, "include[s] every aspect of individual and corporate lives." [23]

People learn best when they experience instruction and enculturation that reinforce each other. In that way the community creates "plausibility structures" for its members, tapestries of meaning that are shared by members of the community and that encourage them to adopt the community's values and ethos. Religious schools have to work hard to create plausibility structures, because people participate in religious schools in staccato fashion, for a few hours at a time and only a few times a week. Camps can create effective plausibility structures because they can use the totality of the social and physical environment to encapsulate and communicate the camp's core values and commitments.

In schools, the classroom and the playground are typically the only physical environments used for learning. Some schools use their environment more fully, taking students to the sanctuary and on field trips in the community or bringing aspects of the community to them. Camps typically have a broader view of the environment, using every nook and cranny of the camp for some educational or recreational purpose. For the school, the challenge is to use more spaces; for the camp, the challenge is to use the spaces educationally. This does not, however, mean simply using outdoor spaces for "indoor education." At one summer camp the Jewish educational program consisted primarily of daily discussions, which were held in an outdoor area known as "the discussion pits."[24] Taking classroom education out of doors is a step toward utilizing the environment, but adapting the educational program so that it takes advantage of the unique characteristics of the physical environment can make education even more effective.

The environment has a social dimension too. Much classroom learning is individual, and students engage in "parallel learning" in much the way toddlers engage in "parallel play." Often, however, classroom educators recognize that learning has a social dimension and that knowledge can be socially constructed. (Constructivist teaching, for example, is based on the belief that people learn better and retain longer when they actively participate in constructing their own understanding rather than being told what they are learning. Some constructivist teaching goes even further and suggests that understanding becomes more sophisticated when people work with others to build their understanding.)

Most camp learning utilizes social groups. Indeed, little of the Jewish learning that takes place in camp is done individually. Campers learn together with their cabin group, their unit, or the entire camp. The question is whether campers are given the opportunity to interact with others to construct their understanding and check it against what others understand, or whether they merely have a similar experience as others—perhaps in the same place at the same time—but with little opportunity to reflect together on what and how they are learning. Significant learning from experience happens only when the experience is reflected upon, and camps need to provide opportunities for shared reflection.

Most educators are aware that every person learns in different ways at different times. And the implication of this proposition is that to help others learn, educators need to provide multiple opportunities for learning, drawing on different senses, different ways of knowing, and different parts of the learner's being.

The simplest understanding of multiple ways of learning is that some people are visual learners, others are auditory learners, and still others are kinesthetic learners. Effective classroom teachers thus provide opportunities for visual and auditory learners, for example, by saying instructions aloud and writing them on the board or at the top of a worksheet. They provide texts and tapes and allow for movement around the classroom. Even with attempts to accommodate different learning styles, most classrooms favor visual learners and neglect kinesthetic learners. Camps, on the other hand tend to favor kinesthetic and auditory learners and neglect visual learners. (There are, for example, few opportunities for reading in most camp programs.)

Howard Gardner and his colleagues in Project Zero have taken the notion of different modes of learning even further and have identified seven types of intelligence: linguistic, logical-mathematical, spatial, bodily-kinesthetic, musical, interpersonal, and intrapersonal.[25] Schools, they argue, focus on only a limited set of intelligences and thereby leave out many children whose talents lie in areas that schools do not emphasize. Daniel Goleman suggests that emotional intelligence is also important.[26]

Robert Sternberg offers a related theory of intelligence.[27] He points to the large number of people who are successful in life but who were not particularly successful in school. By studying successful people who did not test well in school, he developed a tripartite theory of intelligence. The first type of intelligence, emphasized in schools and tested on exams like the SAT, is problem-solving, or "analytic intelligence." But as Dewey is supposed to have said, problems don't walk around with labels hanging from their necks. A second type of intelligence is "creative intelligence," the ability to identify and define problems. Once a problem is identified (using creative intelligence) and solved (using analytic intelligence), the solution must then be implemented in the "real world," using what Sternberg calls "practical intelligence."

Because few if any tests are administered in Jewish education, Jewish schools and camps can help children develop all three kinds of intelligence rather than emphasizing analytic intelligence. They can also recognize children who excel in each area rather than privileging those who excel in analytic intelligence. A Jewish school can, for example, create an environment where students confront "indeterminate situations" involving Jewish values in which they are asked to identify and define problems (using creative intelligence) and then propose solutions (using analytic intelligence). A Jewish camp can provide campers with a series of dilemmas to solve (using analytic intelligence) and then give them the opportunity to put their solutions into practice in the camp community. Encouraging campers to reflect on camp-centered situations can provide opportunities for them to use all three types of intelligence in order to gain a deeper understanding of how Jews live in a community.

In addition to intelligence (which emphasizes the cognitive), education also includes the affective (feelings) and the behavioral (skills). This classic way to understand education is based on a distinction first identified by Aristotle and most recently put into practice in Jewish education in the field of confluent education. Conventional thinking about Jewish education and Jewish identity places identity formation in the affective area. Camps and youth groups are given responsibility for affective development, while schools focus on cognitive development. Recent work on Jewish identity suggests the importance of intertwining all three areas. "[Jewish] identity is best promoted," write Perry London and Barry Chazan, "as an experience that integrates the cognitive, affective and behavioral. This perspective rejects the bifurcation of Jewish education into a 'cultural literacy and cognitive development' branch and an 'identity and affect' part. . . . Jewish literacy training ought to be an important aspect of identity training, providing the content towards which the affects of identity are directed."[28] In this view, Jewish camps that are content to provide children with "Jewish experiences" are less likely to promote Jewish identity than camps that couple experiences designed to enhance Jewish identity with learning of related Jewish content.

Applying Curriculum Principles to Camp

Up to this point I have argued that Jewish camps and Jewish schools are more alike than dissimilar. I have suggested that camps and day schools share much in common and that the lines between camps and religious schools are blurred. I have asserted, therefore, that paying attention to multiple dimensions of the educational situation can make schools and camps more educationally potent. Now I want to suggest several principles of education that have particular and unique application to the curriculum of Jewish camping (though in some instances they may also apply to other forms of Jewish education). I will examine the aims of Jewish camping; the educator as learner; planning and pedagogy; and the three curricula of camp.

Aims

Aims are the broad purposes of an institution. Like goals, they focus the attention of program planners in certain directions. Unlike goals, aims do not address specific lessons or activities; rather, they ask educators to look at the entire camp experience through a "wide-angle lens." When Samson Benderly first conceived of summer camping for American Jewish children, he conceived of the aims of camping as "implant[ing] a love for and interest in things Jewish and arous[ing] in the child a desire for Jewish knowledge."[29] Later, Albert Schoolman viewed the aim of camping as involving a social outcome, namely, a desire "to participate in group activity of a Jewish character."[30] These articulations suggest that the aims of camping are both affective and are focused on stimulating campers to become involved in Jewish learning and living at some later point in their lives.

Many of the UAHC camps refer to themselves as "camps for living Judaism," because they provide environments where campers can experience Jewish living firsthand. They thus make Jewish living a positive experience for campers, with the implied aim that campers continue to practice "living Judaism" when they return home.

Jewish camps do more than just awaken a desire for Jewish learning in the future. They also engage campers in Jewish learning in the present. What, then, should they aim to teach? When Jewish camping first began in America, one of its aims was to help Americanize a generation of immigrants from Eastern Europe. Clearly that aim is no longer valid. Later, Jewish camping became a tool in the battle against assimilation, a form of "pediatric inoculation" that would last from year to year, and, if a child received enough "boosters," would last for a lifetime. This, too, no longer seems appropriate, since there is no evidence that "pediatric inoculation" against assimilation works.[31]

Rather, an appropriate aim for Jewish camps at the beginning of the twenty-first century is to provide campers and counselors with a compelling rationale for Jewish learning and Jewish living. The aim, according to Joseph Reimer, is "to value Jewish distinctiveness by not allowing our heritage to become blended into the American background."[32] Helping campers and counselors understand that Jewish distinctiveness provides a rationale for Jewish living and learning can be difficult, because they are part of an American Jewish community that is characterized by a "coalescence of values."[33] Sylvia Barrack Fishman explains that "during the process of coalescence, the 'texts' of two cultures, American and Jewish, are accessed simultaneously. . . . These value systems coalesce or merge, and the resulting merged messages or texts are perceived not as being American and Jewish values side by side, but as being a unified text, which is identified as authoritative Judaism."[34] In other words, many American Jews hold an ideology that blurs the distinctions between Jewish and American values.

This ideology first developed in the early part of the twentieth century. According to David Ellenson, Jewish immigrants adopted a "melting pot" ideology and "forge[d] a Judaism that was seen as totally compatible with American life and values. They [developed] systems of religious thought and practice—

Reform and Conservative Judaism—that applauded the virtues of democracy and the American way of life. Indeed, an offshoot of Conservative Judaism, Reconstructionism, accorded the status of sancta to such American festivals as Thanksgiving, Labor Day, and the Fourth of July."[35] What better example of coalescence!

Camps miss an opportunity when they echo the messages of coalescence that participants have already absorbed (for example, by teaching American values such as sportsmanship as if they were Jewish values). If Jewish values are perceived to be identical with American values, there is no compelling reason to study, adopt, practice, or live by Jewish values. Elsewhere I have proposed "interaction" as an alternative approach to Jewish education.[36] Through exposure to an education characterized by interaction, young people come to understand how American and Jewish values differ and how Judaism can contribute to their lives and to society.

Ellenson traces the sociological and philosophical reasons why this "new ideological vision [interaction] . . . may be more appropriate [than an ideology guided by coalescence] in guiding our educational and communal decisions in the coming century."[37] He cites three factors. First, he suggests that the rationale for the "melting pot" ideal lost some of its power in the latter part of the twentieth century. He quotes Eugene Borowitz's view that "Today [humanity] needs people who are creatively alienated. To be satisfied with our situation is either to have bad values or to understand grossly what [persons] can do. . . . Creative alienation implies sufficient withdrawal from our society to judge it critically, but also the way and flexibility to keep finding and trying ways to correct it. I think Jewishness offers a unique means of gaining and maintaining such creative alienation."[38] Creative alienation requires an understanding of Jewish distinctiveness.

Second, Ellenson draws on Peter Berger's view that modernity's primary characteristic is the "heretical imperative," the necessity to make choices (which Reform Judaism has exalted in the form of "personal autonomy"). Autonomy is simultaneously liberating (because it "frees people from the shackles of a stultifying culture and tradition that defines roles and expectations in a narrow and confining way"[39]) and bewildering (because people are left without the anchors provided by an authoritative tradition or the certainty that rationalism will provide universal answers). Autonomy places responsibility on the individual for creating a synthesis among the various value systems one confronts.

Finally, Ellenson argues that a coalesced value system is inappropriate in a post-Holocaust world. "Simply put, the Holocaust has rocked the confidence Jews formerly had in the goodness of humanity and the moral progress of civilization."[40] In light of the recognition of the limits of Enlightenment, "Reform Judaism can no longer completely identify and assert its compatibility with the tenets of western or any other civilization."[41] Ellenson does not, of course, advocate a retreat to fundamentalism. He urges Reform Jews to maintain an ideology that incorporates the concepts of autonomy, democracy, and pluralism. But, he says, "in the present situation—both sociologically and philosophically—the task confronting individual persons is not primarily one of affirming autonomy and individual personhood," it is helping Jews understand that "the integrity and wisdom of Jewish tradition . . . can contribute much to individual Jews and the Jewish community in a world that all too often flounders in its quest for values. . . . By providing a model of Judaism that is not identical, but interacts with the larger world of values and culture of which we are a part, Judaism may make its greatest contribution to individual Jews and our larger society."[42]

Interaction calls on Jewish educational institutions to identify areas where Jewish values are distinct from American and western values. For example, Judaism and America take different approaches to individual rights and responsibilities. Elliot Dorff traces the difference between Jewish and American values to the core documents of each tradition. He asks, "Am I, as the Declaration of Independence proclaims, a creature born with inalienable rights, or am I, as Deuteronomy would have it, a person born into a host of obligations?"[43] Camp counselors and unit heads have ample opportunity during the days and weeks of the summer to explore the differences between these two views as they are manifest in the give-and-take of social life at camp. They can point out (and even "heat up") the tension between rights and responsibilities. They can invite campers to explore the dissonance between Jewish and American views and create their own synthesis between these value systems. (It is important to note, of course, that Jewish and American values often have points of intersection, and these too can be taught and modeled.)

Jewish ritual and celebration offer additional arenas where Jewish and American approaches do not overlap. For example, Jewish rituals surrounding meals (*motzi* and *birkat hamazon*, respectively, blessings before and after a meal) differ from American norms, particularly *birkat hamazon*'s individual and communal thanksgiving. Shabbat celebration, with its emphasis on *oneg* (joy), *menucha* (rest), and *t'filla* (prayer), clearly does not have any exact parallel in American culture. Making distinctive ritual and celebration a cornerstone of life at camp provides campers an alternative model for the rhythms of life that reflect values that are distinctively Jewish.[44]

Thus, the aim of Jewish camps should be to show participants a rich tapestry of distinctive Jewish values that can become part of their own lives and that can guide them in their communities. These values can be taught, modeled, experienced, and reflected upon in the context of the camp, thereby giving campers an experience of distinctive Jewish living that includes, but goes far beyond, celebration of Shabbat.

Educator as Learner

One of the unique features of camps is the vast number of young adults who serve in an educational capacity. Counselors are often only a few years older than campers and therefore serve as accessible role models for campers. They are also a vast, under-tapped reservoir of young Jews to be educated. The potential of the camp experience to have a profound effect on staff members is captured by Ian Russ and Hanan Alexander in their evaluation of youth programming serving Jews of Los Angeles. "Being a camper is fun," they write, but "being a counselor is a life changing experience."[45] They echo Bernard Reisman's recommendation to the North American Commission on Jewish Education to enrich the learning of counselors at Jewish summer camps.[46]

The need to focus on Jewish learning for counselors stems from the vast numbers of young adults who are at camps every summer, from the potential to have an impact on their Jewish development, and from the fact that they are the primary Jewish educators of campers. The depth and breadth of campers' Jewish learning is a function of how well educated counselors are. Some of them may bring a rich Jewish background from their childhood or college experiences, but many of them come with meager Jewish knowledge, motivated only by their own positive memories of camp.

One of the most powerful motivators for adults to learn is the need to accomplish a particular task. Adults learn to use computers when the need arises, they learn parenting skills when they have children, and they learn to read Hebrew when their motivation to become a Bar or Bat Mitzvah becomes sufficiently strong. Counselors are often in the position where they need to teach campers. If Jewish learning for counselors is directly related to the Jewish teaching that they will be called on to do, they will come with a strong motivation to learn. In sum, Jewish learning for counselors is a critical part of the mission of Jewish camps.

Planning and Pedagogy

At camp everything seems to happen naturally. When things are working well, one activity flows into the next and learning and doing blend together seamlessly. Campers thus experience an integrated whole that seems to take place effortlessly. But as anyone who has ever been a counselor or unit head knows, nothing happens without a tremendous amount of planning.

Planning at camp calls for attention to incorporating Jewish learning and Jewish living into every activity during the day, not just into designated educational times. Planning thus requires conscious attention to the question of what it means to integrate Judaism into other activities. Integrating Jewish learning into other activities can take a variety of forms:

- Using mealtimes to teach Hebrew by requiring campers to ask for utensils and food in Hebrew, keeping score during games in Hebrew, or referring to places around camp using Hebrew names
- Dealing with behavior problems or issues of group dynamics by referring to Jewish values or texts
- Singing Jewish songs after meals
- Teaching *t'shuvah* (repentence) as part of archery lessons (focusing on the meaning of *chet* [sin] as "missing the mark")

The most significant criterion for selecting which situations are appropriate for integration is whether they allow the flow of the activity to continue normally, or whether the activity stops so that Jewish teaching can take place. If campers are unduly delayed in eating because they can't remember the word for "fork," or if they have very few chances to shoot an arrow because they use all their time discussing *t'shuvah*, these are probably not appropriate times to integrate. But if announcements can be made using Hebrew, Jewish songs can be sung in the midst of a camp song session, and interpersonal issues can be addressed from a Jewish frame of reference while the activity at hand proceeds in a normal way, then these probably are appropriate times to integrate.

Educational planning at camp involves a mix of careful advance planning and an openness to respond as events unfold. Since there are no tests at camp (except perhaps in the swimming pool), planning usually takes place without the specification of objectives, which are the mainstay of classroom planning. Camp programming can be "emergent,"[47] and sometimes the goals of an activity can take shape as the action is unfolding. Also, as Albert Schoolman explains, "Camp learning lends itself also to reversing the traditional practice of beginning with the distant past and never reaching the present. At camp it is easy to start with the functional present and move in retrospect along historic lines that are significantly relevant to the present."[48] This conception of camp programming is similar to Franz Rosenzweig's description of a "new sort of learning . . . a learning in reverse order. A learning that no longer starts from the Torah and leads into life, but the other way round: from life . . . back to Torah."[49] Because of the richness of daily life at camp, Jewish camps can reverse the traditional pattern of studying text and applying it to life and instead move from the life of camp to the study of text. In this way campers can see that Jewish tradition speaks to the realities of their lives, for as Arnold Eisen states in explaining Rosenzweig's thought, "A Judaism which has nothing to say to the lives Jews actually lead . . . is a Judaism that has ceased to be itself."[50] Thus, whatever the programmatic theme is for a given camp session, much of the significant learning will emerge from the daily life of the campers, and that learning will be *Jewish* learning to the degree that the camp staff seizes the opportunity to bring Judaism into everyday moments. The planning task is thus to balance careful advance planning that ensures a richness of opportunities for Jewish living with an openness to the events that occur in daily camp life.

Joseph Reimer uses the metaphor of river rafting to explain the power of Jewish camping. What gives camp experiences their power, he argues, "is that for many these [experiences] are their first opportunities to be *in* the river, to experience Judaism as a live current that carries them along and leaves a lasting impression."[51] Pedagogically, what makes it possible for campers to jump into the river is what Raphael Zarum terms a "'pedagogy of participation,' which emphasizes asking many questions, carefully listening to answers, respecting diverse opinions, empowering individuality, and experiential learning."[52] The participatory character of camp programming invites campers to experience the richness of Jewish life the camp offers. The potential pitfall of the pedagogy of participation, however, is that participation itself is seen as an end rather than a means to an end. Programs can be designed to get campers involved, without equal attention to *what* they are being involved in. The pedagogy of participation is educationally powerful only when it is coupled with careful attention to the content that is being taught.

The power of camp lies, in part, in the Jewish memories that camps create. Sometimes those memories emerge out of natural events that unfold during a camp session, sometimes the memories come from the repeated regularities of camp (such as prayer or song sessions), but often they can be scheduled into a camp session. They require careful planning, attention to detail, creative use of space, coordinated participation by many staff members, and often art, drama, music, or dance. These memorable moments lend rhythm to a camp session and leave an imprint that often lasts a lifetime.

The Three Curricula of Camp

Elliot Eisner explains that every educational institution teaches, and therefore must plan for, three curricula.[53] The "overt" curriculum is the stated content, goals, materials, and activities. The second curriculum is the "null" curriculum, what an institution does *not* teach. Since every decision to include something is in effect a decision to exclude something else, when planners choose a particular theme for a camp session, they are deciding not to expose campers to other themes. When they plan for learners to participate in certain types of learning experiences that call upon and develop certain skills, they are neglecting other skills. For example, if program planners never expose campers to Jewish texts, they are preventing campers from having experiences that may lead them to further text learning in the future. In camp there are many opportunities to pursue purely recreational activities that do not convey Jewish content. As planners set more and more time aside for recreation, there are fewer and fewer opportunities to focus on an overt curriculum of Jewish content. The larger this null Jewish curriculum, the more campers are deprived of experiences that expose them to Jewish culture and religion.

The third and final curriculum, the "implicit" curriculum, is perhaps the most significant in determining what campers will take away from their camp experience. Its teachings are conveyed through the physical surrounding, the social groupings, the hierarchical structures and the policies and procedures that are part of an educational setting. The implicit curriculum is how a camp teaches through its group norms ("how things are done around here"), relationships, use of time, and so forth. In schools, the implicit curriculum is sometimes referred to as "the nonacademic outcomes" of education, the norms, values, and ideas that students learn even though teachers do not directly teach them.

What makes a curriculum implicit is that at a given moment the educator is not consciously attending to it. In a classroom, teachers attend primarily to the flow of the lesson and its impact on student learning, but *secondary consequences* may emerge from the types of activities the teacher chooses. Teachers may sometimes wonder whether the social aspect of the classroom helps or hinders learning, but this is usually a secondary concern. In camp, the focus is reversed. The social structure of a cabin group, the quality of relationships among the campers, and their cohesiveness as a group are often foremost in the minds of counselors and unit heads. The goal is for campers to learn the personal and group skills that will help them socially and will encourage their sense of belonging to the Jewish community. Content is often a secondary concern. For example, in planning a role-play of characters from Jewish history, programmers may focus on helping campers develop a sense of identification with the characters they are portraying rather than how much the campers are learning about the historical context or specifics of the character's life and philosophy. In other words, the aspects of the learning situation that are part of the implicit curriculum in most classroom situations are the overt curriculum in camp, and vice versa.

A skilled teacher plans for the implicit curriculum as well as the overt curriculum, and a skilled educator at camp also pays attention to both curricula. Since the primary curricular concern at camp is often the social learning and Jewish identification that stem from the camp experience, the task of those who plan at camp is to search for an implicit curriculum to support this primary concern. In camp the implicit curriculum might be the Jewish content or the cultural and religious skills needed to support Jewish identification. Jewish schools often teach these skills (for example, praying and celebrating, reading and interpreting text) as their overt curriculum; in camp these skills become the implicit curriculum.

In the 1960s and 1970s the implicit curriculum was frequently referred to as the "hidden curriculum," but from whom is it hidden? If the camp director is aware that part of the "hidden" curriculum is to teach Jewish ideas and values, is it no longer hidden? What if the counselors are aware? What if the campers are aware?

The question of hiddenness points to an important issue in camping education. From time to time, camps employ sociodramas to facilitate their teaching. A sociodrama is a role-play in which campers are unaware that a role-play is taking place. For example, the broadcast of *This American Life* referred to earlier reports on a case where a few counselors in a Jewish camp dressed in costumes and "raided" the camp, pretending to be members of an anti-Semitic hate group. In a similar situation that I witnessed, a unit head ran in to the dining room and reported he had just received a phone call telling him that a group of neo-Nazis was an hour away driving toward the camp. An hour-long discussion of how to respond ensued. In a final example, a camp director gathered the entire camp together and told them that one of the campers had been discovered with drugs, and the camp director wanted the campers' advice about what to do. What unites all these examples is (1) their realism, (2) the total involvement of campers in the role-play, (3) the exciting discussions about "what to do," and (4) the fact that staff members have deceived campers and that campers did not know they were being deceived. It is this final characteristic that makes sociodramas problematic. If campers do not know that they can "opt out," they don't have any recourse if the action gets too intense for them. These situations also violate the trust that campers place in the camp staff. (An alternative to the sociodrama, which is admittedly less engaging but avoids the pitfalls of the sociodrama, is the role-play. For example, campers may build a model of the Temple in Jerusalem and then watch in surprise as staff members dressed as Roman soldiers set it on fire. Although campers may become upset that the Temple that they worked hard to build is being destroyed, the difference between this and a sociodrama is that in a role-play everyone is aware that a "game" is being played. At any moment, campers can choose not to participate.)[54]

A charge often leveled against camp programming is that it is manipulative. The camp staff has the power to control almost every aspect of the camp environment, and it can use that power either to educate or to indoctrinate. Is staging a dramatic, engaging program about the need for a Jewish homeland after the Holocaust education or indoctrination? Is dressing everyone in white, whipping campers into a frenzy during a Shabbat song session, then quieting them down for an emotional healing service education or indoctrination? As in the case of sociodramas, the answer lies in the degree of autonomy campers retain. If they are able to step back, reflect, and think independently about what they are experiencing, they are participating in an educational activity; if not, they are more likely being indoctrinated into a camp "cult."[55]

In order to ensure that programming in a Jewish camp remains educational, the staff who are involved in crafting the environment and programming need to maintain a reflective, self-critical stance toward their work. They need to be guided by more than just pragmatism: "Will this program work?" They also need to ask ethical questions about the work they are doing: "Does our program preserve and enhance the autonomy and dignity of campers? Does it set the stage for their future growth as human beings and as Jews?" These questions do not imply that the camp staff cannot advocate for Jewish living and learning, or that they have to be neutral or take a relativistic stance toward issues of values. Rather, as they are preparing the most engaging and compelling program, they have an obligation to preserve and enhance each camper's ability to think independently.

The Challenges of Success

Jewish camps are undoubtedly one of the great success stories of Jewish education in North America. As Jack Wertheimer concludes in his comprehensive survey of Jewish education over the past half century, summer camps are "perhaps the most powerful vehicle for informal Jewish education."[56] The research on Jewish identity confirms the power of camping and other forms of informal Jewish education. Bethamie Horowitz labels these forms of Jewish education voluntary, because people "*choose* to undertake" them.[57] (By this definition, most Jewish schooling is involuntary, because the decision to attend such schools is made by parents, not the student; most decisions about Jewish camping are either voluntary, that is, made by the camper, or at least shared by the camper and his or her parents.) In a large study of Jewish identity, Horowitz concludes that "adults who came from less intensively Jewish backgrounds were most strongly influenced by later, 'voluntary' experiences during their adolescence and early adulthood."[58] She thus broadens the findings of Bruce Phillips, who concludes that the most potent influences on whom Jews marry are the experiences in which children choose to participate, especially youth groups and camps.[59]

The very success of Jewish summer camps creates challenges for camp educators. The most significant challenge is how to help campers transfer what they have learned to their homes and communities. Some camps deliberately set out to establish camp as a counterculture, a Jewish space and time for "glimpsing Jewish possibilities."[60] They shield out other influences as much as possible and try to keep campers away from contact with the outside world. Steve Plaut suggests that these camps parallel the Zionist endeavor of creating a specifically Jewish culture in a Jewish geography.[61] Even camps that take a less isolationist approach still try to create compelling Jewish cultures and all-encompassing Jewish environments for campers. They often succeed by grafting Jewish culture onto the youth culture of camp[62] and by "making it cool to be Jewish in public."[63]

Campers who have experienced Judaism intensely during a session at camp can have difficulty carrying Judaism back home with them.[64] An oft-quoted complaint from former campers is that it is impossible to do Havdalah back home, because there is no lake! In one poignant story about the difficulties of transferring camp Judaism to the city, a group of campers returned home at the end of one summer and went to services at their temple the following Friday night. They were so disappointed by what they experienced that they picketed the offices of the rabbi and cantor, demanding that they make services as alive and meaningful as they were at camp!

Nachama Skolnick [Moskowitz] argues that the problem of transfer can be addressed only when responsibility is shared by synagogue, home, and camp.[65] Parents can encourage their children to think about their camp experience and continue the Jewish actions they experienced at camp, particularly by celebrating Shabbat. (Camps can help parents by providing them with materials to support their practice at home, including albums of camp music.) Synagogues can ease the transition by holding camp-style services near the end of each summer, coordinating the topics studied in school and at camp, and giving returning campers special responsibilities within the religious school.

Camps bear the most responsibility for helping campers transfer what they have learned and experienced at camp into their lives at home. During the summer, camps can help campers anticipate the problem of transfer and discuss strategies for addressing the problem. They can create connections between campers and community organizations and general Jewish activities in their hometowns. All of these strategies would help campers see that camp is part of a larger set of Jewish involvements and experiences rather than seeing camp as an island, separate from the rest of Jewish experience.

One of the aims of Jewish camping is to create strong Jewish identities. Yet even with all of their power, camps cannot succeed at this task on their own. In summarizing two decades of research on Jewish education and Jewish identity formation, Jonathan Woocher concludes, "More is better; longer is better; and better is better. The more and better quality of Jewish education an individual is exposed to, and the longer the period of time in which she or he is so engaged, the more likely he or she is to be impacted by that education."[66] He goes on to say, "It is critical that we avoid the trap of false choices: more day school or more summer camping. . . . It isn't really either/or. It is equally important that no actor or set of actors believes that it can do what needs to be done either alone or in isolation."[67]

Camping *is* very powerful. But camping alone can't ensure the Jewishness of the next generation or build a Jewish community that is vibrant and alive. By partnering with other institutions (religious schools, day schools, Hillels, etc.), Jewish camps can reinforce what young people learn elsewhere and can become important avenues that lead young people to make Jewish choices in the future. By encouraging campers and counselors to participate in Jewish life and Jewish learning throughout the year, camps can keep young Jews moving on the pathway toward firm Jewish identities that are grounded in a solid understanding of Judaism and the Jewish community.

There are problems that result from the very success of Jewish camping programs. Camp programs are often intense, and many people return summer after summer. Camps often promote a sense of the superiority of the education they provide. "The result," writes Steven Plaut, "is a population of teen-agers and those in their early twenties convinced that they already know all there is to know."[68] At their best, camps awaken in campers the desire to study Judaism and to learn more about their heritage, but at times they convey the message that what they teach is all that is really worth knowing. The challenge for camps is to transmit Jewish knowledge so that campers develop pride in what they know *and* an appreciation of what they do not yet know.

Another challenge revolves around experience rather than knowledge. The experiences children have at camp often have an emotional intensity that overshadows other experiences they have had. Camp experiences often outweigh any *Jewish* experiences they have had, including their Bar or Bat Mitzvah. (These rites of passage are more often peak experiences for parents than for children.) Camp alumni often look back at camp as the Jewish high point of their life. They then struggle to re-create the intensity of Jewish feeling that they experienced at camp. The success of the UAHC Kallah program and the growth of alternative *minyanim* (literally the ten people needed for community prayer, but in practice groups gathering for a more intimate or otherwise "different" worship experience) in Reform temples may reflect the desire of many adults to re-create their camp experience and the desire of those who never attended camp to taste the camp experience. (It is interesting to note that the music at these events is often led by people who are former camp song leaders.) The challenge for Reform Judaism is to create many more venues in which former campers can find sparks of what they experienced as the camp Judaism of their youth.[69]

Finally, Jewish camps are successful because they provide an environment and experiences that make a difference in people's lives. As Reimer suggests, schools should be more like camps.[70] On the other hand, schools provide experiences that shape people's minds and give them a solid foundation of knowledge on which to build their identities, and so camps should be more like schools, too. The challenge for camps is to take on more of the knowledge-transmission functions of schools without also taking on the negative associations that schools often carry. They will not do that by merely using camp space as outdoor classrooms for indoor learning. Nor will they do it by merely providing campers recreational opportunities alongside other Jews. Reform Jewish camps will have to invent a new kind of teaching, a new approach to curriculum, a new vision of what it means to be an educator, and a new way to help campers and counselors encounter Jewish tradition and Jewish knowledge.

For half a century, Olin-Sang-Ruby Union Institute has led the way in Jewish camping. It is poised to continue leading the way as Reform Jewish camping meets these challenges.

Notes

I want to thank the many students with whom I have discussed informal education—in particular, Miriam Cotsen, Tali Hyman, David Lewis, and Avram Mandel. I want to especially thank Avram for serving as research assistant on one phase of this project. I also want to thank Joseph Reimer and Jeffrey Marx for sharing their informal education course syllabi with me.

1. *Shiur-sicha* means literally "lesson-discussion." The technique is to engage the learners in a lesson that triggers small group discussions afterward. The lesson is often a skit or other presentation and rarely a frontal lecture.

2. For a more thorough description of connoisseurship in education, see Elliot Eisner, *The Educational Imagination: On the Design and Evaluation of School Programs,* 3rd ed. (New York: MacMillan, 1994).

3. "Notes on Camp," *This American Life,* 109 (August 28, 1998), WBEZ, Chicago (www.thislife.org). All quotations in this section are taken from the broadcast.

4. "Box 66," UAHC Camp Swig slide presentation, Saratoga, California, n.d.

5. Bernard Bailyn, *Education in the Forming of American Society* (New York: Vintage, 1960); Lawrence Cremin, *The Transformation of the School* (New York: Knopf, 1961).

6. Foundation for Jewish Camping (www.jewishcamping.org). Each "bed" may be occupied by more than one camper over the course of a summer. Even so, Reform Jewish camping reaches only a small percentage (possibly less than 5 percent) of the children who are eligible.

7. Marvin Schick, *A Census of Jewish Day Schools in the United States* (New York: Avi Chai Foundation, 2000). According to Schick, 4,485 students were enrolled in Reform Jewish day schools during the 1998–1999 school year.

8. Samuel K. Joseph, *"Portraits of Schooling: A Survey and an Analysis of Supplementary Schooling in Congregations* (New York: UAHC Press, 1997).

9. Despite the availability of significant amounts of time, especially as compared to religious schools, camp programmers and day school educators often complain that they still do not have enough time for all that they want to do!

10. Quoted in Asher Melzer, "Jewish Community Camps," *Agenda: Jewish Education* 3 (Fall 1993): 21.

11. To learn from models "we must (1) attend to the model, (2) have some way of retaining what [one] has seen in symbolic form, and (3) have necessary motor skills to reproduce" what we have seen. But whether or not we learn from and imitate the model is "governed by reinforcement contingencies." What is so powerful about learning from models at camp is that there are so many opportunities to reinforce what campers learn from their counselors and others. William Crane, *Theories of Development: Concepts and Applications,* 4th ed. (Upper Saddle River, NJ: Prentice Hall, 2000), 196–97. For a more thorough explanation of how people learn from models, see Albert Bandura, *Social Learning Theory* (Englewood Cliffs, NJ: Prentice Hall, 1977).

12. David Resnick, "What If Formal Jewish Education Is Really Informal?" *Agenda: Jewish Education* (Fall 1993): 9.

13. Barry Chazan, "What Is Informal Jewish Education?" *Agenda: Jewish Education* (Fall 1993): 4–8.

14. Ibid., 5–6.

15. Ibid., 7–8.

16. Resnick, "What If Formal Jewish Education?" 11.

17. Jack Wertheimer, "Jewish Education in the United States: Recent Trends and Issues," in *American Jewish Year Book* (New York: American Jewish Committee, 1999).

18. Ibid., 78.

19. John Dewey, *Experience and Education* (New York: Collier, 1938).

20. Ibid., 40.

21. John Westerhoff III, *Will Our Children Have Faith?* (New York: Seabury Press, 1983).

22. Isa Aron, "The Malaise of Jewish Education," *Tikkun* 4, no. 3:32–34.

23. Westerhoff, *Will Our Children Have Faith?,* 49.

24. One former director of a UAHC camp calls this "the *sicha* [discussion] trap." (Harvey Shapiro, "Jewish Educational Camping," paper delivered to the Curriculum Seminar of the Rhea Hirsch School of Education, Los Angeles, March 1988.)

25. Howard Gardner, *Frames of Mind: The Theory of Multiple Intelligences* (New York: Basic Books, 1983).

26. Daniel Goleman, *Emotional Intelligence* (New York: Bantam Books, 1995).

27. Robert J. Sternberg, *Successful Intelligence: How Practical and Creative Intelligence Determine Success in Life* (New York: Simon and Schuster, 1996).

28. Perry London and Barry Chazan, *Psychology and Jewish Identity Education* (New York: American Jewish Committee, 1990).

29. Quoted in Edwin Cole Goldberg, "The Beginnings of Educational Camping in the Reform Movement," *Journal of Reform Judaism* 36, no. 4 (1989): 5.

30. Albert Schoolman, "Jewish Educational Camping—Its Potentialities and Realities," *Jewish Education* 36, no. 22 (1966):77.

31. Jonathan Woocher, "A Jewish Education Strategy for the 21st Century," paper delivered to the UAHC Consultation on Education, Los Angeles, October 1999.

32. Joseph Reimer, "On the Jewish Learner: Entering a New Era," paper delivered to the UAHC Consultation on Education, Los Angeles, October 1999.

33. Sylvia Barack Fishman, *Negotiating Both Sides of the Hyphen: Coalescence, Compartmentalization, and American-Jewish Values* (Cincinnati: Judaic Studies Program of the University of Cincinnati, 1996).

34. Ibid., 10.

35. David Ellenson, "An Ideology for the Liberal Jewish Day School: A Philosophical-Sociological Investigation," paper delivered to the HUC-PARDeS Symposium on Rethinking Integration, Malibu, CA, 1995.

36. Michael Zeldin, "Integration and Interaction in the Jewish Day School," in Robert Tornberg, ed., *The Jewish Educational Leader's Handbook* (Denver: A.R.E. Publishing, 1998).

37. Ellenson, "Ideology for the Liberal Jewish Day School."

38. Eugene Borowitz, *The Masks Jews Wear* (New York: Simon and Schuster, 1973), quoted in Ellenson, "Ideology for the Liberal Jewish Day School," 10.

39. Ellenson, "Ideology for the Liberal Jewish Day School," 15.

40. Ibid., 16.

41. Ibid., 17.

42. Ibid., 20–21.

43. Elliot N. Dorff, "Training Rabbis in the Land of the Free," in Nina Beth Cardin and David Wolf Silverman, eds., *The Seminary at 100: Reflections on the Jewish Theological Seminary of the Conservative Movement* (New York: Rabbinical Assembly and Jewish Theological Seminary of America, 1987.)

44. See Michael Zeldin, "Shabbat Manual for Reform Camps," MA project, Rhea Hirsch School of Education, 1976.

45. Hanan Alexander and Ian Russ, "Good Jewish Youth Programming," *Agenda: Jewish Education* (Fall 1993): 2.

46. Bernard Reisman, *Informal Jewish Education in North America* (New York: Commission on Jewish Education in North America, 1990).

47. Eisner, *Educational Imagination.*

48. Schoolman, "Jewish Educational Camping," 82.

49. Franz Rosenzweig, "Teaching and Law," in *Franz Rosenzweig: His Life and Thought*, ed. Nahum Glatzer (New York: Schocken, 1961), 238.

50. Arnold M. Eisen, "Beginning with Torah," in Sara S. Lee, ed., *Communities of Learning: A Vision for the Jewish Future* (Los Angeles: Rhea Hirsch School of Education, 1977), 20.

51. Joseph Reimer, "Jumping into the Currents: The Art of Informal Jewish Education," *Sh'ma* 31, no. 582 (May 2001): 1–2.

52. Raphael Zarum, "What Page Are We On? Traditional Texts in Informal Jewish Education," *Sh'ma* 31, no. 582 (May 2001): 10.

53. For an elaboration of the three curricula, see Eisner, *Educational Imagination,*

8–10. The elaboration of the three curricula of camp is adapted from Michael Zeldin, "Understanding Informal Jewish Education: Reflections on the Philosophical Foundations of NFTY," *Journal of Reform Judaism* 36, no. 4 (Fall 1989): 30.

54. See Michael Zeldin, "You Be the Nazis and You Be the Jews: The High Risk of Holocaust Simulations in Camp Settings," *Davka* 4, no. 4 (1977): 11.

55. For a further discussion of the differences between education and indoctrination, see Barry Chazan, *The Language of Jewish Education: Crisis and Hope in the Jewish School* (New York: Hartmore House, 1978).

56. Wertheimer, "Jewish Education," 89.

57. Bethamie Horowitz, "Informal Education and Jewish Identity Development," *Sh'ma* 31, no. 582 (May 2001): 8.

58. Ibid., 9.

59. Bruce Phillips, *Re-Examining Intermarriage: Trends, Textures, Strategies* (Boston: Susan and David Wilstein Institute, n.d., ca. 1996).

60. Wertheimer, "Jewish Education," 90.

61. Steven Plaut, "On Zionist Youth Movements," *Midstream* (May 1988).

62. Ed Feinstein, "Jewish Camping," paper delivered to the Curriculum Seminar of the Rhea Hirsch School of Education, Los Angeles, March 1996.

63. I was introduced to this idea by Tali Hyman, a graduate of the Rhea Hirsch School of Education and a rabbinical student at HUC-JIR in Los Angeles.

64. For an exploration of this problem and proposals for solutions, see Nachama Skolnick [Moskowitz], "Outreach and the Jewish Residential Summer Camp," MA thesis, Rhea Hirsch School of Education, 1976.

65. The following suggestions are adapted from Skolnick [Moskowitz], ibid., 15–27.

66. Woocher, "Jewish Education Strategy," 14.

67. Ibid., 21.

68. Plaut, "On Zionist Youth Movements."

69. Some of these efforts are already reaching success, such as full-day and weekend alumni reunions at UAHC camps, including OSRUI. In addition, OSRUI's new Lehrhaus Program brings adults, including many alumni, back to camp to study for several days during the summer as part of the regular camp program. This extremely successful program is reminiscent of Union Institute's first summers, which always included sessions for adults.

70. Reimer, "On the Jewish Learner: Entering a New Era," 13.

1. The Ark in Union Institute's outdoor chapel, emblematic of the camp, was built during the camp's first summer (1952). Here campers and staff are lighting Sabbath candles, circa 1960. Courtesy of the American Jewish Archives and Michael M. Lorge.

2. Union Institute's first promotional brochure (1952). Courtesy of the American Jewish Archives and Michael M. Lorge.

3. The *Bayit*, originally known as "the Big House," was the center of activity during the camp's early years. Here campers and staff are gathering to welcome the Sabbath (*Kabbalat Shabbat*) in the early 1960s. Courtesy of the American Jewish Archives and Michael M. Lorge.

4. Union Institute campers, staff, and faculty in the outdoor chapel in 1956. Courtesy of the American Jewish Archives and Michael M. Lorge.

5. Early publicity photographs, like this one from 1953 that promotes the camp as a "woodland setting for study, worship, work and play," visually demonstrate how campers were enthusiastically engaged in discussion and learning. Courtesy of the American Jewish Archives and Michael M. Lorge.

6. Campers working outdoors on their Judaic art projects in 1959. Arts and crafts director Greta Lee Splansky is third from the left. Courtesy of the American Jewish Archives and Michael M. Lorge.

7. Union Institute's Chalutzim (Pioneers) program is the oldest Hebrew-speaking unit in Reform Jewish camping. Shown here with Chalutzim campers are Sam Alpert (center, with his arm raised), one of the first Israeli emissaries to a UAHC camp, and faculty member Rabbi Hillel Gamoran (right of Alpert with an open-collared white shirt). Courtesy of the American Jewish Archives and Michael M. Lorge.

8. For the first several summers of its existence, Union Institute served as the summer home for the NFTY Institutes. In 1953, Cantor William Sharlin leads NFTY campers in a song session. Courtesy of the American Jewish Archives and Michael M. Lorge.

9. Union Institute campers, staff, and faculty in front of the *Bayit* in 1960. Then-director Phillip L. Brin is standing in the top row, seventh from the left. Courtesy of the American Jewish Archives and Michael M. Lorge.

10. Sidney I. Cole (under the mantle, second from left), Robert J. Cooper, Johann S. Ackerman, and Samuel S. Hollender (from left, faces not showing), founding members of Union Institute's board, participating in an early Founders Day meal in the *Bayit* in 1956. Courtesy of the American Jewish Archives and Michael M. Lorge.

11. Irving B. Kaplan, director of Union Institute from 1963 to 1968, leading a Shabbat song session on Friday night. Courtesy of the American Jewish Archives and Michael M. Lorge.

12. Campers in Union Institute's Kibbutz HaTzofim Unit during the mid-1960s, waiting for Sabbath services to begin. Courtesy of the American Jewish Archives and Michael M. Lorge.

13. In the 1940s, NFTY Institutes and Labor Day Conclaves demonstrated the effectiveness of the camping experience and sparked an interest in acquiring a camp for the Reform movement. Shown here are members of the Labor Day Conclave faculty and student leaders in 1947, including Rabbi Arnold Wolf (top left), Ellie Schwartz (top, second from left), and Rabbi Phineas Smoller (top right). Courtesy of the American Jewish Archives and Michael M. Lorge.

5   The Road to Chalutzim

Reform Judaism's Hebrew-Speaking Program

Hillel Gamoran

Editors' Note: Rabbi Hillel Gamoran has intertwined historical and anecdotal material in order to reconstruct the evolution of Hebrew education and the use of Hebrew language at Union Institute. It is important to note that topics such as Hebrew, the history of Zionism, and the modern State of Israel were accepted subjects of study during the camp's earliest days. This is in sharp contrast to many Reform temples that gave their congregants limited exposure to these topics in the early 1950s.

> *I am not certain when we first raised the Israeli flag at camp but I clearly recall it was long before the tenth anniversary of Israel's Independence. We gathered as always one morning for flag raising and without any previous discussion two flags went up the pole; the American followed by the blue and white. We did not see the Israeli flag that often when we were growing up. Some campers seemed mystified. It wasn't a political statement to us as campers. It was simply one more way that camp made us ask in a personal way, "What does it mean to be a Jew living in America?" It was subtle, but every time I see the Israeli flag to this day, I remember that flag raising. (Sue Ellen Lorge Schwartz, May 18, 2003)*

It is apparent from the education outlines that the founding faculty and other early faculty felt comfortable challenging campers with serious discussions about Zionism and aliyah (emigrating to Israel or returning to Jerusalem). As Gamaron suggests, this may have occurred because of the open environment of camp, which welcomed debate on all matters. Moreover, the campers were surrounded by people who took these issues seriously, including Israelis who were part of the camp staff and who certainly raised the topic of aliyah. These were discussions that many campers never heard in their home congregations.

> We can encourage campers to confront the issue of Zionism, real Zionism, if they confront Aliyah as a necessary and essential part of their life. For evening program we will hold a panel discussion on Zionism in the 20th Century. The discussion should move quickly to Aliyah and two of us will challenge the panel that Aliyah is the only "authentic" Zionist road. I am certain that Dave and others will have no problem countering us. Let it be real. We must show our real feelings and emotions to pull the campers in and to make them challenge their own values from home. For most of our campers Aliyah is not only never discussed at home or in temple, but it would be rebuked by many if suggested. (Rabbi Sheldon Gordon, Union Institute Pioneer Unit Program Book, 1966–1967)

Interest in Israel intensified after the Six-Day War in 1967. Campers arrived infused with new pride in and awareness of Israel. Irv Kaplan, the director of Union Institute at the time, announced his decision to move permanently to Israel after the summer of 1968. His announcement made an impact on some of those who were then at camp and electrified the camp community: "The thought of Irv going permanently to Israel brought out strange emotions. I don't think most of us knew any other close friend who was going permanently to live there. To us he changed a theoretical idea to possibility" (Kathy Bayer Rabinovitz, June 1999).

In 1968 Kaplan and the faculty organized the camp's first trip to Israel for former Pioneer campers. This travel-study program, called Tiyul La'Aretz (A Tour to Israel), was the first of its kind within American Reform Jewish camping. As time passed, the number of campers and staff who considered, endeavored, and in many cases succeeded in settling permanently in Israel grew. It is noteworthy that the garin (a training group for those who intended to live in an Israeli Kibbutz) for the Reform movement's first kibbutz in Israel (Yahel) included several former Union Institute campers and staff. Moreover, this same garin spent considerable time living and working at OSRUI and developing its goals and skills.

In documenting the evolution of Union Institute's distinctive Hebrew-speaking unit, Chalutzim, Gamoran underscores how the educational program of American Reform Jewish camps began to explore innovative and, in some instances, controversial topics that were just beginning to seriously engage Reform Jews in America.

For over four decades, a Hebrew-speaking program known as Chalutzim has been a featured component of Olin-Sang-Ruby Union Institute (OSRUI) in Oconomowoc, Wisconsin, a camp that is owned and operated by the Union of American Hebrew Congregations (UAHC). This program, unique among the Reform movement's summer camps, occupies a noteworthy place in the history of Hebrew language study in the American Jewish community. In this chapter I will explore the early beginnings of Hebrew language education in American Jewish summer camps and follow the chain of events that led to the inclusion of Hebrew in the Reform camps and, finally, to the founding and development of Chalutzim. I will also seek to analyze the Chalutzim program and to uncover its strengths and weaknesses as revealed over the course of the years.

The immigration of Jews from Eastern Europe during the last two decades of the nineteenth century and the first two decades of the twentieth century far surpassed the inflow of Jews in previous times. In 1880 the Jewish community of America numbered about 250,000 people.[1] Between 1881 and 1914 more than two million Jews came to America from Eastern Europe.[2] Many brought their Orthodox religious practices with them to America, but even those who abandoned their religious practices when they came to the new world still maintained that Jewish culture and Jewish peoplehood were central to their lives. Most of the immigrants were fervent Zionists, and many retained a strong bond to the Hebrew language. As these newcomers became the vast majority of American Jewry in the twentieth century, they transformed the American Jewish scene.[3]

Samson Benderly

In 1909 the disparate Jewish organizations of New York formed a community-wide institution called the *kehillah* (community). For the first time there existed a central address for the Jews of New York City. One of the first undertakings of the *kehillah* was to establish a Bureau of Jewish Education to help improve and expand Jewish education in the city. Dr. Samson Benderly, an educator from Baltimore, Maryland, was engaged as the bureau's director.[4]

Born in Safed and educated as a physician in Beirut and Baltimore, Benderly gave up his medical career to devote his life to Jewish education. As director of the bureau in New York, he plunged into his work with energy and creativity. He produced the first standard curriculum for the Talmud Torahs of New York, established several schools that the bureau itself ran, promoted the teaching of Hebrew in Hebrew, started Jewish clubs outside of the classrooms, and introduced music, dance, and drama into Jewish education.[5]

Perhaps Benderly's most consuming goal was to train Jewish educators for the American Jewish community. Between 1910 and 1925 he guided and inspired a score of young men to pursue a comprehensive background in Judaica and in modern education and to make Jewish education their lifelong careers. Isaac Berkson, Barnett Brickner, Israel Chipkin, Alexander Dushkin, Emanuel Gamoran, Leo Honor, and Albert Schoolman were but a few of the many who were known as the "Benderly Boys" and who made major contributions to Jewish education in America.[6]

Camp Achvah

During the second half of the 1920s, Benderly's fertile mind developed a new plan for bringing young people into the field of Jewish education.[7] It was to gather a group of highly motivated young people who would engage in intensive Jewish study for a period of years, winter and summer, and who would thereby be prepared for careers in Jewish education or for leadership roles in the Jewish community. In the spring of 1927, Benderly, together with Joseph Bragin, principal of New York's Hebrew High School, interviewed those high school students who were recommended by their teachers as the most qualified on the basis of scholarship, personality, and leadership. In most cases, Benderly called in the parents of the candidates and introduced them to his plan to train leaders for the Jewish community of the future.

The first group selected (Kvutzah Aleph) consisted of about a dozen young people. Later, a second group (Kvutzah Bet) was organized. *Kvutzah* members met for Judaic studies on Sunday mornings throughout the year and, in the first summer session in 1927, for a period of two weeks in Arverne, Long Island. But Benderly believed that more could be achieved during the summer months. He became convinced that in half a day of study during a full summer, students "could accomplish more than during an entire academic year."[8] Consequently, in its second summer, Camp Achvah (Friendship) was expanded to become a ten-week program. A curriculum based on reading Jewish sources was prepared; teachers from the Hebrew schools were engaged as staff members; and every *kvutzah* member attended the full summer session.[9]

It is not surprising that Benderly entered the field of Jewish camping. He had long believed that children learned not so much by listening as by doing; thus, he taught that the best way to teach a student was to involve the student in an activity. This is why he promoted the arts and a variety of youth activities. Benderly believed that summer camp was the ideal setting for Jewish living and Jewish learning. In fact, in 1919 one of his early students, Albert Schoolman, became the director of Camp Cejwin, the first Jewish educational camp in America.[10]

Camp Achvah was unique in many ways. First, it was created and sustained by the labors of one of the most remarkable figures in twentieth-century Jewish life. Benderly played the central role in outlining the philosophy, planning the studies, recruiting the campers, hiring the staff, and inspiring all connected with it that a Hebrew camp in America could work. Camp Achvah would rise and fall based on the spirit and personality of a single individual.

Another unique feature of Camp Achvah was that "Everything was conducted in Hebrew: eating, studies, conversation, sports, dramatics,"[11] and the rest. Hebrew culture was a natural part of camp life: *kvutzah* members were encouraged to read Hebrew books, and in fact Dr. Benderly brought his own library to the camp. Hebrew singing was an ever-popular activity; discussions and reading circles were an integral part of camp life; a weekly Hebrew newspaper was published; and a Hebrew theater group was formed. All of these activities helped to intensify the Hebrew skills of the young people. As a result of their summer experience, most of the members of the *kvutzah* attained a remarkable fluency in the Hebrew language. Achvah was the first camp of its kind.

In spite of the accomplishments of Camp Achvah, it faced criticism. Some thought that even if this venture could be called a success, it had no application beyond a select group of young people in New York City under the influence of a singular charismatic personality. And because the camp was largely dependent on the energy and enthusiasm of one man, when Dr. Benderly turned his primary focus to other tasks, the camp suffered. Over the years, Kvutzot Gimel, Daled, and Hey were added, but the later *kvutzot* were not of as high a caliber as were the earlier ones.[12] And with the impact of the Depression, financial support for the enterprise became more difficult to sustain. In 1932 the *kvutzot* were dissolved and Camp Achvah lost its distinctive character.

During the years of its existence, Camp Achvah had an enormous influence on the lives of the fifty campers whom it served. More than 40 percent of them entered careers in Jewish education, the rabbinate, Jewish social work, or Jewish organizational work. More than 50 percent of them became very active in Jewish organizations.[13] And it is no small matter that Camp Achvah, the first Hebrew-speaking camp in America, was likely the first Hebrew-speaking camp in all of Jewish history.

Camp Massad

During the last two decades of the nineteenth century, a network of societies called *Choveve Zion* (Lovers of Zion) grew up in Eastern Europe. A few chapters were established in the United States as well.[14] In 1896, with the appearance of Theodore Herzl's proposal for a Jewish homeland, Zionism in America was energized. In 1897, after the first Zionist Congress, many more Zionist groups were formed. By 1900 the Federation of American Zionists boasted 125 component groups, with a total of 10,000 members.[15]

But Zionism did not become a mass movement in America until the time of World War I, when the lives of Jews in Russia were endangered. Public meetings, rallies, and diplomatic initiatives were undertaken to bring aid to the Jewish communities of Eastern Europe, and support was rallied for the creation of a Jewish homeland in Palestine.[16]

It was at this time also that Zionism found expression through greater interest in the Hebrew language. The immigrants from Eastern Europe invigorated the Hebrew movement in America. Hebrew books and journals appeared,[17] and Hebrew clubs were organized in various parts of the country.[18] In 1916 the Histadrut Ivrit of America (National Organization for Hebrew Culture) was founded.[19] In 1937, on the eve of World War II, when the existence of Europe's Jews was threatened and support for Zionism increased dramatically within American Jewry, the Histadrut Ivrit established a youth organ, Hanoar Haivri (Hebrew Youth). This organization maintained that the Hebrew language was "the very soul of Jewish culture" and that instructing children through the medium of the Hebrew language was essential in building a generation of Jews who would preserve the cultural treasures of the Jewish people.[20]

The leaders of Hanoar Haivri saw Jewish children, even those who were receiving a good Jewish education, as facing two worlds: one, Jewish, which included the Hebrew language, and the other—radio, movies, newspapers, books, and sports—all far removed from Jewish life. They were convinced that no matter how excellent a Jewish school was, it could not provide Jewish children with a natural Hebrew environment. What was needed was a place where the Hebrew language would become the lifeblood of the Jewish child, where speaking Hebrew would be as natural as breathing. It was to create this place that Camp Massad (The Foundation) was established.[21]

The leading figure behind the establishment of Camp Massad was Shlomo Shulsinger. A native of Jerusalem, Shulsinger came to the United States at age sixteen and completed his high school education in Brooklyn. When his family moved to Baltimore, Shulsinger entered Baltimore City College and the Baltimore Hebrew Teachers College. His work in Jewish education began with his teaching Hebrew at a Talmud Torah in Baltimore and becoming the director of a Zionist camp in the Baltimore area. In 1939 Shulsinger was invited to join the teaching staff of the Yeshiva of Flatbush. In New York he became an active member of Hanoar Haivri, seeking ways to put the goal of strengthening Hebrew into concrete form. At the conference of Hanoar Haivri in September 1940, Shulsinger addressed the gathering with a rousing speech urging the establishment of a Hebrew camp. The group unanimously passed a resolution to establish a Hebrew camp and directed its executive committee to make the necessary arrangements to implement the plan the following summer.[22]

During the winter and spring of 1941, Hanoar Haivri launched a vigorous effort, laying plans and gathering funds. In April a concert was held on behalf of the camp fund, and friends of the project donated a considerable sum of money. It soon became apparent, however, that it was not possible to launch a full-fledged camp after such brief preparations. It was at this point that the idea of a day camp was proposed. On July 7, 1941, Massad opened as a day camp with twenty-five campers in Far Rockaway, New York with Shlomo Shulsinger as its director. In 1942 Massad became an overnight camp in Monticello, New York, with forty-five campers. In 1943 it rented—and two years later purchased—property in Tannersville, Pennsylvania. This became known as Massad Aleph. Massad Bet, in Dingmans Ferry, Pennsylvania, was added in 1945, and a site in Effort, Pennsylvania, became Massad Gimel in 1966. What had begun as a day camp of twenty-five children in 1941 had grown to more than two hundred campers at Massad Aleph in 1945. During its peak years, 1966 to 1968, it had an enrollment each summer of more than nine hundred children in the three camps.[23]

From its inception, two principles guided the camp's registration policy. The first was that registration would be limited to children who had sufficient Hebrew knowledge to permit some Hebrew fluency in the activities. The second was that registration would be accepted only for the entire nine-week season.[24] There were no formal studies at Massad. The philosophy was that the children would learn Hebrew, not by sitting in a classroom, but by living in a Hebrew environment, that they would build their knowledge of Hebrew by being in a setting where campers, counselors, and staff members all spoke Hebrew. All activities—whether sports or swimming, dance or drama, crafts or gardening, eating, praying, getting up in the morning, and going to sleep at night—were carried out in Hebrew. In short, Massad became a Hebrew place for American Jewish children.

A number of factors led to the demise of Camp Massad. For one thing, when the Conservative movement introduced the Ramah camps, it drew away young people who might otherwise have gone to Massad. For another thing, many of the day schools and yeshivot, which had been the primary source for Massad campers, began to put less emphasis on Hebrew language proficiency. Another problem that arose was the shift to the right within the Orthodox community. All through the years, Massad had, to a large extent, followed Orthodox practice in its food, in its daily services, and in its Shabbat observance. But in the 1970s pressure arose to move further to the right. A *mechitzah* (partition) was introduced at services, and boys and girls were separated for a number of activities. These changes brought about resentment among some in the Massad community. With declining enrollment, it was decided in late 1975 to sell Massad Gimel and concentrate on strengthening the two larger camps, Massad Aleph and Massad Bet.[25]

Perhaps the fatal blow to Massad was the retirement of Shlomo Shulsinger after the 1977 season. When Shulsinger gave up the reins, enrollment fell precipitously, and after the 1979 season, Massad Bet was closed. Campers at Massad Aleph numbered four hundred in 1980, but in 1981 enrollment had declined to three hundred. The 1981 season may have been successful educationally and recreationally, but it was a fiscal disaster. Massad could not meet its debts. At the end of the 1981 summer, Camp Massad had to close down.[26]

For forty-one years Massad had proved that Hebrew camping could work. It showed that it was possible to create a Hebrew-speaking island on the American scene. In the course of its existence, some thirty thousand youngsters had passed through its portals. Massad can count among its alumni hundreds of rabbis, educators, and community leaders. It had a lasting impact on the lives of thousands.

Camp Yavneh

The events that led to the founding of Camp Achvah and Camp Massad—the ascendancy of Jews of Eastern European origin and the growth of Zionism along with Hebrew culture—also came to bear in the establishment of Camp Yavneh.[27] In the early 1900s Boston became one of the major centers for Jewish settlement. A large number of Ashkenazic congregations were established, and Zionist groups flourished.[28] In 1918 a Bureau of Jewish Education was established, and a young educator named Louis Hurwich was invited to be its first director. Hurwich was an immigrant from Lithuania who, in New York, had fallen under the spell of Samson Benderly and decided to make Jewish education his lifelong career. In 1932 he founded the Boston Hebrew Teachers College.[29]

Hurwich believed that summertime should not be vacation time from Jewish learning, but rather a time to be used productively to further Jewish education. In the fall of 1943, he took on the task of raising funds to establish a place for summer Jewish learning.[30] Camp Yavneh opened its doors in the summer of 1944 in Northwood, New Hampshire, with seventy-nine campers. Hurwich's wife, Leah, who came from a strong camping background in New York, served as its director, and Hurwich himself headed the program of studies during the first four years of the camp's existence.

To a large extent, Yavneh was an extension of the Boston Hebrew Teachers College. Each camper enrolled for two hours of classes each morning on such subjects as the Bible, the Talmud, Hebrew grammar, or Hebrew literature. All of the classes were conducted in Hebrew. Examinations and grades were given with credits transferable to the Hebrew Teachers College.[31]

In the afternoons at Yavneh, campers engaged in sports of all sorts and in recreational activities such as music, drama, dance, crafts, and nature study. Hurwich's plan in founding Yavneh was that it was to be a complete Hebrew camp. Not only were classes and activities to be conducted in Hebrew, but Hebrew was also to be the day-to-day language of communication. Knowing that the younger campers would not always know what was going on if Hebrew alone was spoken (unlike Massad, where the campers had to be somewhat fluent in Hebrew in order to be admitted), he instructed his staff to speak to the younger campers in Hebrew and then translate into English. He said that as the season progressed, less and less translation would be needed.[32] Although a strong effort was made to maintain Hebrew as the means of communication, the word around camp, "Studies in Hebrew, but life in English," may have been closer to the truth.[33]

Both Camp Achvah and Camp Massad were pioneering efforts in Jewish education and in Hebrew education, the difference between them being that formal learning was an integral part of the Achvah camp program, whereas at Massad learning was confined to informal activities. Camp Yavneh, then, followed the Achvah pattern in that its emphasis was on classroom education. The educators and academics who led Yavneh over the course of the years—Alvin Schiff (later director of the Board of Jewish Education of Greater New York), Walter Ackerman (later Professor of Education at Ben Gurion University of the Negev), Baruch Levine (later Professor of Hebrew and Near Eastern Languages at New York University), Moshe Avital (later national director of the B'nai Brith Youth Organization) and others—helped Yavneh to fulfill its mission of being New England's place of Torah study.[34]

Unlike Achvah and Massad, Yavneh did not fall by the wayside. It still functions as a Jewish educational camp, serving some two hundred young people from New England each summer. It still offers classes in the morning and recreational activities in the afternoons. But over the course of more than half a century, changes have taken place. In Yavneh's first years, to qualify as a camper one had to know Hebrew to the level of a graduate of a Boston Talmud Torah (equivalent to six years of study, five days a week). Today there is no Hebrew prerequisite for admission to the camp. In Yavneh's early years, only Hebrew-speaking counselors were engaged. Today fluency in Hebrew is considered an advantage for a counselor, but it is not a requirement. In Yavneh's early years all classes were conducted in Hebrew. Today the Hebrew classes for day school students are still conducted in Hebrew, but English is used for other classes, and discussion groups on a variety of subjects take place in English.[35]

A strong effort is still made to keep a Hebrew presence at Yavneh by making announcements in Hebrew, by singing in Hebrew, by praying in Hebrew, by giving dramatic presentations in Hebrew, by giving buildings Hebrew names, and at sporting events by giving cheers in Hebrew. Yavneh today is not a Hebrew-speaking camp; the language of communication at camp is English.[36]

Camp Ramah

Like the Hebrew camps that preceded it, Camp Ramah (High Place) owed its origins to the Zionist and Hebraic instincts within the American Jewish community. But it differed from the other camps in two important ways. One was that its center of gravity was religious; Ramah wanted to teach its campers Conservative religious ideology and Conservative religious practices. The second difference between Ramah and the other camps was that Ramah was created to strengthen and revitalize the Conservative movement.[37]

In 1946 Dr. Moshe Davis, associate dean of the Teachers Institute of the Jewish Theological Seminary, urged that a chain of study camps be organized,[38] and Dr. Simon Greenberg, vice-chancellor of the seminary, asked, "Is it not high time that we have summer camps for the members of our young people's groups and for our school children?"[39]

Meanwhile, Conservative Jews in the Midwest felt the need for a summer camp that would reflect their philosophy of Judaism. Instrumental in putting theory into practice were Reuben Kaufman, chairman of the Chicago Council of Conservative Synagogues, and Rabbi Ralph Simon of Congregation Rodfei Zedek in Chicago. In 1946 the Chicago Council intensified its efforts to establish a camp in the Midwest and in 1947 opened the first Ramah camp in Conover, Wisconsin.[40] It proved to be a great success, and plans were soon made to open additional Ramah camps. Ramah in Maine opened in 1948 but lasted only two summers. However, Ramah in the Poconos opened in 1950 and was highly successful. Ramah entered the scene in New England in 1953, in California in 1956, in Canada in 1960, and in the Berkshires in 1961.[41] Today there are a total of ten Ramah camps in North America.[42]

As conceived by its founders, Ramah was to be a Hebrew-speaking camp. A large portion of the time devoted to learning in Conservative schools was spent on the study of Hebrew. It was believed that Hebrew could be learned more easily in the open air of the camp setting than in the synagogue classroom, and that students would make great strides in their Hebrew learning by spending a summer at a Hebrew-speaking camp.[43]

To a large extent, Ramah was an outgrowth of Massad.[44] Many of the founders and leaders of Ramah in its early years had in fact gained their camping experience at Massad and wanted to create a Massad-like Hebrew environment at Ramah. But there were certain things they wanted to do differently. They wanted less emphasis on Zionism and Israel and more emphasis on living comfortably as a Jew in American society. They wanted Conservative religious practices to prevail rather than the more rigid Orthodoxy of Massad. And they wanted daily study to be included as part of the camp routine.[45]

Though Hebrew education was one of the principal aims in the establishment of Camp Ramah, the question remained as to whether it could succeed in becoming a Hebrew-speaking camp like Massad. Massad, after all, had a distinct advantage; it drew its campers from yeshivot and day schools where youths had gained some measure of Hebrew competency before arriving at camp. The campers at Ramah, on the other hand, came from the afternoon Hebrew schools. Their knowledge of Hebrew was often weak.

Could Ramah, serving the camper population that it did, become a Hebrew-speaking camp? Announcements were made primarily in Hebrew, activities were conducted mainly in Hebrew, and the staff made a maximum effort to speak Hebrew with the campers and to serve as Hebrew models for them. Furthermore, incentives were given for speaking Hebrew, including awards to campers who spoke Hebrew for a full day and further recognition for those who accumulated a number of such days. In spite of all these efforts, however, it had to be admitted that the campers rarely spoke Hebrew.[46] Entering the summers of 1948 and 1949, Ramah had not abandoned its goal of being a Hebrew-speaking camp, but Ramah veterans have acknowledged that from the 1950s on, because the campers knew very little Hebrew and even the counselors were not comfortable with the Hebrew language, Hebrew had lost its primary place among the goals of Ramah.[47]

Today announcements are still made in the Ramah dining rooms in Hebrew; places at camp are marked with Hebrew signs; Hebrew language and literature are among the courses available for daily study; a Broadway musical is still presented in Hebrew; but Hebrew is not the spoken tongue at Ramah, nor is any concerted effort made for counselors or campers to conduct their daily lives in Hebrew.[48]

Hebrew in the Reform Movement

What attracted many American Jews to Reform Judaism in the early part of the twentieth century was that the services were conducted entirely or mostly in English. This meant that to be an active member of a Reform congregation, one did not have to know Hebrew. As a consequence, for a long time Hebrew did not hold a prominent place in the Reform community.

In 1923 there was little Hebrew learning in Reform religious schools. Only 28 percent of the pupils in Reform schools studied Hebrew, and their average study time was only one hour per week.[49] But even in the Reform movement, which had long been dominated by Jews of German origin, the influx of the Eastern Europeans began to be felt. In 1923 the UAHC invited my father, Emanuel Gamoran—a native of Bessarabia, an ardent Zionist, and a lover of Hebrew—to be the Union's director of education. In this role he redirected Reform Jewish education.[50] Instead of dealing primarily with Bible stories and ethical lessons, he turned the Reform curriculum toward customs and festivals, Jewish history, and the Jewish community. Furthermore, he coauthored a series of textbooks for the teaching of Hebrew as a language.[51] When my father began his work with the UAHC, he was the only member of the staff to declare himself a Zionist. The chairman of the Commission on Jewish Education, which supervised his work, was Rabbi David Philipson, an avowed anti-Zionist.[52] But over the years, the Reform movement changed. The "Guiding Principles" adopted by the Central Conference of American Rabbis at its 1937 convention in Columbus, Ohio, included an obligation of all Jewry to aid in rebuilding a Jewish homeland and a commitment to the Hebrew language.[53]

In time, more attention was paid to Hebrew education in Reform schools. A 1948 survey of Reform religious schools showed that between 1923 and 1948 the percentage of students taking Hebrew had grown from 28 percent to 50 percent, and the average study time for Hebrew had risen from one hour per week to an hour and a half.[54] By 1960, 51 percent of Reform religious schools had twice-weekly Hebrew classes, and 4 percent held classes three times a week.[55] By 1975 it was up to 60 percent holding classes twice a week and 9 percent three times a week.[56]

It is clear that as the Jewish world changed, the Reform movement changed too. A third of the world's Jews had been decimated in the Holocaust. The State of Israel had been created. After World War II, Reform Judaism altered its central focus from theology and ethics to peoplehood and culture. Over a period of time, activities dealing with Israel became part and parcel of the life of Reform congregations. The study of Hebrew rose in importance. As the realization took hold that the summer camp offered a magnificent opportunity for educating young Jews and instilling Jewish values within them, it was natural to turn to the idea of utilizing the summer camp for Hebrew language education.

Solel

In the 1950s and 1960s several Reform camps initiated programs that placed special emphasis on Hebrew-language learning. One was the Solel Unit of Camp Swig in California.[57] In the winter of 1953 Samuel Kaminker and Irving Sores, of the Los Angeles Bureau of Jewish Education, and Sarah Kaelter, a local Hebrew teacher and wife of Rabbi Wolli Kaelter, the camp director, took the initiative in starting a camp unit that would specialize in Hebrew-language education.[58] Solel was launched in the summer of 1954 as a twelve-day unit aimed at stimulating the interest of campers in Hebrew as a living tongue. The program included daily Hebrew classes and a multitude of activities that were interwoven with Hebrew. Even though Solel campers ate with the general camp, an effort was made to have the Solel campers sit together for meals so as to encourage Hebrew conversation.[59]

In 1967, because of low enrollment, Solel was on the verge of being cancelled when Rabbi Albert Lewis, of Temple Isaiah in Los Angeles, called Rabbi Joseph Glaser, director of Camp Swig, and objected strenuously to the idea of discontinuing Solel. Eager to maintain the Solel program, Glaser told Lewis that the only way to retain the program was if Lewis would offer his dynamic educational director, Jack Horowitz, to revitalize it.[60] Soon after that conversation, Horowitz was appointed director of Solel and the foundation was laid for

Solel's resurgence. Thirty-seven campers attended Solel in 1967. Over the next several years, under the leadership of Horowitz and Michael Zeldin (now professor of Jewish education at the Hebrew Union College–Jewish Institute of Religion in Los Angeles), a second four-week session was added. Solel Aleph, during the first half of the summer was open to entering seventh- and eighth-graders, and Solel Bet, during the second part of the summer, accepted entering ninth- and tenth-graders. During its "glory days" in the 1970s about 140 campers attended Solel each summer.[61]

Every camper at Solel attended a one and one-half hour Hebrew class each morning. A curriculum was prepared to teach conversational Hebrew centering on a vocabulary that could be used at camp on a daily basis. Hebrew games were a feature of the classes as well as at other times during the day. "Whenever there was an opportunity to play a game, it was always a Hebrew language game." Singing at Solel was Hebrew singing. Campers and counselors were called by their Hebrew names. In Zeldin's words, "Over the course of the summer, [the campers] mastered the vocabulary and sentence structure needed to survive in a dining hall." All of the phrases that were repeated during a normal day were spoken in Hebrew. Campers did not generally speak to each other in Hebrew, but their knowledge of Hebrew increased. As Zeldin put it, "Solel could not be described as a Hebrew speaking camp but rather as a Hebrew environment program."

In the 1980s it became more difficult to find young people who would dedicate four weeks of their summer to a Hebrew program. Enrollment declined to about twenty-five or thirty campers. Solel for ninth- and tenth-graders was reduced to three weeks and for seventh- and eighth-graders to two weeks. Finally, in the mid-1980s, because of the low number of registrants, Solel was dropped from Camp Swig's offerings.[62]

Solel's demise may be explained in several ways. On the one hand, Hebrew usage had grown throughout all of Swig's units. Hebrew songs, Hebrew names, announcements in Hebrew, all became standard fare at Swig. Solel lost some of the glamour of its uniqueness. Furthermore, Swig offered excellent alternatives for teenagers. It had a social action program and an elaborate arts program that competed for registrants with Solel.[63] Finally, it should be noted that by the late 1980s Solel's emphasis on spoken Hebrew may have been outside the mainstream of Reform Jewish education. More and more religious schools were teaching only liturgical Hebrew. Interest in Hebrew as a spoken language within the Reform movement had diminished.[64]

Torah Corps

Another Reform movement program that stressed Hebrew was called Torah Corps. It was started at Kutz Camp in Warwick, New York, the brainchild of Rabbi Henry Skirball, then the associate director of the National Federation of

Temple Youth (NFTY). NFTY had sponsored Mitzvah Corps, a program in which young people engaged in social action projects.[65] Skirball thought there should be a Torah Corps, where young people would focus on Judaic study. Torah Corps opened in 1965 with Rabbi Dov Taylor as its director.[66]

Torah Corps was designed to attract Reform Jewish teenagers to spend a summer engaged in intensive Jewish study and Jewish living. It included three hours of study each morning. The first hour was a Hebrew-language class taught in Hebrew. The second hour was spent studying a Hebrew text, biblical or rabbinic, with the language of instruction being English. The third hour was an English-language class on some aspect of Jewish life. In addition, faculty members met with students individually for Hebrew-language conversations and encouraged the use of Hebrew in the dining room. Twice-daily religious services were conducted entirely in Hebrew, and the Shabbat sermons delivered by the faculty were in Hebrew.[67]

In 1974 Taylor, Rabbi Jerry Brieger and others came to believe that changes instituted at Kutz Camp that placed Torah Corps under a wide umbrella of NFTY programs at Kutz and integrated the living arrangements of Torah Corps campers with the rest of the camp population would work to the detriment of Torah Corps.[68] Taylor and Brieger therefore left Kutz and established a program in Littleton, New Hampshire, independently incorporated as International Torah Corps. The program continued there using the same format as had been established at Kutz, still attracting scores of young people each summer to engage in Judaic study and in Hebrew-language learning.[69] However, over the course of the years, International Torah Corps suffered, partly because of growing competition from Israel programs and partly because it was not a part of NFTY. Although several rabbis from Reform congregations served on the Torah Corps faculty, their youth groups were affiliated with NFTY, and their youth primarily attended NFTY summer programs. Finally, in 1984, with diminishing enrollment, International Torah Corps closed its doors.[70]

Meanwhile, back in Warwick, the original Torah Corps continued under the auspices of NFTY. Scholars still came to teach in the summer, but the emphasis was more on text study than on Hebrew-language learning. Hebrew classes were no longer required of all the campers, and Hebrew conversation was not encouraged as much as it had been under Taylor's administration.[71] In the 1980s Torah Corps, like Solel and International Torah Corps, found that interest in a Hebrew-language summer program had declined in Reform congregations. NFTY study programs in Israel had become more attractive to teenagers than a summer of study in the United States. By 1987 Torah Corps' numbers had dwindled to the point where the program had to be cancelled.[72]

During the years of its existence, the Torah Corps and International Torah Corps had a significant impact on the lives of more than a thousand young people. This included improvement in their Hebrew-language skills.[73]

Olin-Sang-Ruby Union Institute

In the 1950s Hebrew classes at Union Institute in Oconomowoc, Wisconsin, were offered to campers on an elective basis. Campers chose between Hebrew and, for example, swimming or arts and crafts. In the late 1950s Oscar Miller recommended that learning Hebrew should be a regular part of each camper's day. As the majority of the rabbis agreed with him, Hebrew classes for all campers became a regular feature of Union Institute's program.[74]

The Hebrew Coordinator at OSRUI

During Irving Kaplan's tenure as director of Union Institute (1963–1968), he engaged a Hebrew specialist during the summer. Every camper in every unit took a daily Hebrew class.[75] The specialist's responsibility was to prepare material for the counselors and staff members and to guide and assist them in their Hebrew teaching.[76] In 1967 and 1968 Rabbi Donald Splansky was the Hebrew specialist. Splansky was a product of Union Institute and later became part of the faculty of International Torah Corps.[77]

In 1969 and 1970 Fradle Pomp (now Fradle Freidenreich) was the camp's Hebrew coordinator. While serving in that position, Freidenreich instituted the practice that everyone at camp (campers, counselors, office workers, rabbis' spouses, etc.) took a Hebrew class. This meant that at times adults were in the same classes with children. Freidenreich prepared materials to teach Hebrew at camp through games and songs. She met frequently with the rabbis and counselors who taught the classes, many of whom were unfamiliar with this style of Hebrew teaching. Several individuals followed Splansky and Freidenreich in the role of Hebrew coordinator.[78]

In 1984 Etty Dolgin became the Hebrew coordinator, and she has held that position ever since. When Dolgin assumed her role at camp, she introduced many new games and activities and prepared a written curriculum that enabled campers to advance step-by-step, each session and each summer, in their Hebrew education. In addition, she further integrated the use of Hebrew in the life of the camp outside of Hebrew class time, such as in general announcements and sports.[79] She also developed, with the faculty and Gerard W. Kaye, the OSRUI director since 1970, a facility dedicated solely to the creation and operation of the summer Hebrew program throughout OSRUI.

Chalutzim

There is no doubt that by the 1960s educators in the Reform movement sought ways to improve Hebrew learning among young people. The same factors that led on the West Coast to the creation of Solel and on the East Coast to the formation of Torah Corps had their effect in the Midwest. For some time there had been a feeling among the rabbis who supported OSRUI that the Hebrew program ought to be strengthened.

The first plan for a Hebrew-speaking session was made at a meeting of the Rabbinic Advisory Committee in October of 1962.[80] At that meeting it was agreed that a four-week Hebrew-speaking session would be introduced in the summer of 1963 for children from the ages of eleven to thirteen, but the plan was not immediately implemented.[81] When Kaplan was engaged as director in 1963, he became part of the planning for this new unit, and the opening was delayed. The Pioneer Camp was established in 1964 for high school youth, with an emphasis on learning Hebrew.[82] Kaplan's proposal for the Pioneer unit would differ from Torah Corps and Solel in two important ways. First, it was to be a Hebrew-speaking program; counselors were to speak only Hebrew, and campers were to be encouraged to speak only Hebrew. Second, the program would run for a six full weeks.

According to Rabbi Hayim Perelmuter, Kaplan's proposal was hotly debated; some of the colleagues were concerned that campers might return to their congregations too Hebraically oriented. They might demand practices at their home congregations that were not in tune with the philosophies of the congregations. But the majority of the rabbis warmly accepted Kaplan's suggestion. They believed that any push toward more Hebrew that might come back to their congregations from the summer experience would ultimately be to the benefit of the congregations. Rabbis Ernst Lorge, Arnold Wolf, Perelmuter, and Schaalman are remembered as being among those who enthusiastically supported the new venture.[83]

Would it be possible to launch such a program? Would teenagers be willing to sign up for a summer of Hebrew study? Kaplan assured the rabbis that he was not thinking of trying to find fifty or one hundred registrants. Twenty campers would be sufficient to get it started. So the rabbis around the table— Lorge, Perelmuter, Schaalman, and Wolf—each promised to recruit five applicants.[84] They made good on their promise, and in the summer of 1964 Chalutzim opened as a separate unit of the camp.[85]

In one sense, Chalutzim followed the trail blazed by Achvah, Massad, Yavneh, and Ramah. Each of those camps was created by lovers of Zion and lovers of Hebrew culture. Each was supported by a community that believed it was essential to transmit a knowledge of Hebrew to the next generation. Each was built on the conviction that summer camping provided the best opportunity for Hebrew education. Chalutzim (as well as Solel and Torah Corps) came into being later than those other camps, because Jewish peoplehood, Zionism, and Hebrew did not become a central focus in the Reform movement until some twenty to thirty years after these ideals had become central to the other segments of the American Jewish community. When Hebrew was embraced by Reform as an essential component of Judaism, when the Reform movement appreciated that Hebrew was a powerful bond between Jews and their Judaism, then a program such as Chalutzim could be born.

The birth of Chalutzim can also be explained by the presence in Chicago of a remarkable group of rabbis. Herman Schaalman came from a background in Germany where all prayers were said in Hebrew, where Hebrew pervaded Shabbat in his home, and where Hebrew was a basic element of education in the school he attended.[86] Ernst Lorge, the son of a rabbi, grew up in Germany and imbibed a love for the Jewish people from his earliest days. As a young man he was a member of a Zionist youth group and eventually became a group leader. His Hebrew-language education began in grade school and continued through his high school years.[87] Arnold Wolf studied Hebrew on a regular basis with his uncle, Rabbi Felix Levy. From studying the Bible they moved to Maimonides's *Mishneh Torah* and then to modern Hebrew literature, including Bialik's poetry. By the time Wolf arrived in Cincinnati for rabbinic studies, he was already at home in the Hebrew language and possessed a love of Hebrew learning.[88] Perelmuter, a native of Montreal, was the son of two parents who were leaders in the Zionist movement. His father was a Hebraist who believed that a Talmud Torah education would be inadequate for his son, so he engaged a tutor. Hayim studied with his tutor, a Hebrew poet, three times a week from the age of five to the age of twenty. Zionist leaders, including Chaim Weizmann, were guests in his parents' home. Perelmuter was a lover of Zion and of Hebrew from as early as he can remember.[89]

The emphasis on Hebrew in Reform camps came about because of the change that took place throughout American Reform Judaism. But the creation of Chalutzim, the only Hebrew-speaking program among the Reform camps, was a result of the vision and commitment of Chicago's Reform rabbis and the camp director, Irving Kaplan.

Beginnings

The Chalutzim Unit of Union Institute opened for a six-week session in the summer of 1964 with twenty high-school-age campers.[90] Kaplan engaged a young rabbinic student, Donald Splansky, to be the unit head; Rachel Dulin to be the girls' counselor; and the camp's song leader, Sam Alpert, to be the boys' counselor. Dulin and Alpert, native Israelis, were at that time students at American universities. Rabbi Sheldon Gordon volunteered to be the first rabbi for the Chalutzim program.[91]

During that first Chalutzim summer conditions were primitive. A tent was set up for a place to meet. In addition to the tent, there was a little garden in which campers worked. As a result, Alpert remembers that a true *chalutz* (referring to the early pioneers who lived in Palestine) spirit existed the first year.[92]

The counselors tried to teach their classes using only Hebrew, but it was difficult. The campers' knowledge of Hebrew was minimal; there were no standards for admission; there was no theme for the summer except Hebrew; and the program of studies was loosely structured. Nevertheless, the campers were motivated to learn. They measurably improved their Hebrew skills over the course of the summer, and they believed they had started something special, not only for themselves and Union Institute, but for the Reform movement as a whole.[93]

In the summer of 1966 I paid my first visit to the Chalutzim campus. I had come from a strong Hebrew background. My parents were both products of Benderly's passion for Jewish learning and had given me Hebrew lessons every evening after dinner from the time I was a small child until I graduated from high school. I had also attended Camp Massad for five summers, both as a camper and as a counselor. In the Chalutzim program, English was used quite a bit: some of the announcements were made in English, counselors sometimes spoke in English with their campers, and Hebrew classes were taught partly in English. Massad began with campers who already had some Hebrew-speaking ability, and Ramah's constituency came from three-day-a-week supplementary Hebrew schools. Chalutzim campers, however, came mostly from two-day-a-week schools, and, not infrequently, from the one-day-a-week Sunday School.

I volunteered to serve as one of the Chalutzim rabbis for the following summer and for many summers thereafter. During those years a number of innovations occurred. First, a test was developed to determine whether a potential camper could read and write the Hebrew alphabet, had some small basic Hebrew vocabulary, knew a little Hebrew grammar, and knew the meaning of some of the most important Hebrew prayers in the Reform service. The Chalutzim exam achieved its purpose of weeding out those who were not really desirous of learning Hebrew and of promoting Hebrew study among the campers before the start of the season. The test also alerted campers to the fact that Hebrew at Chalutzim was a serious matter.[94]

Study Time

Mornings at Chalutzim were devoted to Hebrew study—normally, an hour of class followed by a half-hour break and then another hour of class time. There were usually six or seven students per class. The counselors and faculty were the teachers. The principle that Hebrew was to be taught in Hebrew was, as a rule, followed. A study book was prepared in advance of the summer that contained readings on the session's theme. It was supplemented with games, songs, and activities of all sorts. Two days a week, the half hour between the classes was used for *du-siach,* a one-on-one conversation in which a staff member or a camper from the highest Hebrew class would meet with one of the Chalutzim, and they would speak only Hebrew for fifteen minutes. *Du-siach* turned out to be a popular and useful activity in helping the campers grow confident in their ability to communicate in Hebrew. In order to find enough volunteers to speak Hebrew with Chalutzim campers in *du-siach,* counselors on days off, office workers, waterfront staff, and rabbis' spouses who could speak Hebrew were recruited.

Motivating Campers to Speak Hebrew

The success of the Chalutzim program depended on motivating the campers to speak Hebrew to the maximum of their ability. All kinds of techniques were used to encourage Hebrew usage among the campers. For example, placed on one wall of the dining room was a calendar with a space for each day of the season (omitting Shabbat). Every evening, after dinner, a faculty member would inquire, "*Mi diber Ivrit kol hayom?*" (Who spoke Hebrew the entire day?). The Hebrew-speakers for that day were then invited to come forward and receive a cup of M&Ms as their reward. The numbers were usually small at the start of the summer, but steadily grew as the season progressed.

Another activity to spur on Hebrew speaking was *milat hayom* (word of the day). Counselors would select a new word each day and present it to the campers in a humorous fashion. They tried to use that word through the day and in subsequent days to reinforce its knowledge among the campers.

Israelis

Chalutzim always depended, to some extent, on having Israelis among its staff members. It has already been said that Israeli-born Rachel Dulin and Sam Alpert were the counselors during the first year of Chalutzim. Both returned for several summers, including as unit heads, and Dulin's tenure included the role of educational director.

Usually, among the six or eight counselors in Chalutzim, two of them had been brought from Israel for the summer. They added a quality to the Chalutzim program that could not be given by the American staff. It was not only in their knowledge of Hebrew, but also in their being able to connect what was happening at camp with the land and the nation of Israel. Several of those who came from Israel for the summer became enthusiastic about Reform Judaism, including Rabbi Aryeh Azriel, who became active in the Reform youth movement in Israel and ultimately entered the rabbinate.

Timi Mayer became a unit head her second year in Chalutzim and ran the unit for six years. During her tenure, Chalutzim reached the heights of its early success because she exerted a powerful influence on campers and counselors to speak Hebrew. Awards for campers who spoke Hebrew all day had to be expanded for campers who spoke Hebrew all week.

Hebrew All Day

Mealtime provided an excellent setting for encouraging Hebrew conversation. With but a small attainment in one's language study, one could learn enough to have the foods passed. However, during afternoon activities—sports, swimming, and *chugim* (interest groups such as music, dance, crafts and drama)—Hebrew often fell by the wayside. To show that Hebrew was a living language, it had to be demonstrated that Hebrew could work on the ball field, at the lake, and in the *chugim*. The program needed staff members who could be not only cabin counselors and Hebrew teachers, but also leaders of *chugim,* people skilled in dance or drama or crafts. If such people could not be found, and if *chugim* became English-language activities, the goal of Chalutzim would be defeated. In addition, a specialist who did not remember that Hebrew was the primary objective might be tempted to give the instructions to the campers in English. In time, sports, waterfront, and arts specialists with a command of Hebrew, or at least a working Hebrew vocabulary, were recruited and hired each summer.

Evening programs were another challenge for Chalutzim. Campers who led these activities were encouraged to lead them in Hebrew. A true test of the success of the program was when campers used Hebrew when they didn't have to. Rabbi Michael Weinberg has said that when he heard campers speaking Hebrew on a canoe trip, he knew that the program had succeeded.[95]

Services were conducted in the wooded Chalutzim chapel morning and evening entirely in Hebrew. Campers were encouraged to supplement the prayer book with creative thoughts and expressions of their own in Hebrew. It is true that the original prayers spoken in the Chalutzim chapel were not as profound as they might have been had the campers been given free range of expression in their native tongue, but this was Chalutzim, and the thoughts were expressed in Hebrew.

There were certain exceptions to the rule about speaking Hebrew in this special program. One was in the cabins after lights-out. Another was the *sicha* (discussion) when campers selected an English-language discussion group of their choice on subjects such as the Bible, Mishnah, Jewish customs, theology, and Israeli history. One more exception to the rule was the *shiur* (lesson). The theme of the summer—for example, Zionism—was used as study material each day in the Hebrew classes. But to more fully teach about the subject, the staff planned a *shiur,* once a week, in which the campers would participate using English.

One memorable *shiur* was Ben Yehudah Day 1967. A camper with limited Hebrew skills was asked to be Ben Yehudah for the day, but not to let his fellow campers know that a *shiur* was in progress. He was to speak only Hebrew all day long, and, in fact, to reprimand those who replied to him in English. The campers wondered at the camper's transformation but did not suspect that it was a *shiur*. The counselors also put on a dramatization of the life of Eliezer Ben Yehudah explaining the importance of Ben Yehudah's life and his battle for Hebrew to become the spoken language of Palestine. Ben Yehudah Day became a turning point that summer and a regular event in Chalutzim. From that day forward it became acceptable for campers to try their best to speak Hebrew. Chalutzim campers often became infected by the Ben Yehudah spirit and grew passionate about their desire to learn and to speak Hebrew.[96]

Viability

There was a period of time in the 1980s when the number of applicants for the Chalutzim program began to diminish.[97] When the numbers fell to the low thirties or to the upper twenties, concern for Chalutzim's future grew. By the 1980s most Reform congregations had come to the conclusion that they could not succeed in teaching Hebrew as a language. Instead they concentrated on teaching students enough Hebrew to participate in the Reform religious service. Could a camp program whose goal was spoken Hebrew survive? The rabbinic community still believed in the importance of Hebrew-language education at camp. Kaye was in full agreement with the rabbis that everything possible should be done to preserve Chalutzim.

One innovation that had a good effect on Chalutzim was the building of a *Merkaz Ivrit* (Hebrew Center). Kaye and Dolgin maintained that there was a center for swimming and a center for art and a center for everything else, so if Hebrew is important, there should be a center for Hebrew. In 1985 the *Merkaz Ivrit* was built—a place in camp, bright and airy, where young people could hear Hebrew stories, create Hebrew art, play Hebrew games, and engage in a variety of Hebrew activities.

The creation of the *Merkaz Ivrit,* along with a general increase in the number of campers, had a positive effect on Chalutzim; registration picked up in the late 1980s and in the 1990s. The threat to the unit's existence had been averted. Chalutzim now has a capacity of about seventy and a waiting list for entry.[98] The success of Chalutzim in spite of the decline in Hebrew language in the schools is due in large part to the role of Chicago's rabbinic community. It took an extraordinary group of rabbis to keep it going for forty years.

Today

During the last few years of the twentieth century and continuing now in the new millennium, there has been a positive development regarding the emphasis on Hebrew in the Reform camps. This may be in part a result of UAHC President Rabbi Eric Yoffie's declaration that "Hebrew is not a tool; it is a part of Judaism's very essence . . . Hebrew literacy is an attainable goal." Though Hebrew as a language is still not taught in most Reform religious schools, the Reform camps are including more Hebrew in their programs. Generally, places in the camps are referred to by their Hebrew names, as are activities and staff titles. Hebrew songs and prayers play a prominent role in all of the camps. Some have Hebrew signs throughout the camp designating the various buildings and places. At Camp Coleman in Georgia, if the campers catch the director using English to announce an activity or place, they get to stay up a bit later that night. At Greene Camp in Texas, two Hebrew-language specialists from Israel are brought to camp each summer. At Goldman Camp in Indiana, except for the high school students, all campers attend a daily Hebrew class.[99]

At OSRUI, teaching material is prepared on several levels for every unit of the camp. During the period before the campers arrive, the counselors are given an orientation on the methods to be used in teaching Hebrew within the camp setting. To operate the *Merkaz Ivrit* and to supervise the Hebrew program in all of the camp units, four Hebrew specialists now spend the summer at OSRUI.

For the last twenty years, since Massad ceased to operate, Chalutzim has been the only Hebrew-speaking camp in America. The campers are still encouraged to speak Hebrew all day long. The goal of Chalutzim is still to create a Hebrew environment for seven weeks so that when the season is over, if the campers have not achieved fluency in Hebrew, many of them will at least be able to carry on simple conversations in Hebrew and have a foundation for achieving fluency with further study. During its forty-two-year history, Chalutzim has served some two thousand campers. Most Chalutzim alumni will testify to the enormous influence the experience has had on their lives. "For a lot of the kids, the Chalutzim experience is transforming. It moves aspects of their Jewish identity from the fringes to their core. . . . To be able to give them the Hebrew at this key moment in their lives . . . helps to give their Jewish identity a framework. . . . And it is not just Bar or Bat Mitzvah Hebrew; it is Hebrew as a language."[100]

The Best-Kept Secret

In Daniel Isaacman's 1976 article on Jewish camping in the United States, he said that Massad was "the *only* [his emphasis] Hebrew speaking camp in America."[101] He gave no consideration to Chalutzim. In Shimon Frost's 1981 essay on the history of Hebrew camping in America, there was no mention of OSRUI or of Chalutzim.[102] Nor did Walter Ackerman include Chalutzim in his 1993 survey of Hebrew-speaking camps.[103] Nor did Alvin Schiff say a word about Chalutzim in his discussion of Hebrew camping in his 1996 book, *The Mystique of Hebrew*.[104] In fact, as far as can be determined, in all of the research that has been done in the field of Hebrew camping in particular or of Hebrew-language education in general, nothing has ever been written about OSRUI's Chalutzim program. It is one of the best-kept secrets in Jewish education. Chalutzim, arguably, one of the most successful and enduring Hebrew-language camping programs in America, is generally unknown in the wider community.

Camp Achvah did not survive; Massad too fell by the wayside; and as for Ramah and Yavneh, although elements of Hebrew still exist in their programs, they may no longer be considered Hebrew-speaking camps. Only Chalutzim, a full summer program for high school youth sponsored by the Reform movement, may today be considered a Hebrew-speaking camp.[105]

Notes

1. Howard Sachar, *A History of the Jews in America* (New York: Alfred Knopf, 1992), 117.

2. Ibid., 138.

3. Arthur Hertzberg, *The Jews in America* (New York: Simon and Schuster, 1989), 168–76, 217–36; Alan Mintz, "A Sanctuary in the Wilderness: The Beginnings of the Hebrew Movement in America in Hatoren," in Alan Mintz, ed., *Hebrew in America: Perspectives and Prospects* (Detroit: Wayne State University Press, 1993), 29–67.

4. Sachar, *History of the Jews*, 406; "Mordecai Kaplan, the Teachers Institute, and the Foundations of Jewish Education in America," in Jeffrey Gurock, ed., *American Jewish History*, vol. 5, part 3 (New York: Routledge, 1998), 67–72; Arthur Goren, *New York Jews and the Quest for Community* (New York: Columbia University Press, 1970).

5. Benderly's contribution to Jewish education has been chronicled in Nathan Winter, *Jewish Education in a Pluralist Society: Samson Benderly and Jewish Education in the United States* (New York: New York University Press, 1966).

6. Ibid., 74. Some of the attainments of these disciples of Benderly were: Berkson— professor of education, City College of New York; Brickner—rabbi of Euclid Avenue Temple, Cleveland, Ohio; Chipkin—director of the American Association for Jewish Education; Dushkin—executive director of the Jewish Education Committee of New York; Gamoran—director of education, Union of American Hebrew Congregations; Honor—director of the Board of Jewish Education, Chicago; and Schoolman—founder and director of the Cejwin Camps.

7. Most of the information about Camp Achvah comes from the article "The Kvutzah and Camp Achvah," by A. P. Gannes and Levi Soshuk, *Jewish Education* 20, no. 3 (1949): 61–69.

8. Ibid., 63.

9. Ibid.

10. See Albert Schoolman, "The Jewish Educational Summer Camp," *Jewish Education* 17, no. 3 (1946): 6–15. Camp Boiberik, the Yiddish camp, opened in 1922. See the Camp Boiberik home page, www.media.mit.edu/~mres/boiberik/.

11. Gannes and Soshuk, "Kvutzah and Camp Achvah," 63.

12. Ibid., 67.

13. Ibid., 68.

14. Sachar, *History of the Jews*, 246.

15. Ibid.

16. Hertzberg, *Jews in America*, 225–36.

17. William Chomsky, *Hebrew: The Eternal Language* (Philadelphia: Jewish Publi-

cation Society of America, 1957), 261–66; Alan Mintz, "A Sanctuary in the Wilderness," in Mintz, ed., *Hebrew in America*, 29–67.

18. Chomsky, *Hebrew: The Eternal Language*, at 266.

19. Ibid.

20. Shlomo Shulsinger, "Hebrew Camping—Five Years of Massad (1941–1945)" *Jewish Education* 17, no. 3 (1946): 16.

21. Information about Camp Massad comes from Shlomo Shulsinger, "Hebrew Camping," 16–22, and by the same author, "What Brought the End of Camp Massad?" (Hebrew) *Bitzaron* 5, nos. 19–20 (1983): 103–06, from the article by Shimon Frost, "Milestones in the Development of Hebrew Camping in North America: An Historical Overview" (Hebrew, with an English summary), in Shlomo Shulsinger-Shear Yashuv, ed., *Kovetz Massad*, vol. 2 (Jerusalem: Irgun Machnot Massad B'Israel and Alumni of Massad Camps in USA, 1989), 17–73, as well as from this writer's personal experience.

22. Frost, "Milestones," 24–26.

23. Ibid., 31.

24. Shulsinger, "Hebrew Camping," 18. Beginning in 1971 this rule was relaxed, and a number of campers were admitted for only half the season.

25. Shulsinger, "What Brought the End?" 105–06, and Frost, "Milestones," 44.

26. Ibid., 105.

27. Information on Camp Yavneh comes from William Furie, "Yavneh," *Jewish Education* 17, no. 3 (1946): 28–30; Louis Hurwich, *Memoirs of a Hebrew Educator* (Hebrew) Part 3 (Boston: Bureau of Jewish Education, 1960), 141–203; Lisa Goodman, *Camp Yavneh—Then and Now* (New York: Jewish Theological Seminary of America, 1994); Frost, "Milestones," 68–73, and from a telephone interview with Yavneh's current director, Deborah Sussman, May 18, 2000.

28. Sefton Temkin, *Encyclopedia Judaica* 4:1264–68.

29. Mordecai Halevi, *Ishe Hinukh be-Yahadut Amerikah* (Haifa, 1972) 83–87.

30. Hurwich, *Memoirs*, 148–49.

31. Furie, "Yavneh," 28–29.

32. Hurwich, *Memoirs*, 162–63.

33. Frost, "Milestones," 70.

34. Ibid., 70–71.

35. Goodman, *Camp Yavneh*, 16–17; Sussman interview.

36. Sussman interview.

37. Information about Ramah comes from Shuly Rubin Schwartz, "Camp Ramah: The Early Years, 1947–1952," *Conservative Judaism* 40, no. 1 (1987): 12–42; Sylvia Ettenberg and Geraldine Rosenfield, eds., *The Ramah Experience: Community and Commitment* (New York: Jewish Theological Seminary of America, 1989); and Frost, "Milestones," 47–63.

38. In his address to a Rabbinical Assembly Conference on Jewish Education. See Schwartz, "Camp Ramah," 15–16.

39. Schwartz, "Camp Ramah," 16.

40. Ibid., 20–21.

41. Burton Cohen, "A Brief History of the Ramah Movement," in Ettenberg and Rosenfield, *Ramah Experience,* 35.

42. Jack Wertheimer, "Jewish Education in the United States: Recent Trends and Issues," *American Jewish Yearbook, 1999* (New York: American Jewish Committee, 1999), 90.

43. Schwartz, "Camp Ramah," 24.

44. Ramah was also influenced by Achvah. See ibid., 17.

45. Ibid., 19–20.

46. Ibid., 27–28.

47. Seymour Fox, "Ramah, A Setting for Jewish Education," in Ettenberg and Rosenfield, *Ramah Experience,* 35.

48. On the decline of the place of Hebrew in Ramah, see Robert Abramson, "The Indispensability of the Hebrew Language," in Ettenberg and Rosenfield, *Ramah Experience,* 71–84.

49. Emanuel Gamoran, *A Survey of 125 Religious Schools* (Cincinnati: UAHC, 1925), 18–19. See also Hillel Gamoran, "Say Kaddish for Hebrew?" *CCAR Journal* (Spring 1997): 83–84.

50. Michael Meyer, *Response to Modernity* (New York: Oxford University Press, 1988), 298–301.

51. The Gilenu Series, with Abraham Friedland, (Cincinnati: UAHC, 1932–1938).

52. Meyer, *Response to Modernity,* 300.

53. Ibid., 389.

54. Richard Hertz, *The Education of the Jewish Child* (New York: UAHC, 1953), 88–91.

55. Samuel Grand's 1960 survey of mid-week Hebrew instruction was published by the UAHC. The data appeared in Hillel Gamoran, "The Study of Hebrew in Reform Congregations," *Yearbook of the CCAR* 86 (1977): 78–79.

56. Ibid., 79.

57. In its early years the Swig camp was known as Camp Saratoga.

58. Telephone interview with Rabbi Wolli Kaelter, September 14, 2000.

59. Ibid.

60. Telephone interviews with Michael Zeldin, July 8, 2000, and with Aviva Kadosh, September 7, 2000.

61. Telephone interview with Michael Zeldin, July 18, 2000.

62. Rabbi Martin Zinkow believes that Solel's end came in 1988 or 1989. Ruben Arquilevich, current director of Camp Swig, believes it came a few years earlier. Telephone interview with Rabbi Martin Zinkow, September 13, 2000, and message received from Ruben Arquilevich, September 25, 2000.

63. Zinkow interview.

64. See Gamoran, "Say Kaddish for Hebrew?" 86–87.

65. The name may have come from Kennedy's Peace Corps. See Meyer, *Response to Modernity,* 378.

66. Telephone interview with Rabbi Henry Skirball, (Congregation Solel, Highland Park, Illinois), September 18, 2000.

67. Telephone interviews with Rabbi Dov Taylor, July 16, 2000; Rabbi Gerald Brieger (Temple Emanuel, Orange, Connecticut), September 18, 2000; and Rabbi Ira Youdovin, September 20, 2000.

68. Brieger interview.

69. Taylor interview.

70. Taylor interview; Brieger interview.

71. Telephone interview with Rabbi Stuart Geller, September 20, 2000.

72. Telephone interview with Rabbi Allan Smith, September 20, 2000.

73. Taylor interview; telephone interview with Rabbi Edward Zerin, July 16, 2000.

74. Interview with Oscar Miller (professor emeritus of economics at the University of Illinois in Chicago), May 21, 2000.

75. Telephone interview with Rabbi Donald Splansky (Temple Beth Am, Framingham, Massachusetts), June 2, 2000.

76. Ibid.; telephone interview with Menaham Kohl, June 2, 2000.

77. Splansky interview (June 2).

78. Telephone interview with Fradle Freidenreich (associate director of the Jewish Education Service of North America), September 11, 2000. Others who served as Hebrew coordinators were Victor Cohen (educational director, Temple Emanuel, Greensboro, North Carolina), Menahem Kohl (cantor and education director at Beth Tikvah Congregation, Hoffman Estates, Illinois), Elliot Lefkovitz (educational director, Am Yisrael Congregation, Northfield, Illinois) and Elyse Azriel (middle school/high school director, Temple Israel, Omaha, Nebraska).

79. Telephone interview with Etty Dolgin (educational director, Moadon Kol Chadash, Chicago), May 23, 2000.

80. Present at the meeting were Rabbis Ernst Lorge, Robert Marx, Hayim Perelmuter, Mark Shapiro, Joseph Strauss, and Karl Weiner. The camp director, Norman Buckner, was also in attendance. (Minutes of the Rabbinic Advisory Committee meeting, October 18, 1962, from the Ernst M. Lorge Collection of the American Jewish Archives, Cincinnati.)

81. Norman Buckner left OSRUI in the spring of 1963, and Irving Kaplan became the new camp director. Debate over the appropriate age group for the new unit delayed the start of the Pioneer Camp.

82. Telephone interview with Irving Kaplan, March 6, 2000.

83. Telephone interview with Rabbi Hayim Perelmuter, April 17, 2000.

84. Telephone interview with Eudice Lorge, May 18, 2000; Kaplan interview.

85. From file boxes stored with the American Jewish Archives.

86. Telephone interview with Rabbi Herman Schaalman, September 11, 2000.

87. Lorge interview.

88. Telephone interview with Rabbi Arnold Wolf, September 11, 2000.

89. Perelmuter interview.

90. It was increased to seven weeks in 1965 and has remained as a seven-week program since then.

91. Telephone interviews with Natalie Gordon, April 28, 2000, and with Rabbi Donald Splansky, April 19, 2000. Rachel Dulin is now a professor of the Bible and Hebrew language at Spertus Institute in Chicago.

92. Splansky interview (April 19); telephone interview with Samuel Alpert, June 5, 2000.

93. Splansky interview (April 19); telephone interview with Rachel Dulin, March 22, 2000.

94. Other rabbis who served in the Chalutzim Unit during the 1960s through the early 1980s in addition to Donald Splansky were Leo Wolkow (Temple B'nai Yehuda, Homewood, Illinois), Simeon Maslin (Knesset Israel Congregation in Philadelphia), Mark Shapiro (Congregation B'nai Jehoshua Beth Elohim), Paul Feinberg, (associate dean of the HUC-JIR Jerusalem school), Michael A. Weinberg (Temple Beth Israel, Skokie, Illinois), and Steven Bob (Etz Chaim).

95. Telephone interview with Rabbi Michael Weinberg, May 17, 2000.

96. Dulin interview.

97. Interview with Jerry Kaye, April 21, 2000.

98. Dolgin interview.

99. Telephone interviews with Bobby Harris, July 3, 2000, Loui Dobin, July 11, 2000, and Ron Klotz, July 4, 2000. Eric Yoffie interview, *Reform Judaism* 25 (Fall 1996), 17–18.

100. Interview with Rabbi Steven Bob, March 24, 2000.

101. Daniel Isaacman, "The Development of Jewish Camping in the United States," *Gratz College Annual* (1976): 116.

102. Frost, "Milestones," 8.

103. Walter Ackerman, "A World Apart: Hebrew Teachers Colleges and Hebrew-Speaking Camps," in Mintz, ed., *Hebrew in America,* 105–28.

104. Alvin Schiff, *The Mystique of Hebrew* (New York: Shengold, 1996), 51–52.

105. Many thanks to all of those who agreed to be interviewed for this article: Samuel Alpert, Rabbi Ramie Arian, Elyse Azriel, Rabbi Stephen Bob, Rabbi Gerald Brieger, Micah Citron, Judy Director, Louis Dobin, Ettie Dolgin, Andrew Dubin, Rachel Dulin, Fradle Freidenreich, Rabbi Stuart Geller, Agatha Glaser, Rabbi Simeon Glaser, Natalie Gordon, Rabbi Suzanne Griffel, Deborah (Schreibman) Grossman, Bobby Harris, Jack Horowitz, Aviva Kadosh, Rabbi Wolli Kaelter, Irving Kaplan, Gerard W. Kaye, Rabbi Ronald Klotz, Cantor Menahem Kohl, Elliot Lefkovitz, Eudice Lorge, Sue Ellen Lorge Schwartz, Rabbi Simeon Maslin, Oscar Miller, Frances Pearlman, Rabbi Hayim Perelmuter, Deborah Sagan, Rabbi Herman Schaalman, Rabbi Henry Skirball, Rabbi Donald Splansky, Deborah Sussman, Rabbi Dov Taylor, Rabbi Michael Weinberg, Rabbi Arnold Wolf, Rabbi Ira Youdovin, Rabbi Leo Wolkow, Michael Zeldin, Rabbi Edward Zerin and Rabbi Martin Zinkow. My sincere thanks also to Adam Gamoran, Michael M. Lorge, and Rabbi Gary P. Zola for reading an earlier version of this essay and for their many helpful suggestions.

6 Creating a Prayer Experience in Reform Movement Camps and Beyond

Donald M. Splansky

Editors' Note: From its inception, campers at Union Institute attended worship services twice a day. Donald M. Splansky's chapter on prayer points out that this was a remarkable fact, because even daily prayer was a "foreign activity" for most Reform Jewish campers in the 1950s.

> *We sat with the campers and discussed the daily schedule. Rabbi Weiner and Rabbi Lorge spoke about the schedule used at the Conclaves. Rabbi Schaalman spoke about the need to have a schedule that included prayer, study and time to build the camp together. After much discussion the committee presented the following schedule. Worship in the morning will be presented by the Rabbis and the evening worship will be conducted by staff or campers. We then began to plan the construction of our chapel. (Rabbi Joseph Buchler, Report on Summer, Union Institute 1953; Program Book 1952)*

Splansky focuses on the evolution of prayer within the Reform movement camps. He demonstrates that worship at the camps was not an open-ended encounter with prayer in which all liturgical expressions were acceptable. Rather, we learn that with oversight from rabbis, educators, and staff, expressions of prayer evolved—ever adapting to the circumstances, experience, and age of the campers. "In the summer of 1957 . . . rabbis challenged us to think in a Jewish way about issues important to youth. These rabbis also prepared readings for us to read after their talks. We each walked alone out toward the lake until we found our own spot to read silently and to enjoy the beautiful mornings. What splendid moments of learning, prayer and the joy of being alive these were for me!" (Rabbi Barton G. Lee, summer 2000).

This chapter enriches our understanding of the evolution of the worship experience over the first ten years of Union Institute's existence. Camp fostered an atmosphere where it was safe to experiment liturgically and where the camp's faculty readily joined in the process. This enabled the development of unique worship experiences in which campers were encouraged to cultivate their own ideas about prayers and express them through words and song. "I was a counselor with the youngest campers. One boy, 9 years old, had written a thoughtful piece about how he wasn't sure God really existed. The camper read the piece and the sky didn't fall in. Three years later I had the same camper in an older group. I'd never seen a teenager more intoxicated with God" (Rabbi Donald Rossoff, June 2001).

Splansky notes that both prayer and worship at camp were often spontaneous. In this context he recounts some humorous moments, which did not diminish the beauty of the worship. We also learn that the unexpected moment or the spontaneous act often provides memorable moments of inspiration. "One of my campers liked to hide, usually in the outdoor broom closet behind the Bayit. One Shabbat morning, as Rabbi [Ernst] Lorge opened the wood-crafted ark for the Torah service, we were astounded to see him curled up inside next to the Torah. What occurred was beautiful. Rabbi removed the Torah from the ark with one hand, and held the other out, inviting the camper to join in the Torah blessing. It was as if it was a natural thing to find a camper in the ark. Like it happened all the time" (Rabbi Ron Klotz, April 4, 2000).

Traditionally, Shabbat is concluded with the Havdalah ceremony on Saturday after dark. Splansky points out that the observance of this traditional ritual at camp constitutes yet another example of how Reform Jewish camping influenced the evolution of ritual practice in the Reform synagogue. Only a few Reform Jews had ever participated in a Havdalah ceremony during the early years of Union Institute's existence. "Things developed at Camp that were not mainstream in the Reform Movement at that time. In 1953 when I was director, we made Havdalah part of every Shabbat at Camp. There was a lot of music to create a mood for the end of Shabbat. One time we floated candles into the lake creating a wonderful mood of Shabbat departing as we did the Havdalah service" (Rabbi Gerald Raiskin, March 2002/December 26, 2003).

Over time, many of those who were emotionally affected by their camp worship experiences pushed their home synagogues to adopt different modes of liturgical music, ritual, and creativity. Splansky theorizes that worship in the Reform movement today may be the most dramatic example of how summer camping has contributed to the transformation of the American synagogue. "There was such enthusiasm in this novel way of living together as Jews that its glow soon was felt in all those congregations and communities" (Rabbi Herman E. Schaalman, June 13, 2000).

Splansky concludes by noting that the legacy of camp worship will always be

its ability to build a compelling community through liberal expressions of
prayer. This achievement may be one of Reform Jewish camping's most endur-
ing contributions to the world of modern Jewish prayer. "It is the creativity and
freedom in prayer that my camping days nurtured ... the understanding of
how to fuse the life within to the object of the natural senses. Oconomowoc for
this Jew was America's link to Jewish renewal and revitalization in prayer and
other Jewish expression" (Rabbi Michael Perelmuter, August 10, 2000).

The subject of prayer at Reform Jewish camps covers a broad range that over-
laps with some other subjects treated in this fiftieth-anniversary volume.
Therefore I have tried to limit the subject of prayer to aspects of its narrow
definition.[1] In addition to my own summer experiences for over forty years at
three different UAHC camps, I have learned from other rabbis and educators
who graciously replied in writing or in telephone interviews.[2] I will deal with
several aspects of prayer at camp: its physical and communal setting, creativity
and books, Hebrew, music, Shabbat, "miscellaneous" contexts, *Tisha B'Av*, recent traditional styles, Jewish identity, "amateurism" in leading prayers, and
the influence of prayer at camp on the Reform Jewish movement.

For most campers the experience of prayer at regular times every day is a
foreign activity. But at camp it becomes natural and indispensable. The ancient
rabbis said, "God says to Israel, 'I commanded you to read your prayers to Me
in your synagogues but, if you cannot, pray in your house, and if you are unable
to do this, pray when you are in your field, and if this be impossible, pray on
your bed, and if you cannot do even this, think of Me in your heart.'"[3] In this
setting the campers (and staff) become habituated to daily prayer at fixed
times.

Perhaps the most wonderful aspect of prayer at camp is how it benefits from
and adds to the sense of community. The campers, staff, and faculty know one
another and live together in a full-time, intensive experience. When they come
together as a community, whether camp-wide or unit-wide, they feel themselves to be among friends. The sense of community precedes the praying. Usually no one has ever had that experience outside of camp (unless they have
spent time on a kibbutz or an Orthodox section of a city, or, occasionally, a
havurah (a group of friends), youth group, regional NFTY Institute, or creative
congregation in our own movement). One respondent, Rabbi Norman Koch,
wrote, "You don't leave the world to go to services. Services are part of the
world." The daily service is led by peers, who are assigned on a rotational basis,
and if someone brings some special skill, such as reading, singing, dancing, or
guitar playing, he or she receives extraordinary praise afterward. Although
guided by rabbis, cantors, and Jewish educators, the camp service tends not to
be "professionalized," but accepting of "amateur" leaders. Even the youngest

and smallest of campers have a turn as prayer leader. The "professionals" blend into the setting, because they too wear camp clothing and have no seat of honor to set them apart. Yet many former campers can still remember some story a rabbi told or some comment during a service that touched them deeply. And most former campers can recall the experience of praying at camp as their foremost time of feeling a sense of close-knit community at prayer.

The setting of formal services in the camp *beit k'nesset*, or synagogue, usually has the form of a U-shape, circle, semicircle, or concentric circles so that the members of the community see each other during prayer. It is a more human and informal setting, and it differs dramatically from the fixed pews in rows that campers know at their home congregations. It helps bind the worshippers together, creates a closer focus, and lends itself better to taking turns. It also encourages more spontaneity, group singing, and discussion during the Torah service. Lawrence A. Hoffman has written extensively about the importance of "sacred space" and its effect on community.[4] Whatever other advantages praying at camp has over praying in home congregations, the sense of community must rank first. The campers engage in prayer with peers, friends, and nurturing adults with whom they live in an intense way day-in and day-out. When this community converges on its *beit k'nesset* for prayer, it is engaging in an especially Jewish activity among many activities in a full daily schedule. The community makes the service unique, and the service reinforces the sense of community. The preeminent power of a community at prayer is in keeping with the observation of Abraham Joshua Heschel: "The Jew does not stand alone before God; it is as a member of a community that he stands before God. Our relationship to Him is not as an I to a Thou, but as a We to a Thou."[5]

The recent development of "Synagogue 2000" and other national discussions seeking to promote a sense of community in Reform and Conservative synagogues examine the worship experience developed in the summer camps. Such features as greeting people at the synagogue door; sitting in semicircles or circles; singing "inclusive," "singable" music; and drawing people into community are all time-tested characteristics of camp worship.

When campers come home after their summer session in the camp community, they usually miss their camp friends. They also miss the sense of community. Their home synagogue with fixed rows of pews leaves them strangely unsatisfied. It is not only the camp service they miss, but also the perceived absence of community. Therefore, as our Reform Jewish summer camps have influenced children for decades (and up to five decades for Olin-Sang-Ruby Union Institute), those children have grown into synagogue leaders. They now push for more community and more synagogue architecture that helps create community.

In addition to camp's emphasis on community, consider the advantage of praying outdoors. Unless inclement weather has forced everyone indoors, the service takes place in an outdoor synagogue in some splendid location. The lofty trees, nearby pond or lake, or lovely views of a camp's grounds add to the worshipper's sense of awe and of praise to a Creator God. "How manifold are Your works, O Lord; in wisdom You have made them all."[6] The words carry increased meaning when one prays outdoors. The benches or logs, however, may feel hard after sitting on them awhile, or mosquitoes may be flying around, but the worshipper outdoors feels himself to be part of creation. He senses a feeling of "creatureliness" and therefore feels indebted to the Creator. Moreover, the view all around usually includes movement: the clouds are passing, the branches are swaying, the moon is glowing, the birds are flying, the breeze is blowing—everywhere the worshipper looks he is reminded of God's creations. Thus he senses what the author of Psalm 24 knew: "The earth is Adonai's and all that it holds, the world and its inhabitants."

One who prays in an outdoor setting cannot help but feel inspired by God's miracle of creation; one becomes filled with awe at the grandeur, orderliness, lawfulness, and goodness of the world God has made. One even senses that the world will not end up in cataclysmic destruction, as perhaps astronomers predict and the law of entropy dictates. The handiwork of the divine Architect will endure, because God is an *adon olam* in both meanings of the term: a Lord of eternity and a Lord of the world.

In our own time the name most associated with this sense of awe, wonder, and need to praise is the name of Abraham Joshua Heschel. He was a great teacher and philosopher to those whom he influenced, while to his detractors and disparagers he was merely a minor poet. Yet everyone in the mid- to late-twentieth century must feel indebted to him for emphasizing the feeling of "radical amazement."[7]

I am reminded of a late afternoon in the summer of 1962 at Olin-Sang-Ruby Union Institute, when a service took place on the hill in front of the Bayit, and the campers, staff, and faculty sat on the ground facing the lake in the distance. The service celebrated God's creation of the universe. With Dvořák's "New World Symphony" being played over a loudspeaker in the background, a reader by the name of Rabbi Gene Levy read the creation story in Genesis, chapter 1. Each day of God's creation fit perfectly into the symphony's various musical themes. This creative service utilized no prayer book, but it filled the worshipper's religious imagination. The trees, lake, earth, sky, and birds attested to God's power and wisdom. For as long as the poetic memory of that service lasted, we *knew* the Architect of nature and drank in the wonders of God's work.

When adults visit camp—whether on visitors' day, Shabbat, some retreat during the academic year, or any other time in which they experience a service outdoors—they sense what they miss in their home congregations (although some synagogues have outdoor "chapels" or grand vistas through windows).

Major thinkers throughout the ages have testified to their own deep inspiration from settings in nature.[8]

Many types of creativity have abounded over the decades. Some campers danced or dramatized a story from the Torah. The liturgy at camp was "age appropriate" for children. Most notably, the campers themselves wrote "creative prayers" that they shared with the camp. Some prayers were "better" and some "worse" than others, from a creative writing point of view, but they all were heartfelt. They prayed for one another; for the end of war, pollution, poverty, and anti-Semitism; and for the future of Israel, of America, of Jewish family life. Often they expressed gratitude for friendship. (Some of the prayers in the Chavurah and Chalutzim programs were written in Hebrew.) Creative prayers tended to be prayers of petition rather than of praise and gratitude, and thus reflected the larger American culture and the "Me generation." Nevertheless, prayers of petition have a long biblical and rabbinic background.[9] And when campers were asked informally which prayer they found the most meaningful, they often replied, "The silent prayer." That too reflected American culture. In fact, sometimes the silent prayer was lengthened to comprise the entire duration of the service, in what used to be called a "Quaker service."

The Quaker service was the exception. The normal service utilized a prayer book, whether the *Union Prayerbook,* the *Gates of Prayer,* another "official" prayer book of the Reform Jewish movement, or a prayer book developed by the camp unit. These books often included "creative readings," illustrations, and song lyrics (or the unit used its separate songbook at services).

The normal service included a lot of singing. It was a congregation of singers. Campers could "sing through the service," meaning they could sing the major rubrics of the Hebrew prayers of the daily service, usually to the accompaniment of guitar, banjo, keyboard, or even accordion. The inclusion of other instruments was encouraged, so other stringed and wind instruments enriched the service too. (Sometimes, when "Band" was a *chug,* the band played some songs at services!) The song leader often taught songs after meals, including prayers for the services. Often the song leader led a choir that sang as the strongest voices of the unit. From those two sources, songs taught after meals and the choir, the entire unit learned the melodies of prayers. Singing prayers rather than reading them was more moving to people, because song has a more direct line to the soul. One respondent, Rabbi Arnold J. Wolf, remembered how he and composer Max Janowski traced music of the *sh'ma* (the first word in the most central prayer of Jewish liturgy) through Schubert, Dixie, the Beatles, and rock 'n' roll. Song leaders such as Debbie Friedman, Rabbi Joe Black, Cantor Jeff Klepper, Rabbi Danny Freelander, and others developed their liturgical melodies at Reform movement camps. Everyone who experienced prayer at camp can remember the *ruach,* the high-energy camp spirit of singing prayers, in keeping with the verse, "Let all that breathes praise the Lord" (Psalm 150:6).

One aspect of prayer at camp, often overlooked, is the feeling of pride that campers experience in building and maintaining the place of prayer. They contributed to the wooden or mosaic artwork on the ark; they cleaned it regularly or at least before the beginning of Shabbat; they might even have worked on repair of benches or replenishment of gravel. Thus, when entering for prayer, they felt proprietorship for the place. And if the unit was small enough, the official photograph of the unit was taken in the chapel or synagogue, which made that location stand out in the memory of the camp experience. In 1953, the first time I was a camper at "Union Institute" in Oconomowoc, I brought gravel in a wheelbarrow to the chapel during the "work period," and I knew that my older brother, Joe, had helped to build the ark there. Those simple acts still fill me with a sense of accomplishment. How many lay leaders of our Reform congregations developed from the ranks of campers who cleaned, painted, and repaired our camps? They must number in the thousands.[10]

In some units of the camp, the distinction between a morning prayer service and morning study time may have become blurred. Sometimes campers might take a prayer book and study materials or a Bible in hand and separate themselves from all others to study for a specific length of time. They received some instructions about what to study and think about, but exactly how they spent their time was up to each individual. One can relate this educational technique to the traditional custom of praying and studying Torah. Every time the Torah is read during a service, the worshipper experiences "time out now for study." For that matter, the prayer book itself was an object of study. This use of the prayer book was of primary educational importance, because in every religion the best single book to study in order to understand the ideas of that religion is its prayer book.[11]

Shabbat services at camp added an additional dimension to all aspects of prayer at camp. Everyone enjoyed seeing all members of the camp community dressed up in Sabbath clothes. Usually they showered and put on clean white shirts and blouses. Every unit looked its best as it gathered its own community into a chapel-synagogue to welcome Shabbat. Many units had their own custom of marching from cabin to cabin as they joined together in one long march and sang Shabbat songs on the way to pray. (Or alternatively, they enjoyed Shabbat dinner before services in order to vacate the dining room and allow another unit in later.) At the Goldman Union Camp Institute in Zionsville, Indiana, they would initiate the Shabbat march with the sounding of a shofar. Shabbat evening and morning services at every camp tended to be more "traditional" in utilizing the prayer book, Torah, and haftarah, but always with singable songs, high energy, and camp spirit. The campers assigned to lead

Shabbat services always felt especially honored and motivated to do their best, whether it was a Friday night or a Saturday morning. Following a late wake-up on Saturday mornings, the campers and all others seemed especially fresh for the duty of praying.

Shabbat services always impressed the campers as very special and different from those they knew at their home congregations. Apart from those few who attended Hebrew day schools, campers lacked the experience of daily prayer services. When Shabbat arrived they could truly compare and contrast the camp service with their experiences at home. They preferred camp services. The sense of community, creativity, music, outdoor setting, age-appropriate and "inclusive" liturgy, and large numbers of peers combined to move their hearts. (People at camp sometimes criticized their home congregations too harshly for Shabbat services. They could quote the old joke about an out-of-town visitor who came to a temple on Friday night and saw a plaque on the wall that said, "In Memory of Those Who Died in Service." The visitor asked, "Which service?!" Such critics never included in their comparisons that the camp Shabbat service enjoyed great advantages from the days and weeks of intensive community-building, individual preparations and participation, and other camp dynamics.) An old saying teaches, "Prayer without *kavvanah* (intention, meaning, spirit) is like a body without a soul."[12] After camp was over, campers understood this very well.

Camp prayers took place at many locations other than the chapel-synagogue, including the dining room, fire circle, cabin, "friendship circle," other sites at camp, and places outside of camp. The dining room as a place of prayer meant mainly the recitation of the *motzi* and *birkat hamazon*. The *motzi* before meals meant either the version without English or with English. If the latter, the prayer started, "*Hamotzi lechem min haaretz*—we give thanks to God for bread . . . ," which actually was a blessing and a half, because it led to repeating the whole blessing. (The Chalutzim Unit, of course, sang the *motzi* in Hebrew only, omitting the English.) Reciting the *motzi* conditioned campers to express in a traditional Jewish way a gratitude to God for food. It marked each meal as an official Jewish meal, although sometimes the prayer for eating bread was recited before any bread could be brought to the table and eaten.[13] The important aspect of this ritual, obviously, was the conditioning of the campers to express thanks to the ultimate source of food. (It also helped them in their manners as they waited for everyone to arrive.) Singing the *motzi* before each meal gave the campers a time-honored Jewish way to thank God and, like other regularly performed rituals, added structure to their lives. Some campers retained this ritual afterward for use at home. The other prayer of the dining room, *birkat hamazon*, was sung regularly after meals. Its abbreviated form appeared in the camp songbook. The leader of this blessing was either the regular song leader or campers (assigned by rotation among cabins or by birthdays or special arrangement). On Shabbat the special insertions were included, especially the beautiful opening paragraph, *shir hamaalot*.[14] Many campers heard this prayer for the first time at camp, and it remained with them, either periodically or regularly, throughout their lives. Those who learned its meaning in Hebrew felt enriched, and those who hummed its melodies felt happy. Reciting this blessing fulfilled the mitzvah commanded in Deuteronomy 8:10, which reads: "When you have eaten your fill, give thanks to the Eternal One, your God."[15] A lengthier series of prayers than the *motzi, birkat hamazon* was sung after the meal was consumed and therefore could be enjoyed more leisurely. Although these prayers were not as old as the ancient rabbis thought, they nevertheless "sounded old," even with the new melodic variations and the table pounding that the campers often gave them.[16] These two prayers at the table may well be the most lasting rituals that campers transferred from camp to home and synagogue.

The fire circle, or *m'durah,* also was used for prayer, especially the Saturday night Havdalah service. This service, separating the Shabbat from the "six working days," was very popular among campers because it appealed so strongly to the senses. The use of the twisted candle, the spice box, and the wine cup lent themselves to the setting of the fire circle. Sometimes other services were held there as well, but the roaring fire seemed most appropriate for the service, which praised God for creating "the lights of fire." (At least one camp used a fire circle for its final program on Friday nights, which contradicted the Shabbat rule that prohibited lighting fire but became a beloved custom at camp. Alas, our movement permits a wide interpretation of traditional Jewish laws. "One man's Mede is another man's Persian"!) The Havdalah service was conducted without the prayers of an evening service (*aravit*).[17] It was short, sweet, and lovely and was usually accompanied by another song session and storytelling. Havdalah at camp made Shabbat memorable from beginning to end.

Prayer in the cabins took place mainly at the end of the day when campers were in their bunks and the counselor was trying to quiet them down and induce thoughts of sleep. Sometimes rabbis and others were invited to the cabins for "cabin prayers." Invariably those prayers included individual expressions of gratitude and the recitation of the *sh'ma.* Traditional prayer books include the *k'riyat sh'ma shel hamitah,* the recitation of the *sh'ma* at bedtime, so the custom at camp had long precedent.[18] It probably worked better as a means of bonding with the rabbi and developing prayerful behavior than it did as a means of quieting the campers down. As soon as the rabbi left, campers wanted to talk some more!

The "friendship circle" used to be a very popular way of ending an evening program, either indoors or outdoors under the stars. Usually, the song leader led a quiet song or two ("*Rad Hayom,*" "Now the day is done," "Day is done," or some other slow song), someone said a closing prayer, and everyone said,

"*Laila tov*" (good night) as the campers dispersed. Did that bit of program count as prayer? I think so. When you compare it to the experience at home today—which has a youngster in a bedroom doing homework, watching television, or on the computer until bedtime—it certainly counts as prayer.

Other locations could be used for services: the waterfront, the lawn, any area of benches or logs, a clearing among trees, and, of course, the main building of the *edah* (unit), especially in rainy weather. Some places were more conducive to prayerfulness than others. Sometimes when bad weather would force a service indoors, the results were surprisingly good. The change of location and the sense of struggle against adverse elements added freshness to the prayers.

Sometimes a camper or staff person would offer a "creative prayer," that is, an innovative prayer, written by someone for a particular service. Some of these prayers were very moving. Often they addressed an issue that had arisen at camp or in the world at large. Such prayers brought the ethereal realms down to earth, in keeping with the view that when prayers are offered, they should be connected with some current events in the life of the worshipper. A popular topic for teenagers, of course, was friendship, and many creative prayers dealt with gratitude for and proper expressions of friendship.

The one holiday that falls during the summer is *Tisha B'Av*. Few campers in the Reform Jewish movement ever experience *Tisha B'Av* outside the camp setting. Most camps appropriately utilize this day as a means to teach about Jewish suffering throughout history, identification with fellow Jews everywhere, and the importance of fasting, praying, and giving *tsedakah* (charity). (Sometimes an "austerity meal" resulted in funds for Jewish and other charities.) Campers learned about prejudice and persecution, and sang songs such as "*Ani Ma'amin*," which produced somber effects. (I remember Rabbi Ernst M. Lorge, teaching and leading the song "*Shiru Lanu Mishirei Tsiyon*" [Sing us songs of Zion], and the campers sang out like captives in Babylonia.) Campers learned about historic Jewish tragedies and heard the haunting melodies of the Book of Lamentations. Most campers had led rather comfortable and sheltered lives, relatively free of anti-Semitism. They learned how different most of Jewish history was from their own experience. Amazingly, they were not threatened by that grim truth, but were grateful for their own lot. They knew that their sadness on *Tisha B'Av* would last only a short while, but a little suffering goes a long way. *Tisha B'Av* made a big impression on campers. I feel safe in saying that without the Reform Jewish camps the observance of *Tisha B'Av* would have disappeared in the Reform movement and would have gone the way of the Fast of Gedaliah.

In more recent years prayer at camp has included some people experimenting with more Orthodox rituals and style. For example, counselors who were influenced by more traditional services at their college Hillels (or perhaps their rabbinic schools) would daven the traditional service (with body motions) while the campers were praying the Reform service. This contrast in styles developed into a problem, because the counselor was not only a worshipper but also a role model. Some campers were imitating this Orthodoxy without any meaningful idea of why or wherefore. Yet, on the other hand, the counselors deserved to pray in the style and philosophy they found meaningful. The camp director addressed the problem by asking the counselor to pray that way in the back of the congregation rather than in the front so that the swaying and the added prayers would be less intrusive and disjunctive to the service. The counselor agreed to do so. This example illustrates how ongoing tension in the Reform movement both invites and resists change and tries, with varying degrees of success, to resolve conflicts between institutional and personal needs.[19]

The prayer experience at camp comes at a formative time in the development of the Jewish child, who, like non-Jewish peers, is working through matters of identity, Oedipal resolution, rebelliousness, and continuity with ancestral traditions. The camper has been told about God but is truly encouraged at camp to think about God as "One who listens to prayer." Earlier religious education is often subjected to more critical evaluation and even rejection by a thoughtful youngster. Psychologist, Gordon W. Allport, wrote:

Usually it is not until the stress of puberty that serious reverses occur in the evolution of the religious sentiment. At this period of development the youth is compelled to transform his religious attitudes—indeed all his attitudes—from second-hand fittings to first-hand fittings of his personality. He can no longer let his parents do his thinking for him. Although in some cases the transition is fluent and imperceptible, more often there is a period of rebellion. Various studies show that for approximately two-thirds of all children there is a reaction against parental and cultural teaching. Approximately half the rebellions come before the age of sixteen and half later. In general the time of insurrection is appreciably earlier for girls than for boys. It takes many forms: Sometimes the youth simply shifts his allegiance to a religious institution different from his parents'. Or he may reach a satisfying rationalism from which religious considerations are forever after eliminated.[20]

The prayer experience at camp, as reinforced by the sense of community, validates the camper's familial faith; it gives considerable certitude to the validity of Judaism. It may be difficult for the camper to articulate the change afterward, and, regarding religion, tests for absolute certainty are lacking. Nevertheless, the positive experience of prayer and the reality of the "One who hears prayer" are convincing to the camper, who has now realized that Judaism "works." This insight is especially meaningful to someone who hails from a rural area where few Jews live (or from an urban area where few Jews live, which was my own case). This insight is not "an abrupt conversion," such as those William James described, but a breakthrough in continuity with one's family traditions.[21]

Before considering the influence of prayer at camp on the Reform movement, I would be remiss not to mention that services sometimes included some very funny, amateurish mistakes. (These times also added to the sense of community!) Someone would open the ark and find no Torah inside, or someone would open the Torah scroll and be unable to find the appropriate place from which to read. Some prayer leader, suffering from allergies to ragweed, would sneeze his way through the *v'ahavta*. A group at prayer would be attacked by mosquitos, or a rabbi telling a story would be pursued by a bee. A camper near the end of the service would announce, "Please rise for the *alulu*," mispronouncing the correct name for the prayer, which is "aleinu." A guitar would be terribly out of tune. A dance group would mess up their dance. Experimental music would prove entertaining at best and ridiculous at worst (e.g., the *sh'ma* set to the musical scale or some popular song). The end of a creative service would have a song for which the leader did not know the melody. (At one service the prayer leader, a rabbi, came to the lyrics of a song that he did not know, so he read the words aloud, including "La, la, la, la, la, la, la"!) The wind would blow away the music sheets. The hard benches would still be sticky with a new coat of varnish. (The rabbi said, "I had hoped to bring you a clear, unvarnished tale.") Perhaps none of these gaffes are as bad as the one in which it is alleged that a camper at a Christian camp once said, "And lead us not into Penn Station."

We Jews keep our good sense of humor when entering a sanctuary for prayer, and that has its pros and cons. On the plus side, a humorous happening keeps things from being ponderous and helps them be, as kids put it, fun. On the minus side, the mood of a service requires a certain seriousness and devotion to task. The camp setting somehow achieves a mood of prayer that is both fun and serious. The campers feel comfortable praying without feeling too self-conscious about it. They feel proud of themselves for participating even though they were not "self-starters"; in other words, the time for praying was built into their daily schedule, and they themselves had no choice whether or not to attend the service.

The real question is, how does the camp experience of prayer translate into praying back home? Related to that question is the more general question, how has prayer at Reform Jewish camps affected the Reform movement?

When campers first return home with great memories of camp and friends and with great "afterglow" for the Jewish experience, they may sing camp songs and contact camp friends, make plans for reunions, and perhaps even want to do the *motzi* (and *birkat hamazon* and Havdalah) at home. The Friday night table rituals may be affected, at least for a few weeks or months. The big difference, however, lies in the loss of community and the style of worship. The home synagogue cannot hope to duplicate the camp worship services. The home synagogue serves people of all ages, not just the camper's contemporaries. Moreover, the camper does not feel the same sense of community, the intensity of a full-time Jewish environment, and involvement. Especially the camper from a small town knows that high-energy Jewish life happens only during the summer at camp. Many rabbis, probably the majority, do not know how to meet the increased Jewish needs of a camper who has recently returned from such an experience. "Can we sing this song at services?" "Can we sit in a circle facing each other?" "Can we do Havdalah?" "Can someone take me back and forth because my parents are busy?" "Can we build a Jewish *omanut* [arts-and-crafts] room in the religious school?" "Why doesn't the youth group do such-and-such activity that we did at camp?" One rabbi told me that he was "afraid" of sending kids to camp because of how they come back "all fired up." (Needless to say, he had never served on the faculty at a Reform Jewish camp in the summer.)

These problems and others were well known to the people in charge of the camps. The minutes of an OSRUI program committee meeting held on March 20, 1956, reflect the situation at that time:

> As the discussion ensued, it became apparent that it was necessary to evaluate the effect that the Institute sessions in the past have had upon our youth. Various problems were brought forth, e.g., as a result of writing their own services at the Institute, frequently when the youth went back to their own temples, they felt that they could not have "living Judaism" through the Union Prayerbook and through the services conducted by their own rabbi. Often their sense of values back in the city was distorted and caused confusion in their lives at home, school, and temple. The rabbi's role at the Institute was minimized to the point where the youth almost felt that we must constantly evaluate the program of the past and use the evaluation for building future programs that will meet the needs of youth in the Reform Jewish movement.[22]

OSRUI has a proud history of rabbinic involvement during its summer sessions and throughout the whole year.

The influence of camp music on the Reform synagogue is treated elsewhere in this book. One of the foremost composers of formal music for the synagogue today, Ben Steinberg, has argued in favor of limiting congregational singing:

> [W]e should remember that the congregation is only one of the voices in a service. If there is a cantor, he/she must also be given special moments to chant in the unique style of our treasured traditions, both Ashkenazic

and Sephardic. If a choir is present, it must do more than lead congregational singing . . . the restrictive, foursquare guitar beat driving a 60's pop melody now obscures those same words—hence the damage done to an entire generation of young temple-goers who have been exposed to little else and who indeed consider camp songs as their sole "tradition."[23]

In the course of time the camp movement has certainly affected Reform Jewish synagogue services. The first and most obvious way is through the growth of "creative" services. (They may be called also "innovative services," "youth group services," or even "camp services.") These usually include printed services handed out to worshippers for use in the synagogue sanctuary, although some other venue may be selected, such as an outdoor chapel. The services are "gender-sensitive" and have certain rubrics of prayer that everyone agrees are important, such as the *barchu, sh'ma, v'ahavta, mi khamokha, avot v'imahot, v'shamru, shalom rav, aleinu,* and kaddish, as well as the required candle-lighting and kiddush. Many of these prayers are sung to melodies learned at camp and without regard to the fact that adult worshippers are unfamiliar with them. (The printed service pages may contain the words but certainly not the notes.) Often the service will have readings interspersed between these prayers, but the readings are not prayers addressed to God. They are expressions on a theme. They create a mood of seriousness about that theme. The themes reflect the concerns of youth culture—for example, friendship, peace, loyalty, hope, Israel, growing up Jewish, ecology, the beauty of nature, being true to yourself, and love. The readings, although often disjunctive to the task of praying, are usually thought-provoking. They are usually anonymous, but those that are quotes of well-known people may reflect a very diverse group of people: ancient rabbis, Mark Twain, John Lennon, Robert Fulghum, Robert Frost, Elie Wiesel, James Taylor, Dr. Seuss, and David Ben-Gurion. Some recent folk song by the guitarist de jour or an older one by John Denver, Debbie Friedman, or Peter Yarrow may also be included. The service usually has a date written on the front page so that everyone will know it was created just for the one occasion and will never be "used" again.

When such creative services were first initiated, the congregational response was almost always enthusiastic, although many wouldn't want it as regular fare. As time moved on, the congregational Worship Committee (or whatever other name it was called) picked up the challenge to create its own services utilizing the style of the camp or youth group service. Some unconventional congregations and Hillel Foundations on college campuses added such creative ingredients to their weekly Shabbat services as well. Those who could afford it printed their own creative prayer books. Sometimes they added other features such as lengthy silent prayers, breathing exercises, eating challah and drinking wine during the service, meditation, Israeli dancing, or even yoga. Some of the main rubrics of prayer disappeared in favor of more of these features. Somehow we all still called ourselves "Reform" and held together as a movement.

Similarly, worship committees and rabbis experimented with the arrangement of seats into a circle or U-shape because of the influence of Reform Jewish camps. Congregations with fixed rows of pews moved the location of the service to a hall, to an outdoor chapel, or to portable chairs under trees. Portable arks were built to house the Torah. Portable lecterns were purchased to accommodate prayer books and even the open Torah scroll. (Large congregations that had an additional small chapel with fixed seats had difficulty justifying such a different location that did not have movable seats.) Worshippers sitting in a circle or a U-shape felt a greater sense of community. Usually a guitarist led singing, and it would not be unusual to see the guitarist looking at a camp songbook for chords. Youth groups would use such locations more often than would the regular congregation.

Until the recent availability of Hebrew software for word processing, these special services appeared with little or no Hebrew in them. English transliterations sufficed, although some committees, rabbis, youth group advisors, cantors, or teenagers made copies from some Hebrew prayer book and cut and pasted the Hebrew prayers into the service. Often these services introduced the changes of "gender-sensitive" prayers to the adult congregation, and they did so long before the congregation invested in buying quantities of the "gender-sensitive" *Gates of Prayer for Shabbat* or *Gates of Prayer for Shabbat and Weekdays.* Congregations would be impressed by how meaningful and upbeat the Hebrew prayers were in this setting. Whether spoken or sung, the Hebrew prayers took on added liveliness.

The music of these "camp services" in congregations made worshippers more aware of how their regular musical menu was slow, disjunctive, and unfulfilling by comparison. The old *Union Hymnal* did not touch their hearts anymore, although the *Union Prayerbook,* with its elegant prose, fared somewhat better. Camp services had energy. They made an effect. At the very least, the music was periodically used by the cantor, soloist, or choir, and sometimes played on the organ. Igor Stravinsky once said, "I haven't understood a bar of music in my life, but I have felt it." So too did the adult worshippers "feel" the camp music at services. I suspect that some congregations, when moving or downsizing, switched from organs to pianos, guitars, or keyboards because of the influence of camp services (although I know of no formal study on the subject). Cantorial search committees (except those of classical Reform congregations), when interviewing cantors and senior class cantorial students of our School of Sacred Music, look for candidates who can play an instrument that lends itself to the music of such services. Increasingly, they look for cantors who appreciate the place of "inclusive," "singable" music in services. This is not to say that cantors and soloists should have only camp-type music in synagogue services, but rather a good mixture of such popular, participatory music together with the esthetic, grand cantorial pieces that continue to inspire worshippers. Which type of music will grow in usage will be decided not only by the professional clergy and lay leaders but also by the worshippers, who will "vote with their feet."

One of the greatest evidences of the influence of prayer at camp on the Reform movement as a whole is the worship service at a UAHC Biennial Convention. Despite the huge numbers of worshippers in one big hall, the service celebrates the Reform Jewish community and breaks down the numbers into smaller groups by means of several strategically placed television screens and by means of singing many camp melodies along with the traditional liturgical melodies. On Shabbat mornings several Torahs are taken throughout the hall in *hakkafot* (circuits) so everyone can see and even touch a Torah. It is not unusual to have group aliyot to the Torah for the recitation of the Torah blessings. Usually the service ends with a camp song during which all worshippers, row by row, place their arms on the shoulders of those next to them. These features reflect the influence of our camping movement. And why not? So many of the movement's leaders themselves attended our camps years earlier and carry much nostalgia for the melodies, the community, the "folk era," and the people they knew decades ago. Delegates of the North American Federation of Temple Youth are given prime space at UAHC conventions in order to participate and show their enthusiasm. And one of the most popular evening programs at UAHC conventions is the concert and sing-along with the great song leaders of our camp movement. These song leaders now find a growing market for "concertizing" in Reform and some Conservative congregations.

The influence of the Reform Jewish camps on prayer in our movement is even greater if we add the fact that the camps have produced so many Reform rabbis, cantors, educators, and Jewish communal service workers. Those who join these professions were once campers, staff, or faculty. They continue to regard the program, prayer, and music at camp to be on the cutting edge of creativity in our movement. Moreover, the regions of NFTY continue to use the camps for their regional institutes, which are enriched not only by the facilities but also by the associations that the youth groupers have with the camps' summer sessions.

Similarly the camps have influenced the Israelis who worked in them for one or more summers. Although I know of no formal study about how working at Reform Jewish camps has later affected Israelis' observances, I know that some Israelis have joined liberal synagogues in Israel (where they sometimes spot a fellow Israeli wearing a T-shirt or sweatshirt from the same UAHC camp where they once worked.) At these camps they gained an appreciation of the strengths of Reform Judaism. Other Israelis, who remained in the United

States, have often found their way into liberal synagogues, Hebrew schools, and non-Orthodox Hebrew day schools.

As I pointed out earlier, it is no exaggeration to say that the camps saved *Tisha B'Av* as a holiday observed in the Reform movement. This summer holiday would not otherwise be observed except in the largest and most traditional of Reform synagogues (and perhaps some located in popular summer vacation areas). A *Tisha B'Av* service made it into the *Gates of Prayer: The New Union Prayerbook,* but unfortunately it was combined with a service for *Yom HaShoah.*[24]

Perhaps the most important influence of prayer at camp upon prayer at Reform synagogues is the increasing recognition that the sense of community must precede praying in a group. Without a sense of community the worshipper comes to the service for some ancillary purpose—for example, saying kaddish—and leaves without meeting anyone. That person is unlikely to return until a year later. ("If he came alone, he leaves alone," Exodus 21:3 says of a Hebrew slave.) But the worshipper who is greeted upon arrival, who joins in the praying and singing, who is recognized in some way (by a fellow worshipper or the leader of the service, or, at least, by the aged custodian) will respond warmly and is more likely to return often. (It is like the old joke that ends, "I don't come to pray. I come to be with Cohen." The truth is that he comes both to pray and to socialize, and the two activities are inseparable.) The sense of community at camp is established within a few days at the beginning of the camp session and is reinforced in every communal activity throughout the day. Praying together is one part of the whole experience. It is the same dynamic that keeps small congregations going and motivates large congregations to break down their membership into smaller groups. It is the same dynamic that creates nostalgia for "the good old days" when the congregation was in its early years, and everyone knew everyone, and they all shared the work of praying and cleaning and cooking and giving.

This heightened sense of community is no small achievement in our larger society that emphasizes individualism. One of the great observers of world religions, Huston Smith, wrote, "Emile Durckheim, the nineteenth-century sociologist, thought religion was entirely a social affair, a reification of the shared values of the tribe. Today our individualistic society comes close to assuming the opposite, that religion is altogether an individual affair."[25] The experience of Judaism, and especially of Jewish prayer at camp, restores the importance of community.

I should put a couple of caveats on this concept that the camps have taught the Reform movement about the importance of community. First, the concept is as old as the ancient rabbis who said, "Give me fellowship, or give me death."[26] In rabbinic literature the term for synagogue as "communal assembly house" (*beit k'nesset*) appears more often than the term for "house of prayer" (*beit t'filla*).[27] In Eastern Europe too the synagogue was the center of communal life, even "the town hall of the shtetl."[28] Second, what has made the place of the synagogue different in the United States in the last quarter of the twentieth century is the general culture's growing emphasis on individualism, privacy, and creature comforts at home. What will bring Jews to synagogue for Shabbat in the era of cable television? I know one Reform rabbi who jokes with his congregation near the end of each Yom Kippur by announcing the date of the following year's Rosh Hashanah! Some congregations are now responding to the initiatives of Rabbi Lawrence A. Hoffman's "Synagogue 2000," which is based on the building of community. Many of its supporters were once campers. Therefore, instead of claiming that the camps have taught the Reform movement about the importance of community, it would be more accurate to claim that the camps are reteaching the movement about community.

A recent influence of camp upon youth culture is that life at camp removes young people from their beloved computers and access to the Internet. Although they still bring their computer games and CDs with headsets, they cannot retreat into the world of "surfing the net" and thus escape the community of their cabin, their unit, or the camp as a whole. Forced to function within the community, they must surrender a good bit of their private entertainment and seclusion.

Despite all of my admiration for the camp influences on prayer in the Reform movement, not all such influences have been positive. For example, the Havdalah Bar Mitzvah has become more prevalent, in part, because of the beauty of Havdalah at camp. (The Conservative movement also faces this unfortunate development.) Whereas at camp Havdalah has community, appeal to the senses, and singing around the campfire, in the synagogue a Havdalah Bar Mitzvah is an artificial, shorter service than on Shabbat morning. Moreover, invited guests usually attend dressed up for the party to follow rather than for a religious service. At a Havdalah Bar Mitzvah no one is in doubt about which is the main event, the service or the party.

Another drawback due to camp influence (although not only camp influence) is the sense that if Hebrew prayers can be sung with great enthusiasm, they need not be understood. One of the hallmarks of Reform Judaism has always been the emphasis on understanding the prayers and therefore praying at least part of the service in the vernacular language of whatever country in which we live.[29] We must know what we are praying. And the increased use of transliterated Hebrew adds incentive neither to understanding prayers nor to learning Hebrew.

To appreciate the influence of UAHC camp services on the services of Reform synagogues, consider the observations of Marc Lee Raphael. In a recent article he described three types of services. The first two were "classical Reform," emphasizing great formality, little Hebrew, rare spontaneity or informality, and "big sermon"; the second type was "middle of the road," with some measure of informality, more Torah readings, a balanced mixture of Hebrew and English prayers, a less formal sermon or discussion, and a mixture of congregational singing and solo pieces. (This was the most common type of Sabbath worship in American Reform congregations.) The third type of service seems like a clone of a camp service (although Raphael does not point out the similarity of the two):

> It is a service marked by informality, abundant Hebrew, maximum congregational participation, Torah reading and discussion, and occasional commentary about, or explanation of, the liturgy by the rabbi. The rabbi hardly needs to give any stage directions, as the worshippers are expected to read the instructions in their book or simply follow what others (more familiar with the service) are doing. The cantor is much more of a congregant, initiating hymns and responses but rarely singing them alone. The rabbi frequently greets the worshippers at the door of the sanctuary prior to services, conducts the service informally, pausing from time to time to explain a prayer or an interesting word within a prayer, clearly trying to choreograph a service with maximizing spirituality. The rabbi will also be more likely to take out the Torah, read it, and discuss the weekly portion with the congregation, or to deliver a talk that permits either responses or, at the very least, questions. The worshippers tend to dress casually; more younger worshippers are present than in the other worship environments; and the rabbi is more likely to come off the bima [the elevated part of the sanctuary from which the service is usually led] (usually not elevated in any significant manner) and read or talk among the congregants, who themselves are more likely to be in chairs that are movable, in contrast to fixed pews or seats in the other congregations.[30]

With the exception of reference to chairs that are movable, this description matches camp services. (Perhaps someday camps too will be able to dispense with hard benches or logs. However, at this point they seem necessary in order to withstand weather year-round.) This type of service is the wave of the future.

The camp influences on prayer have been extremely important. They have built and reinforced Jewish identity. They have emphasized creativity, community, Hebrew, singing, enthusiasm, egalitarianism, and spirituality. They have motivated up to three generations of Jews to care about the values of the prayer book, the synagogue, and the Jewish people. They have inspired us to pray in ways we have not generally found in "classical Reform" or "middle of the road" synagogues, and certainly not in self-help books in bookstores, or in our secular society. Whatever will be the shape of American Reform Judaism in the twenty-first century, our camps will play a major role. "The gates of prayer are never closed."[31]

Notes

1. A good classic introduction to Jewish ideas of prayer is George Foot Moore, *Judaism,* 9th ed. (Cambridge: Harvard University Press, 1962) vol. 2, 212–38.

2. Although grateful to them, I alone am responsible for the observations expressed herein.

3. *Pesikta d'Rav Kahana* 157b.

4. For example, Lawrence A. Hoffman, *The Art of Public Prayer: Not for Clergy Only* (Washington, DC: Pastoral Press, 1988), 197–223, and Lawrence A. Hoffman, *The Way into Jewish Prayer* (Woodstock, VT: Jewish Lights, 2000), 39–102. For the Jewish legal aspects of community at prayer, see Max Kadushin, *Worship and Ethics: A Study in Rabbinic Judaism* (New York: Bloch, 1963), 131–62.

5. Abraham Joshua Heschel, *Man's Quest for God* (New York: Charles Scribner's Sons, 1954), 45.

6. From the daily morning service. See *Gates of Prayer: The New Union Prayerbook* (New York: Central Conference of American Rabbis, 1975), 55.

7. See Abraham Joshua Heschel, *Man Is Not Alone* (New York: Jewish Publication Society, 1951), 11–17. Heschel, of course, did not limit the cause of "radical amazement" to inspiration from nature. See also Joseph B. Soloveitchik, *Worship of the Heart: Essays on Jewish Prayer* (New York: Ktav, 2003), 122–32, especially p. 124.

8. For example, William Wordsworth, "Lines Composed a Few Miles above Tintern Abbey," in *The World's Great Religious Poetry,* ed. Caroline Miles Hill (Westport, CT: Greenwood Press, 1973), 248.

9. For examples of petitionary prayer in the Bible, see Moshe Greenberg, *Biblical Prose Prayer* (Berkeley: University of California Press, 1983), 1–18. For examples of petitionary prayer in the rabbinic period, see Jakob J. Petuchowski, *Understanding Jewish Prayer* (New York: Ktav, 1972), 35–42, and Dudley Weinberg, "The Efficacy of Prayer," in Petuchowski, 121–37, and Bernard Martin, *Prayer in Judaism* (New York: Basic Books, 1968), 12–17. For a classic Jewish analysis of the efficacy of prayer, see Joseph Albo, *Sefer Ha-Ikkarim,* 2nd ed., ed. Isaac Husik (Philadelphia: Jewish Publication Society, 1946), vol. 4, 160–67.

10. Camp director Jerry Kaye has joked that the people who told him they helped build the ark must number in the thousands.

11. See Henry Slonimsky, "Prayer," in *Essays* (Chicago: Quadrangle Books, 1967), 120; full quote in *Gates of Prayer,* 6.

12. Gershom G. Scholem traced this saying back to *Shulhan Arukh of R. Isaac Luria* (1681), p. 31d. See Gershom G. Scholem, *On the Kabbalah and Its Symbolism* (New York:

Schocken Books, 1965), 126. For an introduction to the rabbinic idea of *kavvanah,* see Moore, *Judaism,* 223–27.

13. The Talmud distinguishes between "casual eating," which does not require a *motzi,* and a "fixed meal," i.e., with bread, which *does* require a *motzi.* See Babylonian Talmud *Yoma* 79b. For the Messianic aspects of saying the *motzi,* and for how "the table is an altar," see Lawrence A. Hoffman, *The Way into Jewish Prayer,* 136–40.

14. Psalm 126.

15. See Babylonian Talmud *B'rakhot* 21a, which based the obligation to praise God after meals on Deuteronomy 8:10, which says: "When you have eaten your fill, give thanks to the Lord your God for the good land which He has given you."

16. See Babylonian Talmud *B'rakhot* 48b.

17. Traditionally, the Havdalah prayers were inserted in the evening service before the fourth prayer of the *t'filla.* See Ismar Elbogen, *Jewish Liturgy: A Comprehensive History* (Philadelphia: Jewish Publication Society, 1993), 102. For a scholarly appreciation of "Liberal Halakhah and Liturgy," see Jakob J. Petuchowski, *Studies in Modern Theology and Prayer,* ed. Elizabeth R. Petuchowski and Aaron M. Petuchowski (Philadelphia: Jewish Publication Society, 1998), 169–82.

18. For example, Philip Birnbaum, *Daily Prayer Book* (New York: Hebrew Publishing, 1949), 787–88.

19. Jakob J. Petuchowski wrote, "when all is said and done, *adding* to the inherited liturgy is as much a 'reform' as *omitting* from it." Petuchowski, *Understanding Jewish Prayer,* 14.

20. Gordon W. Allport, *The Individual and His Religion* (New York: Macmillan, 1950), 36.

21. William James, *The Varieties of Religious Experience* (New York: Mentor Books, 1958), reprinted from the Gifford Lectures, 1902, 157–206.

22. Those present at this meeting of the program committee of Union Institute were Robert J. Cooper, Phillip L. Brin, David Gottlieb, and Rabbis Karl Weiner and Ernst M. Lorge. Phillip L. Brin was then the director of the camp. I am grateful to the current chair of the camp board and editor of this volume, Michael Lorge, for bringing these minutes to my attention.

23. Ben Steinberg, "Response," in *CCAR Journal* 38, no. 3 (1991): 20–21.

24. *Gates of Prayer,* 573–89; Hoffman, *The Way into Jewish Prayer,* 162.

25. Huston Smith, *Why Religion Matters: The Fate of the Human Spirit in an Age of Disbelief* (New York: Harper Collins, 2001), 275.

26. Babylonian Talmud *Ta'anit* 23a.

27. Elbogen, *Jewish Liturgy,* 337–38.

28. Mark Zborowski and Elizabeth Herzog, *Life Is with People* (New York: Schocken Books, 1962), 216.

29. For example, Abraham Geiger wrote in a preface to his 1854 prayer book: "nowadays a prayerbook must make provision for the great number of those who either do

not know Hebrew at all, or do not know it sufficiently to find edification in a Hebrew prayer. Yet particularly for that segment of the congregation, a mere translation of the existing prayers does not suffice." Quoted in Jakob J. Petuchowski, *Prayerbook Reform in Europe* (New York: World Union for Progressive Judaism, 1968), 151. And Leopold Stein wrote in a preface to his 1860 prayer book: "We are . . . profoundly convinced that a removal of the Hebrew language from the synagogue would constitute a breach in the very foundations of the structure of our religion; and such attempts have nowhere been successful. However, to allocate a significant area in the worship service to the vernacular *by the side of the Hebrew*—that, under present conditions, is not only permitted, but a duty" (emphasis his). Quoted in Petuchowski, *Prayerbook Reform in Europe*, 158.

30. Marc Lee Raphael, "Sabbath Worship in the American Reform Synagogue, 1970–2000," in *CCAR Journal* 50 (Winter 2003): 47.

31. Deuteronomy Rabbah 2:12.

7 Singing Out for Judaism

A History of Song Leaders and Song Leading at Olin-Sang-Ruby Union Institute

Judah M. Cohen

Editors' Note: Cohen's chapter reminds the reader that music at Union Institute, and at other camps associated with the Reform movement, is tied to meaningful spiritual experiences that go beyond social encounters. Music is intertwined with prayer, Sabbath observance, study, personal religious encounters, and Israel. "We would stand in a line outside of the dining hall, all of Chalutzim [the Pioneer Unit], waiting for our song. Linked hand to hand over our shoulders, we would dance in singing. It was electric. It was energy to our Jewish souls. We were part of something greater than camp itself" (Dean Zemel, July 2000).

One of the most vital, visual, and memorable musical experiences at camps occurs when the camp gathers to welcome the Sabbath. Although over the years the setting has changed, the entire camp has always gathered as a collective community to celebrate Shabbat in song. These Sabbath song sessions are filled with special excitement: "Camp music made Shabbat holy. We would just sing through our Shabbat repertoire with no words of explanation. It was much more than fun, more than even community-building; we were touched by the transcendent, and were never the same again" (Rabbi Mark Shapiro, May 2000).

Cohen emphasizes that song leaders and song leading at Union Institute evolved into a significant mode of Jewish religious expression. Despite the fact that the genre of music changed significantly over the years, the centrality of the communal singing experience never waned.

In 1958 I was hired as a Union Institute song leader. I stressed the themes of brotherhood and universality to match the mood of the country, leading "If I Had a Hammer" and "We're in the Same Boat, Brother." Of course, we sang Hebrew and Israeli songs as well, particularly on Shabbat.

In the mid-70s I came back to camp, not with my guitar, but with my stethoscope as camp doctor. I was struck by the change. Now, there was more singing in Hebrew and more Israeli songs. But the community singing had the same feeling. (Dr. Larry Ross, September 29, 2000)

Regardless of the repertoire, aside from the deep friendships or influential counselors that a former camper might remember, it is the camp's music that lingers with those who spent their summers in Oconomowoc. The experience of community singing; the ever-present song sessions at meals, praying with guitar music at worship, learning Israeli folk songs, and singing into the night with the telling of Jewish stories—all of these have influenced thousands of Reform Jews. "Late at night when we CITs were in bed on the second floor . . . Sam Alpert used to sit downstairs and sing songs in Polish and Russian. Today, I've spent some years in Israel. Yet when I recall Jerusalem in the springtime, my mind plays a time warp trick: I'm still reminded of those summer nights listening to Sam sing" (Rabbi Ron Klotz, April 4, 2000).

Cohen's chapter concludes by demonstrating how the early musical years at Union Institute affected the face of contemporary Reform Judaism. As summer camping grew within the Reform movement, songs and song leading were one of its fundamental components. In each one of the movement's summer camps group singing has been a central feature of the camping experience. Cohen emphasizes that Union Institute in Oconomowoc was an early catalyst for the growth of a new liturgy. From the first decade of the camps, when the Israeli song leader Sam Alpert arrived and opened the door to expansive new folk melodies; to the early 1960s, when Rabbi Howard Bogot set up an electric piano on the gravel floor of the outdoor chapel; to the impact of the remarkable original compositions of Debbie Friedman, Rob Weinberg, Rabbi Joe Black, and others, Union Institute fostered the growth of new and influential modes of Jewish musical expression in America: "I still lead 'Hinei Mah Tov' and 'Bim Bam,' which I first sang at Union Institute in the 1950s and later led as a song leader there. Later I took these same songs to the UAHC camp [Coleman] in Cleveland, Georgia. Make no mistake: group singing is a vital part of what made Jewish camping a powerful 'shaper' of identity. It became very much a part of who I am as a Jew" (Rabbi Ralph D. Mecklenburger, July 5, 2000).

A little after 10:00 AM on June 19, 2000—the commencement of the year-long celebration of Olin-Sang-Ruby Union Institute's (OSRUI's) fiftieth anniversary—all the camp's song leaders brought their guitars to the front gate, joining several other staff members gathered there. Wearing their bright orange OSRUI staff T-shirts, the group began to sing an extended, excited rendition of the song "*Salaam.*"[1] A succession of guitar-accompanied songs continued at various levels of intensity for more than an hour and a half as a growing stream of campers began to arrive. Eventually, the song leaders had to leave to attend to their augmenting units; and by the time the last buses of campers came through the gates, the musical activity had ended.[2] Yet the morning's opening song session had served as background music to many of the incoming young people. It welcomed them into a removed society of living Judaism that harbored a unique sound environment. Several weeks later, as sessions ended and campers prepared to return home, song leaders marked the transition by accompanying a closing friendship circle, leading songs that had obtained particular significance over the summer. These songs would then serve as reminders of the camp experience throughout the rest of the year.

The totality of music heard during the campers' tenures at OSRUI was wide-ranging, coming from numerous different sources and venues: song leaders accompanied Friday night Shabbat *shirah* (song sessions), Saturday night American folk-song sessions, and twice-daily prayer services held throughout the camp; CD and tape players reproduced prerecorded Israeli folk-dance music during dance sessions scheduled on Friday nights and Saturday afternoons; and contemporary American rock and hip-hop music accompanied each unit's once-per-session dance party. Campers and counselors produced covers and parodies of popular tunes for both all-camp and individual-unit talent shows; and unaccompanied group singing took place during services, the blessing after meals (*birkat hamazon*) and informally through spontaneous *ruach*-raising (spirit-raising) chants. Amid this complex of sound, campers explored their Jewish identities, forged relationships, and had a great deal of fun—all within the framework of a Reform Jewish lifestyle. By the time they left, many of the campers had come to feel a Jewish "sense of belongingness" to OSRUI through the sounds they heard and the songs they sang.[3] Such sounds would act as reminders of camp throughout the year and contribute to the campers' desires to return the next summer.

In this essay I will take a closer look at one of the most prominent and visible elements of the OSRUI summer camp "soundscape": the song leader.[4] While certainly not the only musical figure in the camp environment, the song leader has developed in tandem with Reform Jewish camping to become nearly synonymous with summer camp and youth music; thus, to some, song leading has even come to symbolize Reform Jewish music in general. Song leaders, often mediating between popular culture, political activism, and Reform theology, have long served as musical interlopers between faculty, staff, and campers, actively propagating a sound environment that is conducive to the programs and ideologies set out by the camp. Most importantly, however, the song leader has consistently been a focal point for musical expression and discourse within the camp environment. Contemporary discussions of OSRUI's musical history by both campers and alumni invariably center on song leaders and their activities, further suggesting their importance as indicators and negotiators of youth religious identity. Thus, by examining historically the song leading culture at a single camp (in this case the oldest permanent camp in the American Jewish Reform movement), I hope to shed some light on the forces that brought this form of musical expression such distinction in the Reform Jewish camp setting.

For reasons I will discuss later, music receives scant coverage in secondary sources on American Jewish camping. In my research of song leading at OSRUI, I relied upon several different primary sources for information. I used as my basic source the voluminous and (at the time) uncataloged archive of OSRUI materials at the Jacob Rader Marcus Center of the American Jewish Archives (AJA). Although containing a few makeshift scores for the camp's orchestras and choirs, the AJA's most relevant materials for this project were the saved copies of numerous mimeographed song sheets and worship service booklets handed out to campers over the years. Supplementing the booklets were a number of short firsthand accounts of musical activities written by campers and published in camp-produced newspapers, several scattered lists and photographs of participants in music-oriented *chugim* (clubs), and occasional administrative discussions of the camp's music program. These materials, along with copies of two editions of the camp's *shiron* (songbook) obtained at Olin-Sang-Ruby Union Institute, provided a good overview of the camp's documented general activities, song repertoire, and forms of music usage.

To obtain a more detailed understanding of song leading from the "inside"— that is, from the point of view of those who organized, led, and experienced the music—I conducted and transcribed interviews with many former and current song leaders, all of whom served as faculty and campers at different times within the camp's history. Ranging from about half an hour to more than two hours in length, these interviews provided a great deal of information regarding the process of creating musical experiences and meaning at Union Institute and also helped to fill some of the most gaping historical holes in the archival materials.

In addition, between June 12 and July 16, 2000, I spent a period of extended observation at OSRUI, where I worked on the faculty as a music specialist.[5] During this time I experienced a good portion of the camp's current song leading activities in situ. Being on the camp's grounds also helped me visualize the activities I had heard and read about from past years, allowing me to place them in both geographic and demographic contexts.

It is my intention here to provide a broad historical framework highlighting some of the more prominent trends and occurrences in song leading over the first thirty years of the camp's existence, and to attempt an initial interpretation. I hope to make some inroads into studying the areas of both summer camp music and "folk-based" music in the American Jewish Reform movement— the latter of which has rarely been touched outside of polemicized scholarship.

Before Union Institute: A Brief History of Group Singing at Camp

When Union Institute held its first session in Oconomowoc, Wisconsin, in the summer of 1952, American camping had already become, in the words of folklorist I. Sheldon Posen, "one of North American culture's most prolific settings for both structured and spontaneous group singing by children and adults."[6] Taking place at campfires, after meals, on nature walks, and during specifically designated song sessions, group singing served a significant role in propagating a sense of self for Americans during pastoral respites from urban or suburban living. Therefore, in order to understand the means by which such practices took root at Union Institute, it is important to understand first how group singing became a lasting—and in many cases defining—feature of the summer camp experience by the mid-twentieth century.

Posen estimates that group singing at camps may have begun as early as the late 1800s, as an extension of common recreational group singing practices among the urban middle classes (the population at the time most likely to send its children to summer camps). It is hard to tell, however, if camp singing at this time was done with any uniformity or according to an articulated philosophical rationale; more likely, singing accompanied certain activities as an extension of existing urban practices. By the 1920s and 1930s, as summer camping became a more uniform practice, the sing-along began to take a role as a more or less standard part of the camp experience, involving distinct titles (such as the term "sing-along" itself), set-aside times, and designated leaders. For recreational camps such as those founded by the YMCA, according to Posen, group singing was probably incorporated as a way to involve everyone in a "genteel" activity—"civilizing" the participants by endearing campers to popular culture, building a camp identity, and encouraging universal participation.[7] Others, however, saw the persuasive power of group singing as a way to encourage political activism and foster a dynamic of strength among "common peoples." The efforts of this latter group proved a significant impetus to the eventual blooming of the folk song movement.

In the wake of the Bolshevik Revolution, a number of left-wing organizations arose in the United States in the 1920s that promoted populist, socialist, and communist ideals. These organizations established their own summer camps as a way to provide a "congenial atmosphere in which leftists shared ideas and activities, and reinforced their beliefs, values, and political allegiance."[8] Although not explicitly Jewish, some of these summer camps (including Camp Kinderland and Camp Woodland) catered to an overwhelmingly Jewish clientele. Children and teenagers sang songs that embraced political topics, universalism, and the triumph of the working class; and many heard these songs again at workers' rallies and other similar events throughout the rest of the year.[9] The ubiquitous nature of group singing in these environments served to motivate and educate the campers, even inspiring some who came from more conservative backgrounds to join their comrades in lives of political action.[10]

Labor Zionist movements in Europe and America were also important propagators of group singing in the early part of the century. Professing politics similar to many left-wing organizations, but cultivating more nationalistic goals, the Labor Zionists tried to instill in their youth movements a sense of Jewish pride and longing for the establishment of Israel, in addition to a love of the outdoors. In Germany, Zionist youth organizations such as *Blau-Weiß* (Blue-White) produced songbooks for their *Kinderwandern* (scouts) as early as the mid-1910s, and later German Zionist groups such as *Habonim* did similarly.[11] When *Habonim* camping began in the United States in the early 1930s, songs of the Israeli pioneers and other melodies of Zionist import helped imbue young campers with the concepts and ideals of establishing a Jewish state as they sat around the campfire or prepared for the Sabbath.

Christian and Jewish educational camps in America often included group singing in their programs as well. New York's Cejwin camps published songbooks for use by their campers as early as the 1920s,[12] while Surprise Lake Camp articulated in 1936: "Every camp has singing. . . . A very important asset in setting an environment is introducing folk songs and particularly Jewish folk songs and Jewish effects from songs in English and Jewish themes, songs in Hebrew and songs in Yiddish about Jewish life and Jewish situations, etc."[13] In 1939 Rabbis Samuel Cook and Eugene J. Sack used a large Christian camp meeting (the Estes Park Conference) as a model for creating what proved to be the first Reform Jewish camping weekend. Group singing was a part of the experience, though as Sack noted, it did not necessarily come intuitively. "When I rose to teach [the first camp attendees] a song they had never heard," he wrote, "it was evident that they were not used to and did not like group singing, but they tried."[14] Ten years later, prominent synagogue composer Max Helfman assisted education pioneer Shlomo Bardin by providing a songbook of arrangements for group singing at Bardin's new Brandeis Camp Institute in Southern California.[15] Through religious services as well as sing-alongs, the campers learned how to profess their faith as a group in song; and conversely, through group singing, the songs themselves became important emblems of these camps' religious identities.

Thus, by the middle of the century, group singing had become a nearly ubiquitous phenomenon within the summer camp setting, Jewish and otherwise. Conducted in a variety of formats, song helped campers develop a sense of personal worth, philosophical ideals, and camp pride while assisting them in adapting to their new, intensified social situations. When Union Institute joined the world of youth summer camping, it too began with these concepts in mind.

Unifying the Song Leader's Voice: The Creation of a Hybrid Musical Paradigm

Most of the rabbis who played roles in the founding of Union Institute, including Herman Schaalman, Ernst Lorge, and Karl Weiner, were native Germans who had grown up with the Zionist ideologies of *Blau-Weiß* and *Habonim*.[16] Relatively conservative by American standards of Reform Jewish observance, they emigrated to the United States in the 1930s (several of them at the behest of Leo Baeck) and some enrolled as rabbinic students in Cincinnati's Hebrew Union College (HUC). Within the Zionistically ambivalent and "religiously progressive" seminary environment of the time, the German students were known to cause occasional disturbances, advocating actively for broader observance and support for establishing the State of Israel.[17] Many maintained their Zionist youth backgrounds by associating with the American *Habonim* movement, working at camps during the summer, and helping to lead local activities during the year.[18] In the HUC, they lobbied for a more extensive *birkat hamazon,* among other things, in an effort to retain "traditional" texts they saw as important within the fabric of Jewish life.[19] Many of the students harbored visions of using the summer camp experience as an educational tool for Reform Judaism.[20]

By the late 1940s several of these German immigrant rabbis had found positions in the Chicago area. Such geographic proximity made it possible for them to coordinate their visions and make plans for establishing a summer camp under the imprimatur of Reform Judaism. It seems their experiences with Zionist youth groups, as well as their periodic stints as teachers of Judaism at Christian summer camps, became the impressionistic basis for a working model.[21]

From the perspective of Reform Judaism at the dawn of the twenty-first century, the classic image of song leading usually conjures up a group of young people being led in song by a marginally older person with a guitar who had devoted at least some time to developing song leading skills. This image, however, was not the norm at the dawn of Reform Jewish camping. The guitar as an instrument was far from standard during the camp's first sessions. Rabbis generally led singing themselves during the first years of the camp, counting the activity as one of their many responsibilities; and they appeared, moreover, to have little song leading training. Accounts of early song sessions described how leaders of the singing often just "waved their hands and jumped around" to raise and organize enthusiasm, with little regard to method or technique.[22]

Interestingly, this practice appeared to be analogous with that of the Labor Zionist summer camps used as a model by Union Institute's founders: with all their emphasis on group singing, Zionist summer camps appeared to have no tradition of trained song leaders.[23] Song sessions seemed to resemble more the contemporary "hootenanny" culture of the time, primarily oriented on the facilitation of communal (often topical) singing; the centrality and expertise of the person leading these sessions appeared less significant than the actual musical material sung.[24] The subsequent emergence of the song leader and song leading idiom, as well as the creation of a stable song leading repertoire, thus became important developments that would mark the coming-of-age of Reform Jewish camping.

It is difficult to know the musical activities of Union Institute's first few summers, as little archival material pertaining to musical content survives from these years. Singing, however, was probably an important part of the campers' activities. The rabbis likely instituted specific times and places for group singing, and likely led the early campers along with "someone on staff capable of conducting some of those sessions."[25] Chances are the thirty-nine high-school-aged, Chicago-area campers who came during the camp's first summer in 1952 sang songs they knew from their local youth group chapters, folk songs such as "*Die Gedanken Sind Frei*" (My Thoughts Freely Flower),[26] and Israeli pioneer songs such as "*Anu Banu Artza*" (We Have Come to the Land).[27] During services, campers probably used settings of the prayers they knew from their local synagogues: "traditional" melodies, selections from the 1932 *Union Hymnal,* and compositions by Chicago-area composers, such as Max Janowski. Beyond these general parameters, however, the exact repertoire and song leading techniques used are uncertain.

Significantly, although several early participants remembered group singing from the start of Union Institute, they seemed to have trouble recalling these first years as a part of the camp's musical history. Such memories suggest that although singing had a place of importance at these camps, it had not yet become a "skilled" art form. The people who coordinated (and sometimes led) these sessions appeared to place little importance on their teaching strategies or musical programs. Participant and faculty descriptions of singing during those first years were vague; there was even an occasional dismissal of early song leading as an activity conducted by people who "didn't know what they were doing."[28] Maintaining little continuity with the "tradition" of song leaders that emerged in the mid-1950s, this early period appears to be relegated to a self-imposed state of obscurity.

Song leading "traditions" at OSRUI as they are identified today apparently began to take root only after an individual was hired to lead group singing at the camp full-time. Although this did not happen at the regional camp until 1955, a supplementary national Reform camping initiative at the same location began this practice three years earlier, in 1952. The person employed to lead the singing at this supplementary camp, Cantor William Sharlin, would become the progenitor of the Reform song leading tradition; and his successor, Morris ("Morrie") Hershman, would soon bring the traditions he introduced into the regional camp.

On the wall of the staircase leading up to the second floor of OSRUI's *Bayit* (the mansion once known as "the Big House") is a black-and-white photograph of a young Bill Sharlin standing in the camp's dining hall. He wears black plastic-rimmed glasses, shorts, and ankle socks, and he holds a small, classical guitar in his hands. Several dozen teenagers are seated tightly together at tables surrounding him, filling the room. Chalked into the fireplace mantel behind one table of teens is an abbreviated form of the grace after meals written in all capitals: "*Adonoi Oz L'ammo Yiseyn Adonoi Y'vorech es Ammo Va Sholom*" (God will give strength to God's people; God will bless God's people with peace). Four small chalkboards with additional song lyrics rest atop the mantel. And above these hang three banners identifying the event: "NFTY Leadership Institute, '53 Oconomowoc, Wis."[29]

In Union Institute's inaugural summer, two national sessions supplemented the Chicago-area main camp in the Oconomowoc facility. Referred to as Leadership Institutes of the National Federation of Temple Youth (NFTY), the ten-day retreats took place after the main program and brought together promising Reform Jewish high-school-age youths from across the country (as well as Canada and England) for an intense experience of Jewish learning, prayer, and recreation.

During the rest of the year, the classically trained Cantor Sharlin directed the HUC choir in Cincinnati. Song leading was an avocation of his that had begun several years earlier at a camp for handicapped children in New Jersey. Sharlin, who used a twenty-five-dollar guitar purchased specifically for the job, had been impressed at the depth of impact and connection that group singing created between him and the disabled campers. He continued his song leading work in limited venues for the next several years, becoming involved in the NFTY scene through his friendship with Samuel Cook.[30] One weekend, Sharlin spontaneously agreed to take his guitar and accompany Rabbi Cook to a local youth-group weekend conclave. His performance at the conclave clearly swayed Cook, who subsequently hired Sharlin to lead group singing for the fifth NFTY Leadership Institute, slated to take place at the new Reform Jewish camping facility in Oconomowoc.[31]

Sharlin was certainly not the first song leader to work at an NFTY Leadership Institute, nor was he the first to song-lead with a guitar (though the instrument was much less commonly used in song leading at the time).[32] He was, however, a liturgical musician and trained cantor with strong ties to Cincinnati's HUC, and, most significantly, he was given the exclusive responsibility of leading "Instituters" in song that summer. In overseeing the Institutes, Cook had a keen sense for bringing music into the Jewish recreational agenda: firmly believing that the success of the institute concept relied heavily on creating a sense of *ruach*, or spirit, among the campers, he worked hard to develop a program with "less domination by rabbis and advisors and more teen-age participation."[33] Sharlin's addition to the faculty was a manifestation of this plan. Joining Sam Cook's wife, Ray—a prolific Jewish children's songwriter—the young cantor found his main venue after meals in the dining hall, running around the room, playing his guitar, and facilitating a select group of Reform Jewish teens in singing Jewish, Israeli, and American folk songs.

Although Sharlin led his share of what he recalled as "silly" songs, such as "Blue-Tail Fly" and "Joshua Fit de Battle of Jericho," he also saw his role, in concert with the Institute's philosophy, as one of teaching and Judeo-political consciousness-raising. Claiming to use the guitar strictly as a way to provide harmonic backgrounds, he tried to place the focus on himself and his message. At the same time, he saw his job less as "leading" than "joining together" with the attendees to create a sophisticated and meaningful musical environment. Sharlin apparently equated understanding the song's meaning and singing it with a pleasing aesthetic: when a session was going successfully, he recalled, the sound in the dining room would resemble a "sort of choral singing."[34]

Accounts of Sharlin's time at the Leadership Institutes attest to both his enthusiasm and his creativity. Repertoire was sparse at the time: aside from Israeli pioneer songs and some liturgical music, there was little Hebrew repertoire available—and few among the campers understood the language well enough to appreciate it anyway.[35] Thus, in an attempt to provide material for the campers, Sharlin searched the Hebrew music he knew for " 'folk-style' elements" that were compatible with the current group singing aesthetics,[36] and texts that were direct and easy to understand. These songs he modified and introduced in contexts that were meaningful to the participants. Chalking the transliterated lyrics up on blackboards, rather than distributing them on song sheets, Sharlin attempted to keep everybody looking up in the hopes of maintaining a positive group dynamic while minimizing lack of interest and withdrawal among the campers. Over the course of several repetitions, simple Hebrew songs began to transform themselves from a series of nonsense syllables into music with a definite, if at that point only general, meaning. According to Sharlin's successor, a number of songs, including "Bim Bam/Shabbat Shalom," came into the repertoire this way.

Equally significant, though less common at the time, were spirituals and "brotherhood" songs. A specialized repertoire on the margins of the contemporary American music scene, these songs remained an important staple of populist ideology, with a strong emphasis on concepts of universal equality and international camaraderie. The Reform movement, having passed a resolution condemning racial segregation as early as 1946, clearly leaned in this direction; but the more liberal-minded rabbis in charge of the emerging youth movement went further, teaching this ideology as a mainstream element of Jewish belief and professing very early on that the campaign for civil rights was a common task for both Jews and African Americans.[37] In this environment Sharlin introduced one of his first brotherhood songs—Huddie Ledbetter's "We're in the Same Boat, Brother." The overwhelmingly positive reaction to this song among the campers and staff reinforced the camp's position as a place for championing the values of social justice as an integrated part of Jewish ideology.[38]

Campers tended to view Sharlin's work at the Institute as a new approach both to music and to Judaism. According to Mark Shapiro, a future song leader and rabbi who attended the 1952 Leadership Institute:

> [I]t was just eye-opening. . . . People used to [say]: " . . . the music is the highlight [of camp]. Wait 'til you sing with Bill Sharlin." And the way he moved around a dining hall and the kind of sound he elicited from people; and the high, the sense that music at camp was an art, not just the day camp [idea of] "let's sing songs" . . . Sharlin wanted us to sing well, he wanted us to have a good time, he wanted it to be a vehicle for Jewish expression—at that time, not very much on the Hebrew, but just enough to let us know that we were Jewish.[39]

Sharlin's work also helped Instituters explore their identities as Jews and Americans—something that former campers recalled as remarkable. In their lives outside camp, most of the attendees had experienced a strong separation between the music they experienced in Jewish contexts and music they experienced in the rest of their lives. At the Leadership Institutes, however, the separation blurred. During the morning and evening services, Cantor Sharlin would leave his dining hall persona behind and help lead services, intoning many of the prayers and accompanying some with soft chords on his guitar: "Bill would accompany the service with guitar and lead all the liturgy so . . . there really was a link between songs as the community glue in the dining hall—the thing that everybody did all together and enjoyed . . . [and] the liturgical experience, which was of course very, very different for most of us. . . . we'd sure never seen [our synagogue musical leaders] doing anything else that was fun; and [we] never [saw them] having a relationship with us."[40]

This minimization of the sonic distinctions between recreational and worship music at the Institute would remain a dramatic break from the rest of the Reform Jewish world for many years to come. Though at this point the continuity between dining hall and chapel was vested mostly in the song leader figure himself (rather than in the songs), the connection would eventually become a defining feature of the Reform Jewish youth movement.

Rabbi Ernst Lorge's wife, Eudice, noted that the *ruach* "that was created in the atmosphere of these retreats . . . was transferred into the programming of whatever we did at the new camp in Oconomowoc."[41] Lorge's comment also applies to the creator of this *ruach*. Rabbi Schaalman recalled the song leading of the Leadership Institutes and was impressed by Sharlin's energy and ability to engage the campers in song; but he was never able to bring him to the main camp. In 1954 Morris Hershman agreed to lead singing at the main camp the following year.[42] With Hershman in place as Sharlin's successor, the song leading tradition at the National NFTY Leadership Institute transferred over to the organizational framework of Union Institute's regional camp.

Like Sharlin, Hershman had grown up with a Western musical background. After considering a career in music, however, Hershman decided instead to enter the rabbinate, beginning his studies at HUC in the late 1940s. His participation in the HUC choir during this time brought him in contact with Sharlin, and the two became fast friends. The cantor took the young rabbinical student under his wing, teaching him to song lead and play the guitar, providing him with a new repertoire, and (eventually) grooming him to take over the HUC choir directorship. Consequently, when Sharlin was unavailable to lead the NFTY Leadership Institute, he recommended Hershman to take his place.[43]

The paid song leading position Morrie Hershman held throughout the summer of 1955 came with unique privileges: he received his own room in the Big House, and had to participate only in programs directly involving him. In return, Hershman had to prepare and run all the camp's song sessions and religious services, and remain on call the rest of the day to fill dead time or shore up struggling programs. Hershman, too, saw his job at the camp as an educator, a "transmitter of . . . values."[44] Influenced by composer Max Helfman while a camper at Shlomo Bardin's Brandeis Institute in 1949, and then by Sharlin at HUC, he worked to expand the camp's repertoire by using "quality" as a criterion for choosing songs. A quality song, he remembered, had an "interesting chord pattern, interesting rhythm, interesting concept; a song that can stimulate the imagination. It isn't just 'Ninety-nine Bottles of Beer on the Wall.' It's a different kind of camp song."[45]

Notably, this statement hints at the differentiation the song leader perceived between songs that were appropriate for a general "camp" atmosphere and those that were appropriate for Union Institute. In addition to musical value, the songs had to embody a philosophy concordant with "Jewish values" as defined by the camp's director and faculty. Civil rights activism, taught under the guise of "Prophetic Judaism," fit squarely into that area.[46]

While Sharlin had particular talent for introducing and leading Hebrew and Israeli songs, Hershman found his milieu in the newly emerging folk-song movement. The repertoire of Hebrew and Israeli songs Hershman learned from Sharlin continued to be sung in the dining hall. Brotherhood songs also remained part of his agenda, and to this effect Hershman introduced pieces from Hy Zaret and Lou Singer's 1947 collection *Little Songs on Big Subjects,* such as "Close Your Eyes and Point Your Finger" and "It Could Be a Wonderful World."[47] But Hershman delved especially deeply into folk music sources, including issues of the recently published left-leaning magazine *Sing Out!,* for good songs with appropriate messages by the likes of Big Bill Broonzy, Woodie Guthrie, and Pete Seeger. Despite the left wing factions these songs represented, it is a sign of the camp's political tendencies that the songs were not disallowed because of content.

Hershman took great care in the way he introduced new songs, treating his material with reverence. "It was a whole presentation," he remembered. "I sat on my porch . . . for a couple hours, thinking about how I would represent this [song] in a way that would pique [the campers'] interest."[48] "I think that we considered [the introduction] as much of an art form as we considered the music," said Mark Shapiro, Hershman's successor, even suggesting that the process of presentation itself was a sacred act: "[for] the brotherhood songs especially . . . it was a D'var Torah." Hershman illustrated his teaching methods by describing his introduction to "The Hammer Song"—"[I'd start off by asking] 'what does a hammer represent to you? If you had a hammer, what would you do with it?' and so forth. . . . [A]nd by the end of it . . . I'd captured their imagination and their attention. They'd learn the song and they gobbled it up." In this way, new songs found meaningful places within the camp's repertoire.[49]

The campers, for their part, took to the new songs eagerly, though not merely because of content. Union Institute had been succeeding in its founders' vision of creating an overall *ruach* for Jewish education, and inspired teenagers were beginning to associate the songs they sang in the camp setting with the "warm feelings" that flowed through the overall camp experience.[50] Rabbi Ernst Lorge's daughter, Sue Ellen Lorge Schwartz, remembered the clear division she perceived even at a young age between songs she sang in camp and those that were popular in the rest of the world: "I'm sure that a lot of people thought I was probably 'obnoxious' . . . when we would have birthday parties in the city, we would have talent shows. All the other kids were singing popular songs like 'How Much Is That Doggie in the Window' or whatever in the '50s, and I would sing these camp songs, which the kids [didn't know]; this was not their music, but I realize how important to me it was at that time."[51]

This association between camp songs and camp experience was so strong that some campers even expressed surprise when they heard recordings of "The Hammer Song" in a secular setting, with a different chord progression from what they had learned in camp. "Wait a minute! This was, this is our song! What're they doin'—'The Hammer Song' is Jewish! What're [they] doing singin' the Hammer Song?"[52]

Reform Jewish youth music was beginning to seem like its own entity to those outside Union Institute as well, attracting the interest of one of America's most influential Jewish composers. Max Janowski, whose prayer settings were widely known throughout the Chicago area, came up to join the faculty in the summer of 1955. While teaching and leading music programs, he also took a liking to the camp's song leading practices.[53] Soon he had begun a friendly relationship with Hershman; the two would occasionally be seen together, with Janowski at one of the camp's two pianos and Hershman sitting next to him playing the guitar.[54]

Later in the summer, Hershman received a request from Sam Cook to introduce a Hebrew song focusing on the concept of *chai* (life) and turned successfully to Janowski for help. With Mark Shapiro, Hershman traveled to the composer's South Side home. There, Janowski and Hershman found a good text in "*Nishmat Kol Chai*" (Creator of all life), and Hershman proceeded to assist Janowski in composing a new "camp-appropriate" setting for it. That same afternoon, according to Shapiro, the composer also created a new setting of "*Ki Mitziyon*" (For out of Zion [the Torah shall go forth]) specifically for use at Union Institute. With new melodies in hand, Hershman and Shapiro returned to the camp and worked out the guitar chord progressions; that summer, they introduced the Janowski pieces, along with other Janowski compositions, to the campers. The settings caught on, and campers continued to sing "*Nishmat Kol Chai*" and others as a part of the local repertoire for well over a decade.[55]

Hershman did not return to work at the regional camp the next summer, but his presence had helped establish a song leading paradigm that would continue through the rest of the 1950s. Young rabbinic student Mark Shapiro, who had been attending Union Institute programs in several different capacities since its inception, assumed the song leader's post in Hershman's place. Following a nascent song leading tradition established at camp, Shapiro was responsible for introducing an annual brotherhood song; that summer, his contribution was "It's the Same All Over," a song that continued to appear on camp song sheets and songbooks into the 1980s. Shapiro moved into the role of camp program director the next year, and Lawrence Ross, a trained guitarist who had earlier been on the camp's kitchen and maintenance crew, took over the song leading responsibilities in 1957 and 1958.[56]

By the end of the camp's first decade, the song leader's position and activities had been all but formally codified at Union Institute. Rabbis had the option of using the song leader for a brief morning service. Breakfast followed, after which the campers would briefly sing "waking up" songs with the song leader such as "Rise and Shine" before heading to their cabins for cleanup. After lunch and dinner, longer song sessions took place. New songs, frequently having been discussed beforehand with the camp's director, would be introduced and taught during these times, for use both in future song sessions and in services.[57] At the evening worship, the song leader would often provide musical accompaniment for a camper-led "creative" service during the opening, the silent prayer, and the service's closing hymn, plus whatever else the campers requested. Finally, as the day ended, the campers would gather in a friendship circle before going to sleep; swaying to the music, and with their arms around one another's shoulders, they would sing "Days Pass and Years Go By," "Now the Day Is Done," and other similar songs, probably accompanied again by the song leader.[58]

The schedule changed significantly during Shabbat, a time reserved for religious celebration. Friday evening would begin as the freshly showered and dressed campers would gather to greet the Sabbath, singing songs specifically meant for Friday night. A choir of campers joined the song leader in leading the music of the Kabbalat Shabbat service, which ended with the blessings over wine and bread to indicate the start of the Friday evening meal.[59] After dinner, there would be a much longer and more enthusiastic song session, occasionally including songs led by and identified with specific members of the staff. Israeli folk dancing would follow on the adjacent tennis court; and though a record player was sometimes present, song leaders recall also playing guitar in the center of the dancing circle, encouraging the campers to sing along as they went through the steps. A snack, more song leading, and bedtime concluded the evening. The next morning, the song leader sometimes participated in a much longer (and by reports a much more "Classical Reform"–style) service, and helped lead more songs after lunch. As the sun sat in the evening, campers would gather around a campfire, bidding farewell to the Sabbath through a brief Havdalah service and transitioning into a classic campfire, complete with song leader–led campfire songs.[60]

The intensity and frequency of group singing in this setting attests to both the stability of the song leading structure as well as the song leader's clearly developed role within the camp's routine. Song repertoires were stabilizing as well: by 1959, Union Institute was issuing to its campers primitive "songbooks" containing a couple dozen songs in English and Hebrew transliteration, separated between songs for Shabbat and songs for the rest of the week. Together, the songs combined to form a distinct "soundscape" of the camp—a secure musical identity. Filtering songs from numerous settings, and introducing selectively through a well-articulated process established by the song leaders, the camp was fast creating its own special soundtrack.

One other interesting dichotomy is evident on the song sheets that remain from this period, revealing a fascinating political situation facing American Jewry. The transliterations show two different forms of Hebrew pronunciation coexisting in camp life. Ashkenazic Hebrew—the form spoken by most Jews of Eastern European descent at the time, and thus the form used in most American synagogues—was used for the standard portions of the prayer service and a few of the Shabbat songs. Sephardic Hebrew—the form of pronunciation adopted by the Israeli pioneers, and eventually the State of Israel—was used whenever singing Zionist or Israeli songs.[61] The employment of Sephardic Hebrew pronunciation was itself an important and early statement, reflecting the Zionist backgrounds of the camp's founders. Yet outside of the singing there was still little Hebrew spoken in the camp in the 1950s. As Israel increasingly came into the mainstream of American Jewish life over the next decade, the spotlight on Hebrew would become brighter, and music would play a key role in its development.

Hebrew and Israel and Folk Music: The Song Leader as Educator

When an eight-year-old Stephen Hart came to spend his first summer at Union Institute in 1961, he felt he had entered into a completely different musical world from the one he knew at home.

[I] grew up in a very classical Reform environment. The Jewish music that I'd been really exposed to as a child was . . . what we'd call now very 'high church' music: organ, gentile soloists who you never saw. Certainly not a cantor—didn't even know what a cantor really was, because we didn't have a cantor. . . . And that was really more from High Holiday services, because being a classical Reform congregation . . . [it] did not have a Shabbat [service]. . . . it had a late Friday afternoon service, but it was not anything that I ever went to. [It] did not have a Saturday morning service. [It] did not have Bar Mitzvahs. And the primary service of the congregation was on Sunday morning.[62]

Hart's transition from home to camp, while particularly stark, probably bore strong similarities to the experiences of other campers. Union Institute at this time was a place apart for young Chicago-area Reform Jews. Dedicated Reform Jewish youth might attend synagogue services once a week at home, but at camp they attended and led creative worship services twice a day, including the Saturday evening Havdalah service that was generally neglected in home communities but now conjoined with the weekly campfire. Where the *Union Hymnal* represented the standard Jewish musical fare in Reform synagogues, it held only a small part of the service music repertoire at Union Institute, which by that time used everything from Israeli pioneer songs to Sammy Fain and Paul Webster's 1955 "Love Is a Many Splendored Thing."[63] Where older adults seemed to dominate Jewish life and leadership outside Union Institute, the population at camp was young, and becoming younger: once only for high school students, new programs provided experiences for children as young as eight. And where Zionist fervor still seemed somewhat radical in the outside world, at camp it was mainstream. Union Institute was developing a vibrant culture that shared less and less with the values of Jewish life at home. Many synagogues supported Union Institute through donations and camp scholarships and seemed encouraged by their children's enthusiasm. Upon their return from camp, however, the children seemed less connected to the culture of their home institutions than they were to the new culture of their youth groups.

Hart's memories of song sessions in his first year bear subtle but significant differences from those in the 1950s. Pioneer songs with few and easy Hebrew words and settings from the "Song of Songs" remained important parts of the Hebrew repertoire. "Brotherhood" songs, so named because of their importance to teaching civil rights at camp, now lost their luster as an exclusive category and began to fall in with an increasingly political and activist "folk" genre.[64] And although the song leader in 1961 still strode through the dining hall with his nylon-stringed guitar, teaching new songs from mimeographed lyric sheets and drumming up enthusiasm, his identity made him a unique and exciting figure in the camp and was a harbinger of a new musical direction.

Although he was born in Eastern Europe, everyone at Union Institute knew Shmulik ("Sam") Alpert as an Israeli—one of the first many of them had met. The dashing young man put Zionism into a new perspective. Up until this point the Hebrew songs campers sang tended to represent enthusiasm over an abstract land of Israel, "not having a sense that we were really singing any of the music that was actually sung in Israel at the time," remembered Hart. "I think it was much more geared to the pioneering spirit and the early songs of the State."[65] Alpert, in contrast, presented the campers with an image of Israel as a real country with a contemporary modern culture, whose citizens could inspire real crushes in pre-teenaged girls.[66] As the camp's song leader, he brought a repertoire of newer Israeli songs with longer, more complicated Hebrew lyrics, and through his very presence at Union Institute, campers seemed to become inspired enough to learn them.

Alpert held the official title of "music and dance specialist,"[67] theoretically acting as the primary arbiter of two of the camp's major cultural venues; however, he is remembered almost exclusively for his song leading.[68] Endowing his various activities with a voice of "authenticity," he seemed to be part of a concerted program throughout Union Institute to support and promote Israeli language and culture. Since song leading was a medium already being used effectively in creating camp identity and in teaching rudimentary Hebrew, it became an important purveyor of this program. Israeli and American folk music styles shared many of the same features, including a socialist political basis, the use of guitar, and an ethic of group singing.[69] Thus, rather than create a new vessel for disseminating materials on Hebrew and Israel, Alpert helped reorganize and intensify an existing one. Expected like his predecessors to introduce new songs into the camp repertoire, he taught many of the selections he knew from Israel. This greatly expanded the camp's Hebrew base, while providing a strong point of connection with the young Jewish state.

Perhaps spurred on in part by Alpert, the early 1960s saw a standardization of all Hebrew pronunciation to *Sepharadic,* the version spoken in Israel. This adjustment was most apparent in religious services and songs, which earlier were a stronghold of Ashkenazic pronunciation. Transliterations from mimeographed camp materials show the change to be relatively sudden. Before 1961, the Hebrew word for Israel was frequently spelled "Yisroel"; campers would often refer to resting on "Shabbos"; and one of the most popular Friday night prayer songs was called "*Tov L'Hodos.*"[70] After 1961, campers read about "Yisrael"; they would rest on "Shabbat"; and "*Tov L'Hodos*" all but disappeared from the repertoire.[71] Such orthographic transformations indicated unequivocally the symbolic translation of the camp's cultural center from America to Israel. In doing so, however, it also widened the gap between youth and the older generations. Older adults "weren't comfortable" with the change, according to Sue Ellen Lorge Schwartz, in part because "it didn't sound to them like Hebrew."[72] To the youth, however, the break seemed to be a source of empowerment: it unified their camp linguistically, further strengthening the connection between dining hall and religious services, and providing a connection to a hegemonic Jewish culture that until then they had known only in spirit.[73]

Songbooks show how rapidly the camp's Hebrew song repertoire expanded. As in previous Union Institute song collections, the camp's 1963 pamphlet "Songs We Sing at the Union Institute of the UAHC" continued to distinguish songs for Shabbat from songs for the rest of the week.[74] This latter category, however, broke down further according to language. Sixty-one non-Hebrew titles constituted the "Songs We Sing" category; forty-eight "Hebrew Songs in Transliteration" made much of the Hebrew repertoire accessible to the campers; and three "Hebrew Songs in English Translation" completed the book. An additional packet of twenty-one "Songs in Hebrew" displayed lyrics in the original Hebrew text and provided a Hebrew alphabet pronunciation guide, revealing the importance of music program for Hebrew education. Many of the Hebrew songs remained from the camp's earlier years; but some songs, such as Yakov Orland's "*Rad HaLayla*" and Naomi Shemer's "*HaDerekh Aruka,*"[75] presented a Hebrew difficulty level beyond any yet introduced at camp and showed the ambitions of the new initiative.

In 1964, in a groundbreaking publication that was also distributed to several of the other, younger UAHC camps, the Union Institute's new, enlarged *shiron* continued to emphasize Hebrew repertoire; even the name—the Hebrew word for "songbook"—attested to the camp's progress in promoting Hebrew and Israeli culture. Taxonomic divisions remained the same as in the previous year, but the proportions had changed dramatically: the number of songs in the Hebrew section had nearly tripled, coming to comprise more than 57 percent of the material in the book. For the most part, these songs were listed in order according to the Hebrew *aleph-bet,* and appeared on the page in Hebrew, English, and Hebrew transliteration. The songbook probably reflected a hope for greater Hebrew literacy more than an achievement of it, but nonetheless the new publication provided campers with an unprecedented way to integrate Hebrew into their musical, camp, and Jewish lives.[76]

Sam Alpert served as the first boys' counselor and song leader for the camp's Pioneer Unit, which was founded in 1964.[77] In this new environment, where Hebrew songs were seen as a part of the educational program, he supplemented the songbook with several sheets containing the latest Israeli music. Through this, song sessions became a time for coming to terms with a language that was strange to many of the attendees, in addition to raising spirit and forming group identity through a common experience. "[It] seemed that music was really the Hebraic glue for the Chalutzim," suggested Mark Shapiro, who spent several years as a rabbi with the group. "We could build up such a repertoire of songs that then we could go into the classroom and talk about the songs that you already know."[78] Rachel Zohar Dulin, a counselor in Chalutzim, further underlined this: "Breakfast, lunch and dinner always ended with a song session which was connected to our theme and our educational focus."[79]

By this point, the camp was employing at least three song leaders: one for Chalutzim, one for the rest of the camp, and one for Avodah, a work-study program devoted to maintaining the camp's physical plant. Notably, however, the song leaders started to hold a status that was different from their status in the 1950s. No longer separated from the rest of the camp population, they were hired primarily as cabin counselors who held the additional responsibilities of leading their units in song. Director Irv Kaplan made this change upon his arrival a year or two earlier in order to aid the camp's overall educational program: "I felt that specialists as such were not a contributory factor to developing a cohesive staff," he noted. "So long as their load was not much greater than a regular counselor, there was no reason to have an 'elite' factor on staff."[80] While this move deprofessionalized the position of song leader in one sense, in other ways it recontextualized the song leader as a fully contributing member of the "professional" camp community. No longer an avocation solely for those with Western classical training, the art of song leading became a central part of the camp's educational process: emphasizing proficiency with guitar chords, facility with group dynamics, and the ability to create an educational music curriculum for a group of campers. People designated as "music specialists" did occasionally appear on staff lists after this; however, they usually led the camp's choir or orchestra and had little connection to song leading.[81]

The mainstream commercial success of artists such as Bob Dylan, Peter, Paul, and Mary, and Joan Baez further helped bring a new, more "democratic" dimension to folksinging at Union Institute. Inspired by these and other musical artists, campers and staff began bringing guitars to camp in relatively large numbers, and would spend substantial periods of time practicing and exchanging songs during free periods.[82] Song leading was no longer a form of lone minstrelsy, as it had been in the 1950s. Instead, song leaders such as Richard Weiland found themselves sponsoring popular folksinging *chugim* (clubs or electives) where they taught campers "to blend their voices in harmony" and "to express their creativity in music."[83] Following the same taxonomic system as the camp's songbooks, Weiland taught English and Hebrew material in relatively equal portions. The campers took to this approach readily, as a reporter from the camp's newspaper discovered: "A question put to the members of the chug was: 'Do you like to sing English or Hebrew songs better?' The majority of the campers agreed that they like both kinds of songs and enjoy singing either."[84] To these campers, the boundaries between the folk music they sang in their mainstream lives and the folk music they sang at camp were fading quickly.

Friday night was the only time when the whole camp came together to celebrate. Far more than services and weekday song sessions, many campers and counselors considered this time the most spiritual and inclusive experience of the whole camp session.[85] The Pioneer and main camp units would welcome the Sabbath separately, praying and eating in their own facilities. After dinner, counselors and campers would set up extra benches in the main camp's dining hall, and the Pioneers would enter, line dancing to a vigorous setting of "*Yismechu HaShamayim.*"[86] A short grace would follow, after which the entire camp would embark upon a long and energetic song session. Progressing from easier to more difficult songs, the song leaders from the various units helped all voices blend together in a celebration of the Sabbath until their repertoire was exhausted. Toward the end of the evening, the campers would call individual counselors up to lead songs identified specifically with them. Few of these counselors were hired song leaders, yet their turns in front of the campers were highly anticipated.[87] Finally, after repeated rhythmic shouts of "We want Irv!" the camp's director would finish up the festivities with a rousing and nearly bombastic version of "*Chiri-Bim.*" A song leader of sorts himself, Irv Kaplan embodied his vision of the song leader's role: working without a guitar (as he had always done), he would jump on tables and run in and out of doors to create "not song as much as energy" and "a passion of celebrating" Judaism.[88] Of all the musical experiences in the camp, Friday night thus became the event seen as the most "spiritual" and exciting of the camp experience, fostering the creation of a community.[89]

By 1967 the camp's emphasis on Hebrew and education had caused enormous changes to song leading and the song-leading repertoire. Its impact on religious services, however, was somewhat more muted. A creative approach to worship remained the norm as rabbis and campers searched for new and meaningful ways to create spiritually fulfilling prayer experiences. Yet as experimental as these approaches were, they often took place within a less-than-inspiring musical framework.[90] The most fertile areas for musical creativity remained the opening and closing "hymns" (which service sheets were now beginning to call "songs") and the end of the silent prayer. In these places campers tended to import songs they found relevant from the current camp repertoire in order to enhance the service's given theme. Outside of this, however, the "creative" nature of the services was almost exclusively textual. Especially within an environment of ecstatic music making, attitudes toward worship began to feel a little strained: campers from this period consistently saw their most spiritual religious experiences at camp as involving the song sessions, sometimes eschewing mention of t'fillot (prayers) altogether.[91]

On January 12, 1967, Union Institute's Rabbinic Program Committee—which included Rabbis Lorge and Schaalman, former song leader Rabbi Mark Shapiro, and Hebrew program overseer Rabbi Hillel Gamoran—met to address the camp's worship program. Their conversations revealed some concern with current song leading practices as well as the skills of the song leaders themselves. Much of this seemed to stem from what the rabbis saw as a lack of a central focus in the music program that led to poorly learned material. Ernst Lorge, for example, averred that singing in services was "not very effective," in part because "the songs are not taught, and therefore not understood." Schaalman suggested as one remedy that there be one formal song-teaching period per day, "using song sheets with only the songs to be taught rather than the whole songster." Adding to this, Shapiro and Gamoran called for a full-time music specialist to hone a cohesive song curriculum for the camp.[92]

Lorge also criticized another element of group singing that he found disturbing. Most likely speaking to what he saw as an undesirable practice in camp, he noted: "The melody should be emphasized, not the rhythm."[93] Though a relatively vague dichotomy on the face of it, the comparison actually delineated clearly a spiritual musical aesthetic. "Melody" appeared to represent to him the lyrical voices and nylon guitar strings of the 1950s sound of camp song leading. Overemphasized rhythm, on the other hand, he seemed to define as a negative element, which distracted campers from both the mood of the service and an understanding of the prayer songs. This distinction represented one of the first attempts to preserve song leading as a cultural practice and testified to the extent of its development. Notably, the same terms would be used to criticize the state of song leading for decades to come.[94]

Israel's victory in the Six-Day War later that year served as an impetus for further change in the song-leading repertoire. In 1969, as part of an explosion of postwar patriotic musical creativity, Israel held its first in a series of annual Hassidic Song Festivals. Espousing in spirit the Hassidic concept of joy through ecstatic devotion, the event's organizers invited Israel's top musical artists to compete with one another by writing songs that incorporated or interpreted common liturgical texts.[95] As an offshoot of the event, the songs from each festival were collected and released in album form, supplemented by a pamphlet containing melodic lines and chords. These materials infiltrated the American Reform movement almost immediately through the Israeli counselors in the Chalutzim. Many at the camp found the Hassidic Song Festival material to be an exciting find: the imported songs began to breathe new life and interpretation into the prayers, and began to allow campers to see the possibilities of using contemporary popular music styles to set the standard prayer texts themselves.

Songwriting and Superstardom:
Creating a Repertoire from Within

The report assessing the 1966 Union Institute camping year recognized significant changes in the role and demographic of the song leader. Group singing had become a crucial element of a burgeoning Reform Jewish youth culture, prompting the camp to propose hiring additional song leaders to work at "week-end kallahs [retreats for Reform Jewish youth] . . . utilizing the Oconomowoc facilities."[96] Moreover, the popularity of song leading motivated many of the youth group members to aspire to positions of musical leadership themselves. The need to provide training for these individuals in a way that maintained a certain quality standard was likely one impetus for the camp's call to establish a special "Song Leaders Institute" in the same report.[97] While it appears these plans did not immediately come to fruition, the concern expressed in the report to train able song leaders for an increasingly popular and autonomous youth group and camping system was significant, as was the assertion that Union Institute was the place for such development to happen.

As the 1960s came to an end, a closed system developed by which song leading began to sustain itself while keeping camp at its center. Established and aspiring song leaders—now mostly teenagers and college students—had several opportunities to lead singing and services at youth group events and conventions over the course of the winter (many of which utilized the Union Institute facilities). Through these, they had the opportunity to hone their craft with friends and campers from the summer. Learning from other song leaders in their region through a process of oral transmission, they acquired melodies, guitar chordings, and teaching techniques to practice during the "off season." The centrality of Union Institute to this process even included the repertoire: an update of the Union Institute *shiron* came out in the late 1960s, providing Chicago Reform Jewish youth with a core set of songs as well as the movement's most recent "hits."

The summer camp session, however, still remained the central time and place for sharing songs, learning song leading techniques, and gaining a reputation as a facile song leader. By 1970, following in Irv Kaplan's vision, song leaders had become a fully integrated part of the hierarchy of Jewish camping at Union Institute. All campers would learn the English and basic Hebrew repertoire in their first few summers (the "Juniors" program, now called "Kallah"), while also becoming familiar with the camp's song leading aesthetic, supplementary melodic lines (often called "harmonies"), and various accompanying hand and body motions. In Chalutzim, program participants would acquire many classic and new Israeli and Hebrew songs using the same aesthetics. Those who wished to continue spending summers at camp would join the staff during their college years, and those who showed the appropriate musical talent and enthusiasm would be hired as song leaders.

Others who had not spent as much time at Union Institute benefited from post-Chalutzim programs intended to smooth the transition of high school students into staff positions. Both Michael and Robert Weinberg, for example, had been song leaders in regional Reform youth retreats before coming to Union Institute as pre-staff: Michael on Machon (the counselor-in-training program) in 1970, and Robert in Avodah (camp maintenance) in 1971.[98] The time needed to acculturate to the camp music style and repertoire was important: according to Judy Director, a song leader at the camp from 1969 through 1973, Union Institute was a "camp very big on tradition" and generally offered little explicit guidance on subjects such as repertoire, song leading techniques, or various local customs.[99] New song leaders generally had to rely on the "staff week" preceding each summer season to learn the nuances of their craft before the campers came. As the young bearers of what they saw as a tradition, they often began with significantly less experience than the camp's first hired song leaders. At the same time, however, their existing knowledge of a base repertoire, their cultivated passion for the music they knew, and their understanding of its power within the youth group community helped them become well-loved and well-regarded role models within the camp's circles.

Reflecting on one hand the sound worlds the campers experienced in their daily lives and, on the other hand, the particular spirit of community they felt at Union Institute, a relatively rigid system of aesthetics arose surrounding certain aspects of song leading. Guitars had by this point become the unequivocal instrument of choice, now all but required in any song leading environment. Indeed, this was so much the case that a 1969 attempt to bring in an Israeli accordionist to song lead for Chalutzim ended unsuccessfully;[100] and when a song leader broke his finger playing softball in 1971, he retained the aesthetic by employing one of the counselors-in-training to play guitar behind him as he led with a tambourine.[101] A very few song leaders, such as Susie Fox Lorge, performed their role without playing guitar, though with difficulty. Indeed, song leaders also began to value louder instruments—probably partly a result of the growing enrollment at the camp, as well as the recent opening of a new, larger dining hall to accommodate the increased numbers. Judy Director explained that she brought two guitars to camp: "I had a Favilla classical guitar [and] a Martin [twelve]-string. . . . [W]hich one I used depended on the songs, although for large groups, the [twelve-]string or a steel string worked better because they were louder."[102] Perhaps also reflecting the trend toward amplification in the American popular music scene, steel-string and twelve-string guitars eventually garnered the favor of the campers, giving song leaders who played them higher prestige than those who played comparatively quiet, nylon-stringed classical guitars.[103]

In addition to keeping a compendium of the songs used at the camp, Union Institute also made attempts to organize a defined technique for song leading. The 1972 *CIT Handbook,* for example, provided a course of apprenticeship for counselors-in-training who wanted to develop their skills and learn about the concept of "song." Complete with articulated objectives and methods, the handbook outlined the contents of a prospective meeting between the CIT and the unit song leader during staff orientation week. As outlined in an "Example Sheet" accompanying the handbook, the CIT was supposed to understand several concepts regarding song leading at this meeting, from learning about the "progression of songs" in a song session, to understanding how to teach a song, to the CIT's responsibilities to the song leader during a song session. Interestingly, the handbook description made no mention of religious services, perhaps suggesting that song sessions still remained the emphasis of the song leader's job. Although it was probably not followed to the letter, this outline nonetheless illustrated both the degree of refinement the song leading process had achieved at the camp and the interactive nature of the song session. Group singing was not merely created by the song leader alone, but rather required the participation of all staff to ensure a meaningful and successful experience.[104] More importantly, however, it showed that the process of becoming a song leader itself had now been taken in by the camp as a part of its formal educational program.

Yet this formal education entailed mainly the leading of the songs. With the exception of Max Janowski's two pieces from the middle of the 1950s, the song leading repertoire was almost entirely an imported one, adopted from sources seen as appropriate, but not specific to camp. Used with sensitivity and direction, and fashioned to fit with two decades of educational and religious agendas, these songs became prime signifiers of the camp experience—the spiritual excitement, the feeling of community, the intangible yet powerful imprinting of a unique Jewish identity. In 1972 the camp's new director, Jerry Kaye, brought a twenty-one-year-old song leader from St. Paul, Minnesota, to camp, hoping she could use her skills to introduce several more songs to this repertoire. For the first time in the camp's history, however, the songs she planned to introduce would be her own. Her activities within the camp that year would solidify the many musical worlds of this group of Reform Jewish youth into a tangible "style," reaching a point where it could replicate itself organically from within.

By the time Debbie Friedman arrived at camp as the Chalutzim song leader, she was already one of the most accomplished song leaders in the entire Reform movement. Her training, however, took place outside the realm of OSRUI. As with Morrie Hershman in the 1950s, Friedman owed her skills to the NFTY National Leadership Institute. For eight years after leaving Oconomowoc in the 1960s the National Leadership Institute moved around to various locations within the camping system. Finally, in 1965, it moved to a new permanent facility just outside of Warwick, New York.

In 1968, Friedman took intensive group lessons in song leading from Jim Schulman, a well-regarded folksinger and song leader who had been involved with NFTY Leadership Institutes since the early 1960s.[105] Schulman's method was ambitious, exacting, and effective: advocating the breaking down of the song leading process into its component parts. He drilled students on every note, word, and chord of the songs they presented; analyzed songs for meaning; and discussed methods for incorporating other elements such as harmony, hand-clapping, and body motions into the song-teaching experience. Friedman's interest and aptitude in the material must have been apparent, for she was invited back to assist Schulman the next year.

In addition to achieving a high level of proficiency and a knowledge of the National Institute ethos of song leading, Friedman also developed a strong sense of personal taste. While leading songs at a Union Institute conclave in 1968, Friedman had a run-in with that year's camp song leader, Bennett Miller. Miller later recalled, "I didn't know that she was . . . the official song leader for the kids. Because she was *one* of the kids. . . . And I was introduced, I got up, I started . . . to lead the singing. And she didn't like the pace of the song that I was doing. So she stood up at her place and screamed: 'Faster!' and started to [speed up the tempo by pumping her fists up and down]."[106]

As with other song leaders in NFTY, Friedman began to experiment with adding creative melodies to Jewish prayers, embarking upon a complete setting of the Friday evening service according to the *Union Prayerbook* in April 1971.[107] She completed the work, titled "Sing Unto God," early the next year and recorded it with a choral group from her old high school. That summer at OSRUI, as she began her work with Chalutzim, she would be awaiting the first pressing of her new album.[108]

Campers and other song leaders remember Friedman as a strong, intense, charismatic leader who had the ability to inspire people to spiritual heights through singing while at the same time directing the group toward a high degree of aptitude and accuracy. "She brought . . . an extraordinary intensity," remembered Chuck Rosenberg, one of her Chalutzim campers that year. "You didn't just sing to sing: you sang to express yourself. And she really brought that out of us."[109] Many saw Friedman as a person who not only cared deeply about the art of song leading, but who also knew how to invite others to care just as deeply. Her devotion to musical quality and precision invited comparisons to the "professional" song leaders of the 1950s. Mark Shapiro saw her as:

> someone who not only taught songs, but was a teacher. [She] really de-manded, "No, you're not quite singing it right": a discipline in music that maybe we hadn't had since Sharlin. . . . I remember the first summer she was there, at pre-camp orientation where she was just working on songs with the counselors, and I was up there for a few days during ori-entation, and she taught the staff "Sing Unto God." And *really*, it was a twenty-minute experience of her *teaching* this. But not just teaching it so we could have fun singing along, but getting *great*. And she did that with kids too. And in Hebrew. . . . And there was this sense that [we were going] back to the demanding nature of doing music well. It was fun, but you had to do it well. And that was really the first thing she brought.[110]

Indeed, with the release of her first album coinciding with her first summer at camp, Friedman was on the way to a professional song leading career. As opposed to Sharlin, Hershman, or Ross, however, Friedman did not see her activities as supplemental to a background in Western music performance. Openly professing an inability to read Western musical notation—a character-istic that would remain an important cultural marker for her throughout her career—she embodied instead a refined folksinger's aesthetic: a lyrical voice with enough edge to retain control over a group, a keen sense of melody, an ear for idiomatic harmony, and the ability to compose songs in her head and teach them orally.[111] Friedman also showed a passion for transmitting her style of song leading to future generations, encouraging two Chalutzim campers into song leading careers through generous and enthusiastic supervision.[112] Her staunch adherence to these qualities impressed many with whom she worked, and set a new standard for the musical aspects of song leading at the camp.

Premiered in its full form in Oconomowoc on August 11, 1972, after long hours of exacting rehearsal, "Sing Unto God" fulfilled Friedman's ambitions for the summer and opened a new era for religious music at OSRUI.[113] Fried-man led most of the service, remaining front and center throughout the ritual; nearly every prayer had a new musical setting, shattering the traditional model of services at camp; and at least two of Friedman's pieces followed a radical new format, combining English and Hebrew within the same composition.[114]

It was an exciting and revolutionary introduction that would change the face of camp worship for years to come.

The music created at this premiere spurred a new compositional energy throughout the camp, as well as some openness toward music that was newly created at other Reform Jewish camps across America. According to Robert Weinberg, a song leader and 1972 participant in the Machon program: "I really think Debbie more than anybody was the most influential person in stimulating the notion that we could write our own melodies for things. And anybody who was a song leader who had some talent kinda got the idea, 'Well, maybe I could take a shot at this; and maybe I have my own take or my own personal interpretation or my own sense of the meaning of a particular text.'"[115]

Albums emerging from the NFTY Leadership Institutes at Kutz Camp in Warwick, New York, brought a limited amount of new music into the camp, including some music by college-aged song leader Jeff Klepper and a new melody for "*L'cha Dodi*" by Michael Isaacson.[116] Most of the new music at OSRUI, however, came through the guitars and voices of campers and staff. Taking after Friedman and the recent steady influx of songs from the Hassidic Song Festival in Israel, their new camp settings engaged primarily liturgical and rabbinic sources. Suddenly, where once the idea of songwriting was not even considered an option, original songs were being introduced to services, composed often with as little premeditation as simply making the decision to create.[117]

Over the next several years the camp became a testing ground for new local music. Children arrived each summer eager to hear the next melody composed by a friend or counselor of theirs, and enthusiastic to learn it. Following the ethos of the time period, campers seemed to see themselves as agents of change through new musical creations that promoted their own sensibilities. Many of the new songs were short-lived, disappearing almost as quickly as they came into existence once they did not catch on with campers. Others remained unfinished fragments abandoned by those who ran out of inspiration too soon. Eventually, however, the new music coming from OSRUI and the other Reform camps came to supplement or replace the traditional service melodies regularly, causing a musical style to arise that came to be known by some as "American Nusach."[118]

Friedman's more refined presence also indicated a change in approach to the camp singing ethos, orchestrated by camp director Jerry Kaye. Kaye had seen the Friday night song sessions become increasingly spirited in the early 1970s, to the point where he and the rabbinic faculty found them to go beyond the bounds of appropriateness. According to Michael Lorge, a rendition of Michael Isaacson's "*L'cha Dodi*" would occasionally spark several of the female campers to start standing on the benches, forming kick lines, and shaking their behinds, much to the dismay of the rabbis who were present.[119] During another Friday evening, Rabbi Arnold Wolf stopped the campers in the middle of the *birkat hamazon* because he found their overly energetic singing disrespectful to the meaning of the words they sang. To remedy this, Kaye began to integrate Friedman's more disciplined style, which focused more on the words, the melody, and the beauty of "the singing voices blending."[120]

Kaye's approach was also evident in the way he ended Shabbat evening song sessions. In contrast to Irv Kaplan's manic "*Chiri Bim*," the new director (who never fashioned himself a singer) concluded the event by telling a story, while everyone else hummed a melody to the prayer "*Mah Tovu*" in the background.[121] The aesthetic he promoted through this was a more subdued, more "spiritual" one. Song leaders, under Kaye's leadership, were hired and trained according to this philosophy.

By the mid-1970s, song leaders at OSRUI had become a community of star figures and role models to the campers. Using their guitars as symbols of authenticity, they served as arbiters of spirituality—not only by introducing songs of recreation and worship to the camp, but now by writing some of them as well.

"Only a Beginning"

In reflecting upon her time at the camp, Debbie Friedman seemed to express the sentiments of many campers, song leaders, and staff when she wrote: "[My summers at OSRUI were] a time when my own experiences and the spirit of the Institute came together to allow me to create in the finest educational and spiritual moment of my life. That is when I knew that SING UNTO GOD was only a beginning."[122]

By the 1970s song leading had seen many beginnings at OSRUI: from Sharlin's introduction of guitar-led styles into Reform Jewish camping in the early 1950s, to Sam Alpert's forging of the Israeli folk connection in the 1960s, to the democratized approach to song leading advocated from the mid-1960s. Friedman's comments, however, held deeper significance in a number of ways. First, they indicated the song leader's emergence within the Reform movement as a person who not only transmitted musical culture, but who also created it. Second, they suggested that the musical values fostered at OSRUI had to some extent solidified into a unique, recognizable, and idiomatic style. Most importantly, however, Friedman's comments implied that this style was maturing into an important indicator of identity within the Reform Jewish youth culture—the voice of an empowered and idealistic young population. Providing relevance and meaning to prayer, spirit, and community, the sounds became an emblematic part of the camp experience; and with the help of Friedman and the many song leaders hired by OSRUI since, the style was able to grow into a deep and substantial genre.

While OSRUI, as the UAHC's first camp, was also the first camp to develop a song leading culture, it certainly was not the only camp to do so. The model was replicated—with local variations—in each of the regional Reform movement camps as they were subsequently founded. And in several cases, these camps' early song leaders had received significant prior experience at OSRUI. William Sharlin went on to become the first song leader at Camp Saratoga (later Camp Swig) in Northern California, and remained a presence there for many years. OSRUI-trained song leaders Michael Weinberg, Robert Weinberg, and Stephen Hart spent one or more summers leading campers at the UAHC camp in Zionsville, Indiana. Debbie Friedman, meanwhile, spent significant amounts of time at a number of Union camps, introducing her songs and instructing students in the art of song leading wherever she went. Together with song leaders from other parts of the country—such as Jeff Klepper, Loui Dobin, Merri and Ramie Arian, and Leon Sher, among many others—OSRUI song leaders thus triggered and energized the formation of a national song leading network, style, and repertoire. Their efforts helped give rise to a new American Jewish sound that, while a product of its time, continues to renew itself as a voice of tradition and authenticity with each generation of campers within both UAHC camps and member congregations.

Notes

1. "*Salaam*" is a song written by the Israeli/Arab group Sheva. Though few who sang it on opening day had probably heard the original recording of the song, it appears as track 10 on the group's first album, "Celestial Wedding" (1997). I should note here that whenever possible, I will mention individual songs throughout this essay along with the names of their authors. This is mainly to place these songs in context.

2. Personal observation, Judah and Rebecca Cohen, June 19, 2000.

3. Jenna Weissman Joselit, "The Jewish Way of Play," in Jenna Weissman Joselit and Karen S. Mittelman, eds., *A Worthy Use of Summer: Jewish Camping in America* (Philadelphia: National Museum of American Jewish History, 1993), 26. Joselit's term applies to the more general field of Jewish summer camping, and, in my opinion, works effectively here.

4. "Soundscape" is a term coined by Kay Shelemay in her *Soundscapes: Exploring Music in a Changing World* (New York: Norton, 2000), based on Arjun Appadurai's "Global Ethnoscapes: Note and Queries for a Transnational Anthropology," in Richard G. Fox, ed., *Recapturing Anthropology: Working in the Present* (Santa Fe, NM: School of American Research Press, 1991), 191–210.

5. I held the music specialist position for one unit only—Tiferet, the camp's arts unit—as a person with responsibilities that did not include being the unit's song leader. Thus, I was able to act as a disinterested observer of song leading activities over the course of the session.

6. I. Sheldon Posen, "*Lomir Zingen Hava Nashira* [Let Us Sing]: An Introduction to Jewish Summer Camp Song," in Joselit and Mittelman, *Worthy Use of Summer,* 29–36.

7. I. Sheldon Posen, "Song and Singing Traditions at Children's Summer Camps." MA thesis, Memorial University of Newfoundland, 1974, 37–41. See also Randall R. Tillery, "Touring Arcadia: Elements of Discursive Simulation and Cultural Struggle at a Children's Summer Camp," *Cultural Anthropology,* 7, no. 3 (1992): 374–88. Tillery focuses more on the summer camp as a holistic experience, though his background also applies nicely to music within the summer camp setting.

8. Robbie Lieberman, '*My Song Is My Weapon': People's Songs, American Communism, and the Politics of Culture, 1930–1950.* (Chicago: University of Illinois Press, 1989), 18.

9. Posen, "Song and Singing Traditions," 43–44. According to Lieberman, however, these songs were not really accepted as "anthems" of the working class by its organizers until around 1940 ("*My Song Is My Weapon,*" 25–66).

10. Lieberman, "*My Song Is My Weapon,*" 18.

11. Typically, the existence of "songbooks" is a strong indicator of the presence of group singing. One fine example of this is the "*Blau-Weiß Liederbuch*" (Berlin: Jüdischer Verlag, 1918), a "comprehensive" book (second edition) of German, Hebrew, and Yiddish songs for Jewish Zionist youth collected from the country's *Blau-Weiß* chapters. Consisting of notated melodies with underlaid lyrics and piano chord symbols, as well as translations in the back, the book served as a comprehensive source of songs for the "*Jugendwandern.*" Notably, the first song in this collection is "*Kol od balewaw p'nimah,*" which later became known as "*Hatikvah.*" For a wonderful discussion of this and many other German songbooks from this time period, see Philip V. Bohlman, "Folk Music and Emerging National Consciousness," in *"The Land Where Two Streams Flow": Music in the German-Jewish Community of Israel* (Chicago: University of Illinois Press, 1989), 47–78.

12. Posen, "*Lomir Zingen Hava Nashira,*" 36 (photo).

13. From Mordecai Kessler, ed., Twenty-Fourth Session, "Minutes of Camp Counselors' Training Course," for Surprise Lake Camp, 1936. Quoted in Posen, "*Lomir Zingen Hava Nashira,*" 30.

14. Eugene J. Sack, "We Discover the Camp Meeting—And Religion." *The Youth Leader: A Magazine for Jewish Clubs* 8, no. 3 (February–March 1940): 9.

15. Helfman (1901–1963) was a major voice in twentieth-century American Jewish music, with a career that spanned both coasts. His illustrious list of posts included engagements as music director of Congregation B'nai Abraham in Newark, New Jersey; faculty member at New York's Hebrew Union College School of Sacred Music; music director at the Brandeis-Bardin Institute; and dean of the School of Fine Arts at the University of Judaism. For more, see Philip Moddel, *Max Helfman: A Biographical Sketch* (Berkeley, CA: Magnes Museum, 1974).

16. Edwin Cole Goldberg, "The Beginnings of Educational Camping in the Reform Movement," *Journal of Reform Judaism* 35, no. 4 (1989): 7; interview with Eudice Lorge, June 12, 2000.

17. E. Lorge interview.

18. Composited from interviews with E. Lorge; Herman Schaalman, September 7, 2000; and Goldberg, "Beginnings of Educational Camping." For more on the "disturbances" caused by German refugee students at Hebrew Union College, see W. Guenther Plaut, *More Unfinished Business* (Toronto: University of Toronto Press, 1997).

19. E. Lorge interview.

20. Other German Reform rabbis who took important roles in the youth camping movement included Wolli Kaelter, one of the founders of Camp Saratoga (later Camp Swig) in Northern California (see Wolli Kaelter with Gordon Cohn, *From Danzig: An American Rabbi's Journey* [Malibu, CA: Pengloss Press, 1997], 119–38); and Alfred Wolf, founder of the Wilshire Boulevard Temple camps (including Hess Kramer) in Southern California.

21. Goldberg, "Beginnings of Educational Camping."

22. Interview with Rabbi Morris Hershman, August 30, 2000.

23. I come to this conclusion after examining several sources on the Habonim camps, including: David Breslau, ed., *Adventures in Pioneering: The Story of 25 Years of Habonim Camping* (New York: CHAY Commission of the Labor Zionist Movement, 1957); David Breslau, ed., *Arise and Build: The Story of American Habonim* (New York: Ichud Habonim Labor Zionist Youth, 1961); and J. J. Goldberg and Elliot King, eds., *Builders and Dreamers: Habonim Labor Zionist Youth in North America* (New York: Herzl Press, 1993). While all of these sources mentioned singing, none discussed it in much more detail, suggesting its status as simply a part of the program that required no special skill set to lead. Evidence regarding German youth groups is rather more scant; the German *Blau-Weiß* songbook mentioned earlier in this essay contained special instructions on providing chordal piano accompaniment, though such instructions appear to address the general public rather than any specialized individuals.

24. Lieberman, "*My Song Is My Weapon,*" 115–17, provides a detailed description of this phenomenon using as his source a 1940s manual from the New York organization People's Songs called "How to Plan a Hootenanny."

25. Schaalman interview.

26. This song was considered a specialty of Rabbi Ernst Lorge. According to his daughter, Sue Ellen Lorge Schwartz, Lorge used a version of the song with English lyrics by Arthur Kevess and Gerda Lerner (see *Sing Out!* 1, no. 6 [1951]: 3). The song was also reportedly used by the "White Rose" student resistance movement in Nazi Germany, further underlining the significance it must have had to Lorge when he led it (interview with Sue Ellen Schwartz, June 2000).

27. Schwartz interview.

28. Interview with Rabbi Arnold Wolf, June 4 and 6, 2000.

29. This photograph is reproduced in *American Judaism* 3, no. 2 (1953): 12.

30. According to Hershman, Sharlin had song led at a B'nai B'rith conclave in Starlight, Pennsylvania, before his stint with NFTY.

31. Telephone interview with Cantor William Sharlin, September 5, 2000.

32. See, for example, Helen and Larry Eisenberg, *How to Lead Group Singing* (New York: National Board of Young Men's Christian Associations, 1955), 20–23. The Eisenbergs favored piano, organ, and accordion as instruments to lead group singing. Guitar, seen as "softer-toned," was mentioned only later.

33. Eugene B. Borowitz, letter to the editor, *Journal of Reform Judaism* 37, no. 2 (1990): 71–73.

34. Sharlin interview.

35. Pioneer songs constituted a repertoire attributed to the Israeli settlers (known as Chalutzim, or "pioneers") of the 1920s–1940s. These songs typically have simple Hebrew lyrics, often depicting pastoral scenes, and promote an agrarian work ethic.

36. Hershman interview.

37. Wolf interview.

38. Interview with Rabbi Mark Shapiro, June 6, 2000. Notably, few seemed to know about the song's authorship by Huddie Ledbetter, known as "Leadbelly."

39. Shapiro interview.

40. Ibid.

41. E. Lorge interview.

42. Hershman interview.

43. Ibid. The next year, Sharlin helped open an extension of the School of Sacred Music in Los Angeles.

44. Ibid.

45. Ibid.

46. Schwartz interview.

47. Hy Zaret and Lou Singer, *Little Songs on Big Subjects* ([New York]: Argosy Music Corp., 1947). Though marketed as a mainstream publication, complete with Tin Pan Alley–style piano and vocal scoring, this collection sported an introduction by Progressive poet Louis Untermeyer.

48. Hershman interview

49. Shapiro interview and Hershman interview.

50. E-mail correspondence from Linda Steigman, April 6, 2000.

51. Schwartz interview.

52. Shapiro interview.

53. Rabbi Arnold Wolf remembers doing a program with Janowski he called "*sh'ma* around the world." In the middle of a religious service that focused on the *sh'ma* prayer, Wolf and Janowski presented several versions of the *sh'ma* as it might have been sung by the Jews in other countries, including singing the *sh'ma* to the tune of "La Marseillaise" to represent French Jewry, and to "Dixie" to represent Southern Jewry (Wolf interview).

54. Hershman interview. Hershman remembers that Janowski especially loved the song "Hey, Ho, Nobody Home," calling it a "perfect melody." Says Hershman: "We'd get that in a round [during a dining hall song session] . . . so then Janowski would close his eyes and you could just see him compose in his head. It was incredible."

55. Hershman, Shapiro, and Schwartz interviews. Hershman recalls that Cook might have requested a *chai*-themed song to mark NFTY's eighteenth anniversary. While the time frame is close, it does not seem to work exactly.

56. Notably, Ross was the first camp song leader who was not either clergy or clergy-in-training.

57. Schaalman interview.

58. This description is based on a composite of data from interviews with Schwartz, Hershman, Ross, and Shapiro, as well as material from Box 1 of the OSRUI collection.

59. *Kabbalat Shabbat*, the name of the service for "receiving the Sabbath," has become the most prominent religious service in twentieth-century American Reform Judaism. Typically, this service is also the ritual with the most elaborate music, in part due to the mystical associations initially attached to it. (Jeffrey Summit, *The Lord's Song in a Strange Land* [New York: Oxford University Press, 2000], 28–31.)

60. It is worth noting that the Havdalah service was a foreign concept to almost all the campers and thus bore no model outside camp.

61. Ashkenazic and Sephardic Hebrew differ mainly in a few key sounds. Two of the most significant are: (1) the letter *Tav* is pronounced [s] in Ashkenazic pronunciation, [t] in Sephardic pronunciation; and (2) the *patach-yud* combination is pronounced [oy] in Ashkenazic Hebrew, and [ai] in Sephardic Hebrew. Other, less-pronounced differences combine to give the two forms of pronunciation distinct sonic characters.

62. Interview with Rabbi Stephen Hart, June 24, 2000.

63. This appears on the mimeograph of a service in the American Jewish Archives OSRUI Collection, Box 1: Union Institute Program Book, 1960.

64. It is worth noting that of the people I interviewed, only those present at camp in the 1950s mentioned brotherhood songs. Anyone who came in afterward referred to these songs within the more general folk genre.

65. Hart interview.

66. Schwartz interview.

67. "Staff Recruitment Procedure Book, 1961," OSRUI Collection, Box 1.

68. Not once during interviews with Schwartz, Hart, Director, or Perelmuter was he seen as anything but a song leader.

69. The accordion, perhaps at least as common in early Israeli music as the guitar, did not share the same popularity in the United States.

70. See OSRUI Collection, Box 1. *Yisroel* appears, among other places, in the closing song of worship service #7, in the "Junior Session" section of "UI Program Book '59"; *Shabbos* appears several times in "Union Institute in Review," in the "Intermediate Sessions" section of the same book; for "*Tov L'Hodos*" see "Procedure—Kabbalat Shabbat, August 7, 1959," in the same section.

71. See OSRUI Collection, Box 2.

72. Schwartz interview.

73. Sue Ellen Schwartz illustrated this beautifully by describing a NFTY send-up of the "My Fair Lady" song "The Rain in Spain," in which the Eliza character was sing-

ing "*Toras Emes Noson HaShem B'Sinai*" in Ashkenazit, while the Professor Higgins character corrected her in Sepharadic: "*Torat Emet Natan HaShem B'Sinai.*"

74. "Oconomowoc '63, Program Book I," in OSRUI Collection, Box 1.

75. The song is actually called "*Zamar Noded.*"

76. Yiddish was fast becoming a forgotten language by this time. In the song "*Chiri Bim Chiri Bam,*" located on page S-8 of the *Shiron,* for example, the variant "As Ich vel zo-gen" ("When I say . . .") appears to have been automatically translated just below as "When I sing."

77. For more on the Pioneer (later Chalutzim) Unit, see Hillel Gamoran's chapter in this volume.

78. Shapiro interview.

79. Rachel Dulin, e-mail communication, September 28, 2000.

80. Irv Kaplan, e-mail communication, September 25, 2000.

81. See, for example, Robert Baruch in 1967, or myself (the "music specialist" for Tiferet) in 2000.

82. In 1964, for example, Gail Hartman wrote: "[The song leader] was overwhelmed by the number of guitars brought to camp. She said that about nine or ten accompanied the campers." "1964 Program Book I," OSRUI Collection, Box 1.

83. Betty Berman, "Folk Singing," "1964 Program Book I," OSRUI Collection, Box 2.

84. Ibid.

85. Interview with Ann Lidsky, June 13, 2000. Lidsky, a counselor who spent her first year at Union Institute in 1966, recalled that her "first calls home were about the song sessions." Even though the Jewish songs were unfamiliar to her, she said she felt immediately pulled into the community during the singing.

86. Telephone interview with Dr. Hillel Gamoran, September 25, 2000.

87. Telephone conversation with Michael Lorge, October 2, 2000. Lorge said that when he spoke with people about song leaders during the 1950s and 1960s, they usually associated the song leaders with a particular song, stating, "I remember so-and-so singing their song."

88. Lidsky interview.

89. Ibid., e.g.

90. Kaplan e-mail communication.

91. See for example, interviews with Director, Hart, and Lidsky.

92. "Notes from Rabbinic Program Meeting, Jan. 12, 1967," in "1967 Procedures" folder, OSRUI Collection, Box 3.

93. Ibid.

94. See, for example, interview with Michael Weinberg, June 2000.

95. See Edwin Seroussi and Motti Regev, *Popular Music and National Culture in Israel* (Berkeley: University of California Press, 2004), 126–29.

96. "1966 Summary Report," OSRUI Collection, Box 3, File 4.

97. Ibid.

98. R. and M. Weinberg interviews, June 2000.

99. Director interview, October 2000.

100. "I think the kids really didn't give him a chance, because of the stigma of that instrument," one song leader later recalled (Director interview). It is interesting that the song leaders who mentioned the accordion player valued him both because of the different sound and because he taught them a lot of new repertoire (Director, Miller, M. Weinberg interviews).

101. M. Weinberg interview.

102. Director, e-mail correspondence, September 27, 2000.

103. Rachel Rosenberg interview, September 27, 2000.

104. *CIT Handbook*, OSRUI Collection, Box 4, Folders 41–42.

105. Interview with Jeffrey Klepper, March 14, 1998; Miller interview.

106. Miller interview.

107. "Rising Star," *Reform Judaism* 1, no. 6 (1973): 2.

108. Interview with Rabbi Donald Splansky, May 11, 2000. One of the songs from this album, "*L'cha Dodi*," appears on the first NFTY album, "Songs NFTY Sings," which was also produced in 1972. This shows the strength of Friedman's connection with the "East Coast" song leaders.

109. C. Rosenberg interview, September 27, 2000.

110. Shapiro interview.

111. Twenty-eight years later, Friedman still mentions this with a degree of pride.

112. C. Rosenberg interview.

113. This is an educated guess based on a service order from that night that contains almost all the songs from her album. "Program Book 1972," OSRUI Collection, Box 4.

114. These two songs were the "*Sh'ma*/And Thou Shalt Love" and "Let Us Adore."

115. R. Weinberg interview.

116. Ibid. These songs were likely introduced through Friedman herself; queries to other Olin-Sang song leaders about their origins reveal little more than the fact that they appeared in camp somehow.

117. One good example of this came from Rob Weinberg, who described the process of writing a setting of "*Oseh Shalom*": "I was I think a freshman in college, so this would've been probably spring of '73. . . . I was standing under the dome of the rotunda [at OSRUI] singin' to myself, enjoying the sound of this big twelve-string guitar [I had borrowed from my brother]; and it just kind of occurred to me, to try to write a song. And I just did it" (R. Weinberg interview).

118. This title first appeared at a 1986 concert in College Park, Maryland, at the Conference for Alternatives in Jewish Education. Some artists, such as Jeff Klepper, still occasionally use this term to define their work. Simply put, *nusach* is a term often used in the Reform movement to denote the traditional melodies or melodic fragments underlying liturgical texts. In this context, then, "American *Nusach*" was used to express the transformation of melodic prayer settings (and their accompaniments) to reflect what was seen as a distinctly "American" idiom.

119. Telephone conversation with Michael Lorge, October 2, 2000.

120. R. Rosenberg interview.

121. M. Weinberg interview, *inter alia.*

122. Jacket notes to Debbie Friedman, "Not By Might—Not By Power" (San Diego: Jewish Family Productions/Sounds Write Productions, 1974).

Postscript

Reflections on Olin-Sang-Ruby Union Institute

Gerard W. Kaye

Union Institute, as it was first known, was clearly an experiment in Jewish teaching. The assembly of many rabbis and educators in a free environment created a kind of idea bowl that did not lend itself to one fabric. As a matter of circumstance, what evolved is more closely akin to a basket of yarns than it is to one single skein. Some of the early teachers emphasized worship, others thought Hebrew to be the real challenge, while still others sought to underline history or literature. What reinforces the legend of Union Institute is that each of the original faculty members and their successors maintained that whatever was undertaken in this place was the best model that could be developed. So it was that the reputation was planted and grew.

Now that there are thirteen Reform camps across North America, the models created in Oconomowoc show in even greater relief. While a kind of boilerplate camping emerged throughout the system, Olin-Sang-Ruby Union Institute has drawn out individual threads that have marked the educational landscape.

Hebrew is high on the list of innovative commitments that OSRUI maintains. Although Hebrew is taught throughout the camp to each child each day, the Chalutzim program is unique in Jewish camping. A wide variety of camps from various streams of Jewish life have expressed interest and commitment to Hebrew. Only Chalutzim remains as a hallmark of Hebrew informal education.

This is not to diminish the experience of the Ramah camps, which maintain Hebrew as a staunch base of their teaching. However, Chalutzim and Ramah are substantively different. Chalutzim sets the bar by establishing a written admissions test and making Hebrew the language of campers (now seventy teens) virtually all day and every day of their seven-week summer. Camps Massad, the Ulpan of Tel Yehudah, and their counterparts around the country have fallen away, while Chalutzim has grown and flourished.

To define the reasons for this success and the others' evaporation is not so simple. However, the maintenance of Chalutzim through very difficult days in the mid-1970s, when no more than forty or so teens would sign up for this challenge, contributed to the idea of purpose-driven Jewish learning tied to renewed Reform education. And this purpose trickled down through the entire camp. Hebrew announcements made to eight- and nine-year-old campers by their senior staff demonstrated that Hebrew counts. Creating a *Merkaz Ivrit* (Hebrew Center), a physical location that put Hebrew on the literal map of the camp, made it clear that this Hebrew counts.

Each of the elements of the camp day stand out in their own right; however, prayer and learning have become dominant throughout the movement. While OSRUI regularly uses the prayer book of the movement, new expression is constantly explored. Perhaps an overriding theme that has emerged concerning worship at OSRUI is the sharp line distinguishing novelty from creativity.

All too often, Reform youth seem to believe that almost anything can be identified as Jewish prayer. When rabbis, educators, and cantors teach that the commonality of Jewish worship throughout the world counts, then campers understand that part of their prayer life is the forging of links with Jews everywhere.

OSRUI has encouraged creativity by a better understanding of the foundations of Jewish worship. Likewise, individual campers are encouraged to share their own thoughts and insights with their peers by writing inspirational annotations that they read.

Maybe the best example of the centrality of worship here is the presence of many Torah scrolls. And OSRUI is one of the few camps in the world to treasure a Shoah scroll in our safekeeping. This scroll reminds the community that several of its founding rabbis were themselves rescued from the Shoah. These Torah scrolls must, of course, have an appropriate physical place in the camp. OSRUI has understood since its founding that prayer can capitalize on the miracle of nature each day with outdoor chapels. Campers learn that God resides in those chapels as sure as the birds and the crickets provide the choir.

Shabbat emerged from the first days of camp as yet another hallmark of the vitality of worship within their Jewish life. Now, more than seven hundred children and adults come together in one common hour to pray and converge on the Shabbat table in one voice. No matter how many different models have been explored in worship at camp, *Kabbalat Shabbat* (welcoming the beginning of the Sabbath) sees campers coming from every corner to share kiddush, challah, and the camp traditions that everyone believes must happen in order for it to be truly Shabbat.

Implicit in the world of worship is music. Olin-Sang-Ruby Union Institute is the home of *Hava Nashirah*. This remarkable workshop brings together a dazzling faculty who invests itself in the lives of more than 150 song leaders, cantors, music teachers, and choir leaders from around the world for nearly a week each spring. Now more than a decade old, these participants help make *Hava Nashirah* resonate throughout the country.

All of these elements—prayer, music, and Hebrew—join together to accent Olin-Sang-Ruby Union Institute as a laboratory of Jewish learning. More than forty faculty members come to Oconomowoc during the summer for at least two weeks to be part of every unit and to work directly with staff and campers.

Over the years a wide variety of projects have been tried. Many are now staples of camp life, while others have waned away. Programs like *Ma'ayan* in the 1970s, a four-month residency for high school students graduating after the first semester of their senior year, inspired a number of teens to go on to the rabbinate and other Jewish professions. Others continued as dedicated congregants. This program diminished and folded when high schools were less accommodating to provide early graduation.

Other all-camp events have become staples of the summer excitement. On Israel Day, the entire camp learns about the land and people of Israel. This program is crafted by the Israelis on staff. Games, presentations, and competitions complement the learning that is presented for everyone.

The OSRUI Judaica Bowl is an opportunity for campers of all ages to test their Jewish knowledge both in their unit and in front of the whole camp. One night each month teams of five campers represent their unit in this quiz-bowl format. It is a contest of general Jewish knowledge with prior mini-bowls in each unit to select the participants for the all-camp event. The level of knowledge that many campers have is remarkable. The questions are random and topics scattered.

Jewish learning is not limited to children during the summer, though. New projects are always percolating and looking for a test of their validity. *Lehrhaus,* a learning and recreational program for adults, now occupies the month of July and creates a parallel community to the kids in their units. Here adults of all ages can come to camp to study with some of the most remarkable teachers of our communities. Although they are separated from the camper facilities, many parents tie their pickup dates to a few days of study. Others with no children find the youth presence to be invigorating and inspiring.

Today, Olin-Sang-Ruby Union Institute enjoys considerable support from the Reform Jewish community in many ways. Not only have we come to serve some one thousand youngsters each summer, but adults and families are included in all of our work. Year-round activities such as a weekend for fathers and sons and for mothers and daughters emphasize the importance of the Jewish family. Programs for Hebrew learning, arts, and a variety of other events round out the calendar. In addition, dedicated rabbis and educators bring their congregational groups virtually every weekend for study and community building. A substantial group of cantors has built a program for their junior choirs to come together in the joy of music.

Since the first twenty-five years of the camp's existence, major financial support has come from families, individuals, foundations, and congregations. Endowments and grants have provided the wherewithal to build new facilities and rebuild existing ones. The grounds are a true source of pride and portray the notion that Jewish camping values the beautification of mitzvah.

Everywhere you go in the Jewish world, alumni of Olin-Sang-Ruby Union Institute recall their friendships and experiences on these few acres in southeastern Wisconsin. They will tell you the truth about how the farmer down the road helped build the benches for the chapel in time for the first Shabbat, and they will tell you about the day that the clouds spelled the word *sh'ma* (the first word in the most central prayer of Jewish litany) in Hebrew or how they discovered their *bashert* (a Yiddish term for the one intended to be your spouse), who was sitting at a quiet campfire humming a melody. But they all know that no matter how impressive the building or how wonderful the "stuff," the most important thing that OSRUI has is a log—just a simple log on the ground, with a camper sitting on one end and a rabbi or teacher or caring counselor on the other end, with nothing between them. Here is where the real magic takes place and the legend expands to yet another Jewish child.

Appendix

Directors of Olin-Sang-Ruby Union Institute, UAHC 1952–Present

Rabbi Herman M. Schaalman (February 1952–December 1952)
Rabbi Gerald Raiskin (January 1953–October 1953)
Rabbi Daniel E. Kerman (November 1953–September 1954)
Rabbi Irwin M. Schor (December 1954–November 1955)
Philip L. Brin (December 1955–December 1960)
Norman Buckner (January 1961–December 1962)
Irving B. Kaplan (February 1963–September 1968)
Rabbi Allan L. Smith (November 1969–Spring 1970)
Gerard W. Kaye (Spring 1970–Present)

Board Chairs

Johann S. Ackerman
Robert Cooper
Sidney I. Cole
John Altschuler
Erwin Greenberg
David Roth
Dorothy Waterman
Daniel Haskell

Donald Garfield
Lawrence Sherman
Judith Kamins
Sandra Brottman
Clive D. Kamins
Michael M. Lorge
Richard Courtheoux
Mark Gershon

Contributors

Judah M. Cohen is a Dorot assistant professor/Faculty Fellow in the Skirball Department of Hebrew and Judaic Studies at New York University. He has conducted extensive research on Jewish life and history in the Caribbean, which was the subject of his first book, *Through the Sands of Time: A History of the Jewish Community of St. Thomas, U.S. Virgin Islands* (Hanover, NH: Brandeis University Press, 2004).

Hillel Gamoran served as rabbi at Beth Tikvah Congregation, Hoffman Estates, Illinois, for thirty-four years, during which he served several weeks each summer on the faculty of Olin-Sang-Ruby Union Institute in Oconomowoc, Wisconsin. Rabbi Gamoran currently teaches rabbinic literature at the University of Washington. His scholarly articles have appeared in the *Journal of Near Eastern Studies,* the *Jewish Law Association Studies,* the *Hebrew Union College Annual,* and other academic journals.

Gerard W. Kaye is the ninth director of Olin-Sang-Ruby Union Institute and has held this position since 1970. He teaches and writes on matters of youth and Jewish education.

Michael M. Lorge is an attorney with Laser, Pokorny, Schwartz, Friedman & Economos in Chicago, Illinois. He is a member of the national board of The Union for Reform Judaism and a vice chair of its national camping commission. He has chaired the board of Olin-Sang-Ruby Union Institute and serves on its faculty. He has lectured and written extensively on both legal and Jewish issues.

Jonathan D. Sarna is the Joseph H. & Belle R. Braun Professor of American Jewish History at Brandeis University and chairs the academic advisory and editorial board of the Jacob Rader Marcus Center of the American Jewish Archives. Author or editor of more than twenty books on American Jewish history and life, his most recent book, *American Judaism: A History* (New Haven, CT: Yale University Press), was published in February 2004.

Donald M. Splansky was ordained at Hebrew Union College–Jewish Institute of Religion, New York, in 1968 and received his PhD at the Cincinnati campus in 1981. He has served as rabbi at two congregations in Cincinnati and now serves as rabbi at Temple Beth Am, Framingham, Massachusetts, and also as lecturer at St. Mark's School in Southborough, Massachusetts. He has served on the staff and faculty of several UAHC summer camps, including Olin-Sang-Ruby Union Institute.

Michael Zeldin is professor of Jewish Education and director of Day School Initiatives at Hebrew Union College–Jewish Institute of Religion in Los Angeles. He has written extensively on informal education, Jewish day schools, mentoring, and Jewish educational leadership, and is currently senior editor of the *Journal of Jewish Education.*

Gary P. Zola is the executive director of the Jacob Rader Marcus Center of the American Jewish Archives, as well as an associate professor of the American Jewish Experience at Hebrew Union College–Jewish Institute of Religion in Cincinnati, Ohio. His most recent publication is *The Dynamics of American Jewish History: Jacob Rader Marcus's Essays on American Jewry* (Hanover, NH: Brandeis University Press, 2004). He has served on the staff at Olin-Sang-Ruby Union Institute and on the faculty of several UAHC summer camps.

Index

Conservative Judaism: educational camping, 40–42; emergence of summer camps associated with, 19; youth groups, 40. *See also* Camp Ramah

constructivist teaching, 99

Cook, Rabbi Samuel, 42, 54, 64, 67, 178, 181, 182, 186

Cook, Ray, 182

Cook County Sunday School Association, 8

Cooper, Robert J., 58, 65, 67, *121*, 171n22

Cos Cob, Connecticut, 9

counselors, 98; as accessible role models for campers, 105; heart of camp experience, 89; need for Jewish learning, 105; rabbinical students as, 37; Union Institute Counselor-In-Training (CIT) program, 75

Counts, George, 24n49

creative alienation, 103

Cremin, Lawrence, 91

Cronbach, Abraham, 55, 64

"cultural transfer," from Europe to America, 36

curriculum: "hidden," 109; holistic view of, 88; "implicit," 108–9; of Jewish summer camps, 107–10; "null," 107–8; overt, 107–8

Davis, Moshe, 18, 133

denominational Jewish camps, 28, 34

Depression, federal aid during, 36

Dewey, John, 4, 24n49, 98, 100

"*Die Gedanken Sind Frei,*" 180

Dimock, Hedley S., 31

Director, Judy, 195

Directory of Summer Camps Under the Auspices of Jewish Communal Organizations, 29

Dobin, Loui, 201

Dolgin, Etty, 138, 144

Dorff, Elliot, 104

Dudley, Sumner F., 29

Dulin, Rachel Zohar, 140, 142, 191

Dushkin, Alexander M., 16, 35; and Camp Modin, 16, 32, 33–34, 35, 40; executive director of Jewish Education Committee of New York, 146n6; influenced by

Columbia University's educational Progressives, 24n49; influence of Benderly on, 127

Dushkin, Julia, 16, 33–34

du-siach, 141–42

Eastern European immigrants, 19, 134; Americanization, 14; experiences in European Zionist Youth movements, 15; invigorated Hebrew movement in America, 129; urban living conditions, 12

education: confluent education, 101; educational planning at camps, 105–7; educational theories emphasizing the link between learning and play, 4; educator as learner, 105; experiential learning, 38; family camps, 29; family education, 91; goals of Jewish camping, 29–30; informal education, 91; multidimensional education, 96–101, 97, 98–99; non-school forms of, 91; "null" curriculum, 107–8; pedagogy, 106–7; Progressive educators, 4, 11, 16, 31; sociodrama, 86, 109

Educational Alliance Camp, 12, 29

Ehrenreich, Bernard C., 14, 23n44, 31

Eisen, Arnold, 106

Eisenberg, Azriel, 37

Eisendrath, Rabbi Maurice, 27, 43, 54, 56, 57, 60, 61

Eisner, Elliot, 107

Eliot, Charles B., 19, 31

Ellenson, David, 102–4

Emin, G. H., 59

Ephraim, Miriam, 32

Essrig, Harry, 55

Ettenberg, Sylvia, 33

European Jewish youth movements, 15, 46n11

Federation of American Zionists, 128

federation-sponsored camps, 29

Feinberg, Paul, 150n94

Fishman, Sylvia Barrack, 102

Folkman, Jerome, 55

folk music, 191–92; brotherhood songs, 182–83, 184–85, 186, 189; group singing, 177, 178

Hull House Camp, 6
Hurwich, Leah Konovitz, 32, 33, 131
Hurwich, Louis, 37, 131
Hyman, Tillie, 24n50

Illinois Federation of Temple Sisterhoods, 60
immigration. *See* Jewish immigration
instrumentalism, 4
intelligence, theories of, 100
International Sunday School Association, 8
International Torah Corps, 137, 138
Isaacman, Daniel, 28, 29, 30, 145
Isaacson, Michael, 199
Israel: founding of, 78; Hassidic Song Festivals, 193–94; kibbutzim, 34; study programs in, 137; trips to, 91
"It's the Same All Over," 186

Jacob Rader Marcus Center. *See* American
Jewish Archives
James, William, 162
Janowski, Max, 156, 180, 186, 196, 204n53
Jewish Board of Guardians, 33
Jewish Chautauqua Society, 57, 58
Jewish community centers, 91; camps, 29;
emergence of summer camps associated with, 19
Jewish day schools, 91–92, 96; formal institution of Jewish education, 91; founded
between 1940 and 1950, 35; intensive
interpersonal interactions, 93–94
Jewish education: defensive response to
adversity and a form of cultural resis-
tance, 36; dramatic expansion of, 35–36,
45; as multidimensional education, 96–
101; opportunity for multiple intelligences, 100–101. *See also* education
Jewish Education, 37, 39
Jewish identity: compartmentalized, 17; development of, 101, 110
Jewish immigration: at end of nineteenth century, 126; and "melting
pot" ideology, 102
Jewish museums, 91
Jewish Publication Society, 36
Jewish religious schools, 91–92
Jewish rituals, 104
Jewish scouting movement, Germany, 57

Jewish social welfare organizations, establishment of summer camps, 12
Jewish summer camping: aims of, 29–30,
46n9, 111; camp rituals, 89, 90; challenges of success, 110–13; class levels, 29;
crucial decade for the growth of, 17–18,
29, 35–39; curriculum principles, 101–10;
denominational camps, 28, 34; difficulties in transferring camp Judaism to
the city, 110–11; early history of, 28–31;
educator as learner, 105; elements of
both formal and informal education,
95–96; emergence of camps serving religious movements of American Judaism, 17–18; emergence of educational
camps, 13, 14–17, 29, 31–35; emphasis on
Hebrew today, 144–45; environment, 98–
99; fusion of cultural phenomena, 11;
goals of early camps, 30, 49; group singing, 177–79; ideologically based camps,
16; intensive interpersonal interactions,
93–94; Jewish learning integrated into
other activities, 93, 105–6, *119;* lasting
influence of educational movement,
44–45; magic of, 89–91; outgrowth of
Settlement, Fresh Air, and other social
reform initiatives, 12; philanthropic
camps, 29, 30; planning and pedagogy,
105–7; plausibility structures, 99; privately owned camps, 12–13, 29; in the
Reform and Conservative movements,
40–44; role of economics in, 33; roots in
1880s, 52; seven varieties of before 1940,
29; similarities to Jewish day schools,
91–94; sponsored by social welfare organizations, 12; three curricula of, 107–
10; view of as informal education, 91;
Yiddish camps, 29, 45, 48n45; Zionist
camps, 13, 18, 25n53, 29, 45, 48n45. *See
also* Reform Jewish camping
Jewish Theological Seminary, 31; and
Camp Ramah, 41; "Ten Year Plan to
Reclaim Jewish Youth to Religious and
Ethical Life," 40
Jewish Welfare Board, 29
Jewish Working Girls' Vacation Society of
New York, 11, 29
Jewish youth organizations, emergence of
summer camps associated with, 19

Schoolman, Albert P., 31–33; aim of camping, 102; concept of camp programming, 106; founder and director of Camp Cejwin, 16, 127, 146n6; influenced by Columbia University's educational Progressives, 24n49; influence of Benderly on, 127

Schoolman, Bertha, 32, 33

Schor, Rabbi Irwin: departure from Union Institute, 67, 169; first full-time director of Union Institute, 65; recommendations for faculty's role at camp, 67–68

Schulman, Jim, 197

Schwartz, Shuly Rubin, 40

Schwartz, Sue Ellen Lorge, 123, 185, 190

scouting camps, 9

Sepharadic, 187, 190, 205n61

Seton, Ernest Thompson, 8–9, 10

settlement houses, 6, 12

Shabbat, 34, 157–58, 173; at Brandeis Camp Institute, 38; celebrated in camp and day schools, 92; as distinctive Jewish ritual, 104; ending with Havdalah ceremony, 152; as part of "camp magic," 90; as way to transfer camp activities to home, 111

Shabbat shirah, 175

Shapiro, Rabbi Mark: call for a full-time music specialist at Union Institute, 193; and Chalutzim Unit, 150n94, 191; on Debbie Friedman, 198; on Shabbat, 173; on Sharlin as song leader, 183; as song leader at Union Institute, 73, 185, 186

Sharlin, William, 120, 181–84, 201

Sharon Camp, 39

Shemer, Naomi, 190

Sher, Leon, 201

Sheva, 201n1

shir hamaalot, 159

shiron, 176, 190–91

"Shiru Lanu Mishirei Tsiyon," 160

shiur, 143; shiur-sicha, 113n1; sicha, 143

sh'ma, 156, 159, 204n53, 212

Shoah scroll (torah rescued from the Holocaust), 210

shofar, 157

Sholem Aleichem Folk Institute, 16

Shulsinger, Rivka, 33

Shulsinger, Shlomo, 16, 37, 38, 39, 129, 130

Simon, Rabbi Ralph, 41, 133

Sinai Temple of Michigan City, 71

Sing Out!, 185

"Sing Unto God," 197, 198

Sisterhoods, midwest region. See Women of Reform Judaism (WRI)

Six-Day War, 125, 193

Skirball, Rabbi Henry, 136–37

Skolnick, Nachama, 111

Smith, Huston, 167

Smith, Rabbi Allan, 77

Smoller, Rabbi Phineas, 56, 123

Social Gospel movement, 2

social reform, in response to the negative consequences of urbanization and industrialization, 2, 12

sociodrama, 86, 109

Solel (Pathfinders) Hebrew program, Camp Swig, 87, 135–36

Solel Aleph/Solel Bet, 136

song leaders, 120, 156, 173–208; changes in the role and demographic of, 194; as educators, 188–94; effect of Hebrew on, 192–93; position and activities at Union Institute, 186–87, 191; system of aesthetics, 195–96

"Song of Songs," 189

Sores, Irving, 135

special needs camps, 21n21

spiritual formation, and organized camping, 6–8

Splansky, Greta Lee, 119

Splansky, Rabbi Donald M., 74, 76, 138, 140, 150n91–93, 151

Steffens, Lincoln, 10

Steinberg, Ben, 163–64

Sternberg, Robert, 100

Stravinsky, Igor, 165

Summer Camp Institute, 16

Surprise Lake Camp, 12, 13, 23n39, 29, 178

Swig, Ben, 56, 64

"Synagogue 2000," 154, 168

Talbot, Winthrop T., 5

Talmud Torah school, 32

Taylor, Rabbi Dov, 137

Temple Beth Israel, Chicago, 71